Criminal Justice Internships

Criminal Justice Internships: Theory into Practice, 9th Edition, guides the student, instructor, and internship site supervisor through the entire internship process, offering advice and information for use at the internship site as well as pre-planning and assessment activities. With more and more programs offering or requiring internships as a graduation requirement, McBride offers students a means of enhancing their credentials and gaining a foothold in a very competitive job market.

Students learn basics such as choosing an internship site at either a public agency or a private firm, résumé writing techniques, effective use of social networks, interviewing skills, and the importance of setting and developing goals and assessing progress. The book also serves as a reference tool for professors and supervisory personnel who assist and supervise students during their internships. Divided into four sections— Pre-internship Considerations, Professional Concerns, Role of the Organization, and Assessment and Career Planning—this book offers resources to enrich the experience of the student and lay the foundation for future professional success. Suitable for all Criminal Justice, Justice Studies, and Pre-law undergraduate programs, *Criminal Justice Internships* is useful as well in Social Sciences programs with a service-learning component.

R. Bruce McBride is Professor Emeritus of Criminal Justice at Utica College. He has also served as Commissioner of University Police for the State University of New York. At Utica College, prior to his time at SUNY, he served as chair of Criminal Justice and coordinated the department's Internship Program which allowed for semester-based study placements in the United States and overseas. Dr. McBride holds bachelor and master's degrees from the State University of New York at Oswego and master's and doctoral degrees from the University at Albany. He is past president of the Criminal Justice Educators Association of New York State.

Criminal Justice Internships: Theory into Practice is a welcome addition to our Learner Researchers' repertoire as they begin their exploration into internship opportunities. In his latest edition, Bruce McBride has done a fabulous job providing insight into this daunting and often intimidating world of social and criminal justice, as practitioner and internship host.

Lonnie C. Croal, *MA, CEC, CACE, School of Justice &*
Public Safety Professional Programs, Columbia College – Calgary

Criminal Justice Internships: Theory into Practice is noteworthy for its comprehensive coverage of all aspects of academic internships with a focus on the unique issues of experiential education in criminal justice. Dr. McBride addresses a wide range of important topics pertaining to the internship process, including timely concerns not commonly discussed in comparable texts, such as social media and networking, political, economic and legal factors and ethical concerns. The book serves as a relevant and useful text for courses dealing with careers in criminal justice.

Jay S. Berman, *Ph.D., Department of Criminal Justice, New Jersey City University*

Criminal Justice Internships
Theory into Practice
Ninth Edition

R. Bruce McBride

Routledge
Taylor & Francis Group

NEW YORK AND LONDON

Ninth edition published 2017
by Routledge
711 Third Avenue, New York, NY 10017

and by Routledge
2 Park Square, Milton Park, Abingdon, Oxon OX14 4RN

Routledge is an imprint of the Taylor & Francis Group, an informa business

First edition published by Taylor & Francis 1984
Eighth edition published by Taylor & Francis 2015

Library of Congress Cataloging in Publication Data
Names: McBride, R. Bruce. | Gordon, Gary R. Criminal justice internships.
Title: Criminal justice internships : theory into practice / R. Bruce McBride.
Description: Ninth Edition. | New York : Routledge, 2016. | Revised edition
   of Criminal justice internships, 2015. | Includes bibliographical references
   and index.
Identifiers: LCCN 2016028446| ISBN 9781138231658 (hardback) | ISBN 1138231657
   (hardback) | ISBN 9781138231665 (pbk.) | ISBN 1138231665 (pbk.) |
   ISBN 9781315314372 (E-ISBN master) | ISBN 1315314371 (E-ISBN master) |
   ISBN 9781315314365 (web pdf) | ISBN 1315314363 (web pdf)
Subjects: LCSH: Criminal justice, Administration of—Study and teaching
   (Internship)—United States. | Criminal justice, Administration of—Study and
   teaching (Internship)
Classification: LCC HV9950 .M336 2016 | DDC 364.973071/55—dc23
LC record available at https://lccn.loc.gov/2016028446

ISBN: 978-1-138-23165-8 (hbk)
ISBN: 978-1-138-23166-5 (pbk)
ISBN: 978-1-315-31437-2 (ebk)

Typeset in Utopia
by RefineCatch Limited, Bungay, Suffolk

A Companion Website for this book is available at www.routledge.com/cw/mcbride

To My Family—
Barbara, Robbie, Megan, and Brian

Contents

Illustrations

Figures

Tables

Preface

This book is directed to the Criminal Justice student who is undertaking an internship with a public agency or private sector organization. It is also intended to be a reference tool for professors and field supervisory personnel who instruct and supervise student interns during the experience. The objective of the book is to direct attention to professional and personal issues that occur during an internship program. This is important because the majority of Criminal Justice programs in the United States have designated the internship as either a requirement or a major elective.

In 1984, this book was the result of a project that began to guide students through their internships. Finding there were few available materials on the subject, these materials were created with former co-author Gary Gordon to give specific attention to the placement process and the internship experience. What you find here is the culmination of decades of experience in using these materials with students.

This book is designed to be used as an introduction to the internship, as well as a course text while at the agency site. A student who is considering an internship will find several chapters helpful in conceptualizing what the experience will entail. Very often, the book is used in senior seminar and program capstone courses the semester before an internship begins to focus attention on site selection, how to obtain a placement, the role of the student and preliminary insight into the nature of organizations. Once in the field, a second reading will help to clarify, explain, and promote an understanding of the experience through specific assignments particularly the formation of educational goals.

A great deal of thanks goes to the hundreds of students I supervised through the years both as a faculty member and criminal justice administrator. Every semester they enhance the understanding of internships by raising questions and sharing their experiences. Much appreciation needs to be given to the many internship coordinators and instructors who have used this book over the years. Their comments and views on internships in this avenue of experiential learning are important.

I would also like to thank faculty members Bill Virkler, Jim Brown, Ray Philo, Zachary Lewis, and Greg Walsh, and career services director Halina Lotyczewski, of Utica College for their thoughts on internship trends and guidance on national internship and career opportunities. George Curtis, who also retired from Utica College, is also acknowledged for helping to keep tabs on the ever-changing legal environment for student interns. Finally, thank you to Ellen Boyne and the staff of Elsevier (formerly

LexisNexis Matthew Bender and Anderson Publishing) for continuing to support this concept and for publishing this new edition of *Criminal Justice Internships: Theory into Practice.*

R. Bruce McBride
Delmar, New York

Online Resources

Interactive resources can be accessed for free by registering at www.routledge.com/cw/mcbride

Pre-Internship Considerations

Introduction to Internships

1

This book is designed to maximize the internship experience for students enrolled in criminal justice degree programs. This chapter presents the background to criminal justice internship programs and the important reasons why a student should consider interning. Upon completing the chapter, the reader should be able to review the internship program options at his or her campus in terms of program requirements, the number of credits that might be earned, and a general range of the number and types of placement sites that are available. Additionally, the main learning goals that could be derived from undertaking an internship are introduced in the areas of knowledge acquisition, knowledge application, skills development, personal development, and professional development.

What Is an Internship?

An internship is a formal course undertaken in an academic program whereby the student is allowed to observe and participate in a variety of organizational operations under the guidance of a field supervisor and a faculty supervisor. During this time, the student completes a number of academic and intern site assignments that introduce the operations of the workplace and, when possible, show the integration of theory, concepts, and practice. At the same time, an internship should assist the student in making future career choices complementary to his or her abilities. In summary, and as stated by the National Association of Colleges and Employers (NACE), "An internship is a form of experiential learning that integrates knowledge and theory learned in the classroom with practical application and skills development in a professional setting" (p.1).

Why Intern?

You are probably considering an internship in a criminal justice or related field because you have determined that learning outside the classroom is an essential component of your education and, possibly, because it may be required for your degree. There is always some apprehension about leaving the safe environment of your college or university to venture into the real world.

Why should you consider an internship? What are the academic, personal, and professional advantages to an internship? What type of internship would be best for you? How can you be sure of selecting a good field site? How can an internship help you clarify your career goals? These are just some of the questions you may be asking and they are addressed in this chapter.

One result of a good internship experience is that you will develop self-directed or experiential learning in an organizational setting. This is part of the college experience whereby learning occurs outside the classroom environment in many ways including volunteering, participation in student and community organizations, study tours, research with faculty members, work-study, and independent study assignments. An internship will also increase your knowledge and enhance your understanding of the complexities of the criminal justice system and its component parts. You may find that you better understand and appreciate what you have learned in the classroom once you have applied your knowledge in a professional setting.

Many students are often uncertain about working in the criminal justice field or about what area of the field best suits their personal and professional goals. An internship experience will help to self-evaluate how you may fit into the field after graduation.

If you do decide on a criminal justice career, the internship experience will prove invaluable. In addition to gaining work experience, which is always a positive résumé item for future employment, you will develop social networks with practitioners who can help you set your future career goals, and possibly assist you in procuring future employment. They may help to identify job openings, write letters of recommendation for you, or possibly call their colleagues to recommend you. The internship may even lead to employment at the internship site if there is an available opening and you are an outstanding worker.

Background of Internships

The development of internships can be traced to the Middle Ages, when the teaching of skills and competencies for most professions and trades was accomplished by a young person serving an apprenticeship with a skilled mentor. The first professional field to adopt this model was in the medical sciences, as future doctors and nurses learned their skills under senior instructors. As discussed by Perlin (2012), this concept continues today in diverse academic areas such as law, journalism, social services, public administration, and education. In fact, some states require some kind of field training before the student may be granted a license or certificate to practice in certain professions.

How does this apply to criminal justice? From the disciplinary perspective, criminal justice is a general term that denotes interdisciplinary scholarly teaching and research in the behavioral and social sciences (including law and public administration), focusing on the social problems of crime (Myren, 1982). It is hypothesized that during the early years of the discipline, the idea for a field experience component in many college programs may have been passed along by faculty in fields in which such a tradition already existed. The real boost for internships in criminal justice occurred in 1968 when the Law Enforcement Assistance Administration (LEAA) provided stipends for full-time students to serve in an agency for 8 weeks or more. The goals of the program were to give students direct hands-on experience as part of their course of study, and providing training for future professionals and additional personnel on a limited basis to agencies. Although this program was phased out in 1980, along with the entire LEAA apparatus, the internship component remains very strong in most programs. Studies of criminal justice academic programs throughout the United States find that the majority have some form of internship offering, varying from 3 credit hours on a part-time basis to 15 credit hours for a full semester (Stichman & Farkas, 2005). Internships today are considered to be part of elective opportunities for upper-level students as presented in certification standards by the Academy of Criminal Justice Sciences (2005). Many organizations actively recruit interns for formal semester or summer programs. Examples include the major federal law enforcement agencies, various state police and criminal justice-related agencies, a wide range of county and local agencies dealing with law enforcement, courts, corrections, public administration, probation and parole, homeland security, private security services, and corporations dealing with fraud and cybersecurity issues. For this text, this wide range of public- and private-sector organizations will come under the academic rubric of "criminal justice."

Your career services office will have reference books as well as links to a number of web sites that post internship possibilities, including www.findinternships.com and www.cei-internship.squarespace.com. Directories and web sites have to be approached with caution, as they generally provide information only on major companies and private-sector agencies. Nevertheless, they all offer the student great leads and ideas in seeking placement in a particular field or location. Most internship coordinators would advise you to review a wide number of organizations before deciding on a particular internship site.

The term "internship" is used throughout this text, but the field experience program at your college may appear under a different title, such as "fieldwork," "practicum," or "cooperative education." These terms are often used interchangeably to denote either full- or part-time work experience in which the student is assigned definite tasks and responsibilities. Most internship programs are credit-bearing and directly relate to your program curriculum. The completion of an internship usually earns a student college credits, the number of which generally depends on the length of time in the field. The standard 40 hours of fieldwork equates to 1 credit hour. During this time, the student is required to complete various academic assignments as well as the assigned tasks at the field site. Some agencies provide a monetary stipend for students, but most programs are unpaid, especially those in the public sector.

Cooperative education programs are not the same as internships. Often termed "work experience education" or simply "co-op," the student in a cooperative education program works in the field for a designated period of time, as part of the regular degree requirements. Usually, this work is done in addition to credit-bearing coursework and, as a member of the organization, the student receives a salary or stipend.

Today internships are an integral part of many academic programs in the United States. According to State University of New York (SUNY) Chancellor Nancy Zimpher, student internships are often recalled as the most valuable experience of students' education. "Students are more engaged with the curriculum, likely to graduate on time, and they acquire the hands-on experience that ensures them a competitive edge in today's job market" (Bump, 2016, Para 3). The SUNY system, as well as other major academic institutions, has encouraged all students to take an internship during their course of study by creating articulations and data bases with business and not-for-profit organizations.

Discussing the role of higher education in today's job market, Selingo (2016) in *There Is Life After College* writes that internships taken during the college experience have become a de facto requirement in many industries particularly in finance, technology, and scientific services. This trend has impacted hiring trends for many graduates in that employers not only want to see completion of the degree but some evidence that the candidate has actually some experience and has applied skills in the workplace (p.16).

Educational Goals

According to standards determined by the Academy of Criminal Justice Sciences (2005), the formal education goals for most criminal justice programs center on the following:

- Gaining information on criminal justice theory and practice through various courses such as justice administration, criminal procedure, investigative practices, juvenile justice, criminal behavior, correctional alternatives, cybersecurity, and global crime.
- Increasing competency in oral and written communication.
- Developing skills in research methods and application of quantitative methods to field problems.
- Increasing the ability to critically think and apply information to problems.
- Helping to understand how ethical issues relate to criminal justice operations and policy.
- Learning specific skills in such areas as forensics, investigations, counseling, cyber analysis, and computer applications.

In reviewing the descriptions of various intern programs, the following are generally cited as educational goals: knowledge acquisition, knowledge application, skills development, personal development, and professional development.

Knowledge Acquisition

At this time, a good portion of your academic learning probably involves sitting in a classroom or logging into an online platform, undertaking readings from books and articles, taking notes from a lecture, or discussing issues in a seminar or discussion forum. Much of what you learn depends on the nature of the course, the instructor, specific assign-ments and discussion threads, readings, and, at times, other students in the class. Of course, what you get out of the traditional classroom or online environment also depends on your efforts regarding preparation and involvement.

In an internship program, self-direction is essential to a valuable learning experience. According to Segroi and Ryniker (2002, p. 188), internships are a form of experiential learning whereby ". . . the student takes significant responsibility in the learning process." While many students are apprehensive about this approach to learning because it is not the usual way, for many, the knowledge acquired through an internship is most satisfying. "For the first time, I really know how to conduct an investigation and put a case together," remarked one student. Another stated, "I learned a great deal about probation and the way an agency operates. It was more than I could ever gain from a textbook." Most students who intern find that they gain a great deal of firsthand knowledge about the criminal justice system that cannot be learned in the classroom environment. The day-to-day interaction with staff, clients, and the community at large provides a rich educational experience.

Knowledge Application

Although closely related to acquiring knowledge, knowledge application refers to applying theories learned in the classroom to actual practice. Your formal coursework in criminal justice is based on a theoretical framework, a conception, or a model of how the system or a specific agency operates. Through textbook and classroom studies you have learned and discussed such concepts as authority, discretion, deterrence, public policy, routine activi-ties, socialization, and social control. During an internship, you will see certain theories in practice, while others will never become apparent. As Ross and Elechi (2002) write, "The internship experience brings forth the practical realities of criminal justice operations in comparison to what is presented in the curricula." Students often write about the applica-tion of theory and how certain concepts may or may not apply to a specific social setting. An internship is usually the first time you are afforded the opportunity to test various theories in a field setting.

Skills Development

While a college education assists in the development of job-related skills, an internship provides an excellent arena for further acquiring and developing such skills. Seeing the immediate application in job-related tasks, many students even improve their academic skills through internships, especially in the areas of written communication. Because report writing is an important part of what professionals are required to do in many agen-cies, many students realize that good writing skills are a necessity and that the coursework taken in a program has much relevance. As one former intern recently wrote, "One thing that I did take away was the importance for good report writing. This is especially important because the majority of the cybercrime case I worked had a strong probability of eventually leading to legal prosecution."

Another area of improvement is oral and interpersonal communication. Many students can acquire good listening and interviewing skills by dealing with clients. Some placement sites require intern candidates to have research and computer skills that may be applied to a project for the improvement of the organization. These skills are then further developed during the internship.

Personal Development

At your field site you will often be in situations that force you to clarify your values and develop the confidence and self-reliance necessary to solve problems. Working in a criminal justice organization will bring you into contact with people who think, believe, and act differently than you do. Their conception of what is right and just may differ dramatically from yours. In this context, you may feel the need to defend, justify, and reappraise your values and reject those of others. Because we believe the issue of ethics as related to internships is so important, an entire chapter of this book is devoted to it (see Chapter 8).

Very often, students express some concern about how they will cope in their internships. Many lack self-confidence about meeting new people and entering into new situations. Their questions tend to center around, "What will I do if presented with this situation?" Worries or self-doubts of this nature are natural. In fact, academic supervisors become concerned if a student feels that he or she can handle everything and anything that could happen in the organization. One of our students had concerns about being able to handle himself in situations involving death. Another, concerned about controlling his temper, presented the question, "What will I do if some guy calls me a so-and-so when I am with an officer?" Another student, assigned to a law office, expressed doubts about whether her writing and research abilities would be acceptable, as there would be law school interns in the same office. The author is aware that situations of this nature can be stressful, but they serve to contribute to the development of your confidence and self-reliance. For many students, working in a criminal justice organization is their first "professional" job. Thus, certain personal goals include time-management (getting to the site on time and meeting deadlines) and adapting to various rules and regulations such as dress, computer access and use, parking, and dealing with confidential information.

Professional Development

Your internship should help you evaluate your interest in pursuing a career in criminal justice or related field. This is preceded by a difficult question, "Why are you studying criminal justice or a related area such as financial crime investigation, emergency management, homeland security, forensics, or cybersecurity?" Many students enroll in these programs because they have a notion about careers or postgraduate work related to the field. Most students realize that they will have to spend time in an entry-level position before moving upward in an organization. Therefore, many view the internship as an opportunity to see if they really wish to enter the field and to gain experience at the entry level. Most students complete their experience satisfied with their career goals; others find that the area they chose does not suit them. One striking example involves a student who was interested in criminal law as a career. After one semester in a law office, he changed his mind.

Another student in major sheriff's department wrote, "I was unsure what I wanted to do after graduation. To see various aspects of the system and department allowed me to gain a better focus and grasp on what I want to do for a career."

Many students see the internship as a vehicle for job placement. There are cases in which students obtained a job with their organization either during or immediately following their internship. In these cases, there was an opening, the student enjoyed the work, and the placement site agency wanted to hire the student. In some cases, the students were granted probationary status for civil service purposes. To be candid, this only occurs in a small number of placements. While the internship experience may or may not lead to immediate employment with the host field site, it provides valuable experience as well as insight into how one goes about procuring employment in a specific field of criminal justice. Additionally, you can begin career networking by developing important references and contacts.

Many organizations would like to hire successful interns but are unable to at the immediate time of the placement conclusions because of budget considerations and civil service requirements. While this may be frustrating, students should never treat the internship experience as merely a temporary obstacle to be overcome on the way to graduation. Students who are not successful in their internship can be negatively affected when it comes to future recommendations or pre-employment background checks. Academic and field supervisors may have to respond, "I do not recommend" or "No comment" for interns who displayed unethical behavior or exhibited serious personal and/or professional problems during the internship. Therefore, you must bear in mind that the internship can have a direct effect on your future employment and educational opportunities. From the beginning of your internship, you must perform with professionalism and an eye to the future.

About This Book

This book is divided into four parts: Pre-Internship Considerations, Professional Concerns, The Role of the Organization, and Assessment and Career Planning. In Part I, Chapter 2, "Preparing for Your Internship in the Age of Transparency," has been added to address the increased use of blogs and the popularity of social networks and online video web sites. You are encouraged to review this before you begin your internship search, as your participation in these technologies may affect the process.

Chapter 3, "The Placement Process," discusses how to obtain a criminal justice internship placement. Although the process varies from school to school, there are some common concerns faced by all students. The internship should be looked at as a dry run for postgraduate employment so information is included on résumé writing, telephone and e-mail etiquette, background investigations, and how to conduct yourself in an interview. The chapter also presents several resources for finding an appropriate site, including your college's career services office and various Internet sites.

Part II: Professional Concerns discusses some major issues that can arise during an internship. Chapter 4, "Setting Goals and Identifying Educational Objectives," focuses on setting your learning goals before beginning your internship. You may be asked to set goals in the following areas: knowledge acquisition, performance assessment, personal development, and professional development. Although your goals may change during your internship, they provide a foundation for your performance and understanding of issues at the internship site.

The four stages of an internship experience are discussed in Chapter 5, "Your Role as an Intern." Critical issues presented include role conflict, social isolation, and interpersonal relations. Chapter 6, "Being a Participant-Observer," provides a methodology for recording your experience. Supervision during an internship is dealt with in Chapter 7, "Intern Supervision." The supervisory process, which involves both academic and field supervisors as well as peers, is an important facet of the learning process. Chapter 8, "Ethics in Practice: Guidelines," is an important chapter because many interns are confronted with real-life ethical and moral dilemmas. In light of major scandals in business and criminal justice, it is important that you begin to identify and distinguish between personal ethics and emerging professional ethics.

Part III is about the role of your internship site. Chapter 9, "Organizational Characteristics: Formal and Informal Structures," reviews the basic tenets of organizational structure. Your success in the internship may depend on how well you adapt to the formal and informal structures of your agency. Two agency case studies, the Flanders County District Attorney's Office and the Northwest Frontier Bank Corporation, are used to illustrate these concepts. Recent trends in organizational dynamics, such as total quality management, reengineering, and ethical issues, are also presented.

Chapter 10, "Political, Economic, and Legal Factors," discusses the ways in which the day-to-day operations and personnel are affected by those factors. The effect of trends in globalization and the aftermath of the September 11, 2001, terrorist attacks on criminal justice, fraud management, and corporate security units are examined. Also covered is the role of public policy and its impact on organizational decision making. In Chapter 11, "Organizational Goals and Relationships," discusses organizational effectiveness and its relationship to the overall criminal justice system, including the system of checks and balances. In Chapter 12, "Using Information and Technology as Crime-Fighting Tools," we discuss how the use of technology in the prevention, detection, investigation, and prosecution of crime continues to change. Progressive public agencies and organizations in the private sector use technology to assist in the day-to-day operations of fighting crime. As a result, interns are exposed to more technology and are able to apply the skills they have learned in the classroom to the tasks at their site.

In Part IV: Assessment and Career Planning, Chapter 13, "Assessing Your Experience," will aid you in evaluating your progress, as well as your total internship experience. It is divided into two parts: assessing your performance and assessing the organization. Factors to consider in seeking post-graduation employment are discussed in Chapter 14, "Career Planning."

Highlights for the Ninth Edition

Criminal Justice Internships: Theory into Practice continues to be a widely used text for internship courses offered in associate and baccalaureate degree programs, and as a benchmark reference book for curriculum planning and review. The following updates have been made to reflect current policies, practices, and trends affecting all organizations in the criminal justice ecosystem.

Chapter 1 gives an updated overview of the nature and purposes of a criminal justice internship in the academic setting. Discussion includes the relationship of an internship with the overall academic goals of criminal justice programs and their importance for future career goals.

Chapter 2 presents more information on the impact of the Internet including the "Internet of things" and social media for internships. Further encouragements and cautions are given here, as potential employers often look at social media sites for intern placements and employment.

Chapter 3, on the placement process, updates the steps for résumé development and intern placement. It also discusses the current issue of pay and related lawsuits that have arisen over nonpaid internships. Recent court rulings are also presented to determine whether an internship placement should be paid.

Chapter 4 updates the process for setting goals and objectives for an internship experience based on general education objectives for most criminal justice programs. Attention is also given to the applications of theory and various criminal justice concepts as a part of knowledge acquisition.

Chapter 5, on the role of the intern, reviews the main steps to becoming a participant-observer.

Chapter 6 presents further discussion of the participant observation and ideas on conducting structured and unstructured interviews.

Chapter 7, on supervision, updates the role of the student, faculty supervisor, and internship field supervisor. More attention is given to when things go wrong and what to do.

Chapter 8 reviews the ethical issues that students face and greater attention is paid to the need for confidentiality and maintaining appropriate interpersonal relationships. The author includes a short list on how students can get into trouble during their internship.

Chapter 9 updates the trends that continue to occur in the post-recession economy. New types of organizational structures are presented as well as some dysfunctions that occur in organizational settings.

Chapter 10 outlines current political, economic, and legal trends that impact criminal justice agencies including those agencies that provide compliance for federal and state laws.

Chapter 12 updates the role of technology in criminal justice agencies for crime detection, investigation, and prevention. Further discussion focuses on the expansion of cyber-related offenses that agencies must deal with.

Chapter 13 gives updated examples of assessment issues that students should review before and after their placements including dealing with clients and customers.

Chapter 14 gives general guidance on career planning and how the internship experience can be used to guide postgraduate career planning. Updated Department of Labor hiring and compensation regulations and trends are presented as well as the author's observations on successful careers.

This book, which is based on the author's experiences as an intern coordinator and supervisor, is designed to maximize your internship experience—an essential component of any criminal justice degree program. I wish you well in your endeavors and trust that this book will be a valuable resource for you before, during, and after your internship.

Conclusion

This chapter presents the background to criminal justice internship programs and the important reasons why a student should consider interning. Having completed this chapter, you should be able to:

1. Apply the definition of internship to the course or program that exists at your institution.
2. Review with your academic advisor the internship program at your campus in terms of program requirements, the number of credits that might be earned, and the numbers and types of agency sites that are available. Is the program offered during the regular semester or just during the summer session? What academic requirements in terms of credits earned, required classes, and grade point average must be completed for internship program candidacy?
3. Make a list for yourself of three benefits of undertaking an internship.

4. Ask yourself the following: What job experiences do I have? What actual skills do I have that can be applied in a professional work setting? Do I really wish to work in criminal justice or a related field? What are the names of three people who can appraise my performance related to professional skills? What have I done thus far in terms of being active in clubs or professional associations for networking purposes?

2

Preparing for Your Internship in the Age of Transparency

As predicted by Schmidt and Cohen (2013), communication technologies continue to expand, especially through the global reach of the Internet. By 2025 most of the world will have access to a wide span of information, especially through mobile handheld devices. It is reported that those ages 18 to 30 outpace older Americans in virtually all types of Internet and smartphone use. For this discussion a smartphone is a mobile phone that has a number of services including Internet, texting, and various applications. They are more likely to have their own social networking profiles, to connect to the Internet wirelessly when away from home and work, and to post video and pictures of themselves online.

The purpose of this chapter is to encourage students to use digital tools to meet professional needs, but cautions about the potential pitfalls if such tools are not used in a professional manner. Upon reading this chapter, the reader should be able to discuss at least one advantage and disadvantage of reading and writing blogs, taking part in social networking web sites, uploading videos to YouTube and related sites, and posting a résumé online.

First Phase of the Digital Age

When the first edition of *Criminal Justice Internships* was published in 1984, the Internet was unknown to the general public. The World Wide Web was first introduced in February 1991 by computer programmer and inventor Tim Berners-Lee (World Wide Web Foundation). Since that time, the amount of readily available information has grown exponentially, as has the technology with which to access it. This chapter first appeared in the 2008 edition of this book, when the use of social media was focused more on interactions with friends. Since 2008, the use of social media has exploded and expanded to a wide range of professional, business, and social applications.

Participation in online social media (blogs, social networking sites, and free video-sharing web sites) has become the norm. The power of the social media continues to impact all aspects of society, including politics, business interactions with consumers, marketing and advertising, distribution of news and information, public protests, and social demonstrations. It has become a powerful communications tool, allowing for enhanced networking, job searching, and discussion of topics germane to specialized groups. Students are using social media to search for internships, communicate with peers during the experience, and find job opportunities.

So-called digital natives comprise the generation described as Millennials (ages 18–29), which includes most of the readers of this book. As a "digital native," you will take full advantage of the benefits of social media before, during, and after your internship. Unlike your parents, and many professors and field supervisors, who are called "digital immigrants," you have grown up in a digital world. There probably has not been a time in your memory when the Internet and its associated technologies did not exist. As a group, digital natives are comfortable with technology, tend to utilize current technologies in greater numbers, and are early adopters of new technologies. Your use of technologies differs significantly from other generational groups: Gen X (1965–1980), Boomer (1946–1964), and Silent (pre-1946).

As a digital native and member of the so-called Millennials generation, most of you will be able to leverage your knowledge and skills to search for internship opportunities, gather information on experiences of past interns in particular settings, develop a personal brand to share with prospective organizations that have intern opportunities, and network with alumni and professionals in the field. Blogs, social networking sites, and free video-sharing web sites have become a part of our culture and, as such, offer both advantages and disadvantages in our personal and professional lives.

Added to these developments is the "Internet of things." This term has come into play in recent years simply because various devices can now link into each other. The development of the Internet and smart phones and the wide use of credit cards is also bringing forth monitoring and operating technologies for homes, vehicles, watches, unmanned aerial vehicles, restaurants, taxis (Uber), appliances, and other devices. The information from these devices is often able to interconnect with each other and not be dependent on human input. This creates a massive amount of data that can be used for personal lifestyle improvement and management but also for hacking, identity theft, and misuse of demographic and personal data. This all has an impact on the creating of the individual brand (the student intern) discussed in this chapter.

Perhaps the biggest challenge you face, as you prepare for your internship and subsequent professional career, is achieving a balance between the benefits and detriments of creating a digital fingerprint.

Entering the Blogosphere: Encouragements

A blog is basically a site where self-published commentaries are presented by individuals, including journalists, who write in the current mainstream media. Whether you are an experienced blogger, a neophyte, one who has never participated in a blog, or something in between, you need to be aware of what blogging can do for you. An Internet search for benefits of blogging nets dozens of hits concerning blogging by small businesses, corporations, real estate agents, teachers, the media, tourism, home businesses, and the like. The web sites regarding benefits of general blogging universally cite communication and community, both of which lead to the sharing of ideas and networking. This is certainly evidenced by several organizations that provide blogs for student interns.

Blogs such as these are a good source of information for those considering an internship. A search for "student intern blogs" on Google turns up many blogs by individual students, as well as some that advertise internship opportunities. Such a search will expose you to many points of view and opportunities. As with any Internet search, it is important to evaluate the reliability and authority of the web sites that you access. That said, student intern blogs can provide you with some insights into what you may be about to experience.

A blog search can also provide you with internship opportunities, although you will have to spend a bit of time sifting through the results. Several organizations post their programs and provide information regarding the experience and the application process. One immediate issue to be aware of is that many blogs are several years old and not up-to-date.

Entering the Blogosphere: Cautions

Any blogging that you have done through college or while you were in high school may still be accessible to those who Google you. Going forward, you should think about what you write, especially from the viewpoint of a future employer. Employers are being encouraged to look for blogs written by potential employees, as a means of getting to know them better and how they conduct themselves, including a review of grammar and spelling. Thus, you should think about how you present yourself in your blog, just as you think about presenting yourself in your résumé, on phone calls, and during job interviews. Your blog is a part of your digital fingerprint, one that you should consider public.

Once you have an internship position, and looking to the future when you are employed, you must think carefully before you begin or add to a blog regarding your internship sites. Some interns have found that there are policies regarding employee and intern blogging. Corporate blogging policies are discussed in Chapter 8. Once you have been hired, you must be aware of and conform to such policies (or do not accept the internship). In all cases, you must not blog about confidential information or occurrences related to the internship site.

Social Networking: Encouragements

Social networking allows a person to link with others and to share information through postings, e-mails, pictures and videos. Social networking has also been adopted by many organizations as a means to present their mission and products, while dealing with misinformation that occurs after a major incident. Today, many organizations use social media as a means to attract the best students for employment and for internship programs. As a result, many are changing their recruiting practices to keep pace with our ever-evolving society. Searching Facebook, LinkedIn, and Govloop may provide you with internship opportunities, as well as connect you with others who have had an internship experience or are in the process of procuring one. Twitter, Yik Yak, and others provide another opportunity to network digitally. While it was initially used for day-to-day communications with friends and colleagues, it has evolved into a collaboration tool to draw individuals to a site to share information, ask questions or seek advice from others, share breaking news, and draw attention to events. Social media websites continue to grow based on communities of interest. At this time, it is estimated that there are more than 200 media sites spanning a wide range of interests.

Social Networking: Cautions

In terms of internships and employment, there seem to be more cautions than encouragements about using social networking web sites. While many criminal justice programs give the "clean up your act" advisory during first-year or transfer orientation, many students have sites with inappropriate and, at times, criminal behavior. For example, the Internet abounds with a number of "party school" sites that show students in various situations. Although no names are presented, the address of the sites often give a clue as to the person responsible for the submission. In one case known to the author, police investigators were able to successfully investigate a sexual abuse case that originated on such a party site.

Schawbel (2012) reported that data collected by Jobvite indicated that 92 percent of employers used social media for recruiting and another 73 percent checked applicant profiles. He reported that many employers were not focused on party behavior but more concerned about grammar and spelling and general presentation. Interestingly enough, some employers were suspicious if the applicant did not have a social profile as ". . . you won't seem relevant and companies might think that you're hiding something." Some states have enacted legislation that forbids review of social media sites for employment consideration. The reality, however, is that you need to think about how it could affect your future.

The main caution that can be offered here is to remember that it is much easier to post something on your Facebook, Twitter, MySpace, Instagram and other pages than it is to remove it from the many places it may subsequently be posted. Just as you must be wary of what you write in a blog, you must be aware of the pictures and information that you post on a social networking site. Even if you limit access to a handful of people, the potential for your personal information to be widely circulated cannot be understated. Because Twitter tends to be more public and because of its viral nature, you must think twice before sending a negative tweet. These tweets can be an embarrassment to you and your agency.

Online Videos: Encouragements

A search for "internships in criminal justice" on YouTube will find videos concerning internship opportunities in the criminal justice field, particularly from colleges and universities. Increasingly, criminal justice agencies post videos that tout their internship programs, including testimonials from interns. These can be a valuable resource not only in finding an internship site, but also in learning about the internship experience in general. You can also find videos about the employment process, such as writing a résumé and preparing for an interview.

Online Videos: Cautions

Anyone who has a camera cell phone or digital camera can take a video that can be posted on the free video-sharing web sites, tweeted, or sent by text message. You may not even be aware of being filmed and may only find out when someone you know sees you in an online video. Again, you should be careful about what you and/or your friends post. "In the information age, life has no chapters or closets; you can leave nothing behind and you have nowhere to hide your skeletons. Your past is your present, and it catches up with you like a truck backing over what it left behind" (Seidman, 2007, p. 38). In like manner, many organizations have policies regarding the posting of materials with department logs without prior approval. The posting of information by employees, including interns, has become a developing human resource administration issue. Interns in high-security clearance situations may expect prohibitions against posting anything related to the organization and there may be prohibitions against participating in social networking.

What If?

The logical question that comes to mind after reading the cautions concerning the use of digital media is: "What if I've already done that?" Everyone makes mistakes, and many of those occur during the high school and college years. Mistakes that your parents may have made are not likely to be public, unless they want them to be, or unless they are running for political office and are under unusual scrutiny. In the age of transparency, mistakes may be as close to the surface as a Google search. How can you diffuse or minimize their impact on your future?

Just as transparency makes those mistakes obvious and public, it can help you to mitigate them. First, whether or not you think that there may be something about you circulating in cyberspace, perform a Google search on yourself. Check the cached files and if you need to, go to www.archive.org, which catalogs web pages from 1996 forward. Knowing what someone else might find out about you is essential. Second, be honest. If you posted something foolish on YouTube that has circulated throughout the Web and that you feel your internship coordinator and/or a prospective employer should learn about from you, tell him or her. You can do that without going into detail. It is enough to inform them that you were indiscreet in your younger years, that you were caught up in a moment, and/or that you and your friends were having a good time without knowing about the future consequences. If, however, your blogging, Facebook, or YouTube indiscretion is not widely available, rather than bringing it to anyone's attention, it is enough that you know about it, so that if and when you are asked, you can explain and apologize.

Posting a Résumé Online

There are many web sites on which you can post a résumé. The obvious advantage of an online résumé is that it will reach a large number of employers and recruiters in a short period of time. It eliminates the need for mailing your résumé or for writing a cover letter. Certainly, circulating your résumé over the Internet is an easy way for you to gain some exposure.

However, there is a very real danger of exposing yourself too much. Your personal information can fall into the wrong hands or be included in an information breach. You are putting yourself at risk for identity theft if you include too much information in an online résumé. You should never include your Social Security number. You should avoid listing your date of birth or any information that can lead someone to your age, such as the year in which you graduated from high school or college. You should not include your home address but city, state, and zip code would be appropriate. It is best to use an e-mail address that you have created solely for your job search.

Online video résumé services provide a unique way to present yourself, but their usefulness is debatable. Employers are not sure of their legal ramifications, such as the possibility of lawsuits alleging discrimination based on personal appearance. Job searchers are warned against making a video that does not present them in the best light. Not everyone is cut out for the video camera; body language, slang, stuttering or stammering, and the like can elicit a negative response from a potential employer. Many, if not most, employers do not have, or want to take, the time involved in watching video résumés. While the age of transparency and its attendant technologies provide you with many opportunities that those before you did not have, you need to make prudent decisions about using them.

■ ■ ■ ────────────────────────────────────

Preparing for Your Internship

1. Google yourself. Spend some time looking through the pages, especially if you have a common name. Do this on a regular basis.
2. Think about your Facebook, LinkedIn, Twitter, or other social media pages. Now is the time to update them, so that you are represented as a mature, responsible adult who is about to embark on the first step to professional employment.

3. Be aware of friends with digital cameras or cell phones at times when you may find yourself in an unguarded moment. Talk to your friends and acquaintances about the repercussions of appearing in unauthorized Web postings.
4. Spend some time searching for internship blogs, recruiting videos, and other online information that will familiarize you with internships in general and may make you more comfortable as you begin the placement process.
5. If you do not have a LinkedIn account, consider creating one. Talk to your friends and professors about how you might utilize them to contact alumni or professionals in the field about internship and job opportunities.

3

The Placement Process

The main steps in achieving an internship are selecting the field site, knowing the academic requirements for internships at your campus program, and successfully completing the placement process based on your academic and career goals. There are several factors for both the student and agency to consider in the placement process. Choosing and finding an appropriate internship, writing a résumé, undertaking the internship interview, and going through background screening and selection are crucial to this selection process. It is the responsibility of the criminal justice faculty and the internship coordinator to approve only those organizations that have high standards of professional performance and that are willing to work to provide a worthwhile and educational experience. In turn, the student is responsible for presenting him- or herself in the best light: from a complete, professional résumé and cover letter to professional appearance and performance during the internship interview.

At the end of reading this chapter, you should be able to identify the main parts of a résumé and then prepare a résumé for review by the internship coordinator. Additionally you should be able to list five main areas that are important for a pre-placement interview and at least five questions that may be asked of you at the interview. In this chapter, current issues involving internships are presented, in particular with regard to recent standards promulgated by the federal courts for paid placements.

Choosing an Appropriate Site

If your college program is one that allows you to select from a variety of field placements on a statewide or regional basis, perhaps the most important thing you will have to do is to plan ahead. Previously it was advised that you should review the program and possible placements with the internship coordinator or your faculty advisor in the semester prior to the one in which you plan to do your internship. In retrospect you should probably start this discussion at least two semesters before your internship; the reason being that some placements are very competitive and may require background checks that take a great amount of time. You should be informed about the overall program including the placement process, deadlines regarding submission of application materials, and the school's academic requirements regarding prerequisites for interns. This often requires the completion of core courses related to the major and a minimum grade point average. Certain programs require students to complete a pre-internship seminar course or series of meetings prior to beginning the internship.

Some programs allow interns to set up their own placement sites. In many programs, students work with an advisor to select appropriate placements. Other colleges are stricter, in that the coordinator handles all communications concerning the student and the agency; students are assigned to field sites based on faculty review and field site availability. A major issue for most students is the number of college credits that may be completed and the amount of time that is expected in the field. The normal requirement is one credit hour equates to 40 hours of field work. Again, you must be aware of your program's policies regarding student communication with potential internship organizations for placement purposes.

Once you have learned about the program, you will have to decide which set of organizations would be best for you. You may be interested in applying for acceptance in a formalized, competitive internship program, such as those offered by private-sector companies, legal aid societies, university law clinics, and federal law enforcement agencies. Such programs have rigid application procedures and deadlines. Often, the deadline for filing the application may be a year before the scheduled placement in order for background investigation procedures to be completed. It is a good idea to explore several alternatives. Just as you applied to more than one college, and will probably apply for more than one full-time job once you graduate, you should consider several possible internship sites. As you grapple with what type of internship to choose, you should consider the following factors.

Post-Graduation Career Goals

For example, if you wish to become a probation officer after graduation, you should consider a probation agency as a field site. Students considering law school might want to intern with the office of a district attorney, public defender, or private law firm. A student having an interest in cybersecurity may wish to review internship possibilities in both the private and public sectors. Ideally, your internship should provide experience that is applicable to future career goals, as consideration of employment opportunities are an important outcome.

Monetary Resources

Many interns desire out-of-state or overseas placements if the school provides such opportunities. However, additional financing may be required, especially if the placement site is not able to offer a stipend. Additional costs associated with the internship include housing, transportation/parking, wardrobe, meals, and so on. Realistically reflect on the costs associated with a distant internship to determine if your resources permit such a placement. In recent years, many students have opted to live at home to reduce internship-related costs. The issue of paid versus nonpaid internships is discussed further later in this chapter.

Geographic Location

Issues that arise include whether you will be living at home, on campus, or elsewhere. Consider the amount of travel involved; scheduling and transportation must be part of your plan. If you are considering a foreign internship, you will have to educate yourself or work with the campus office of overseas programs regarding visa requirements and applying for a passport. You will also need to consider opening an account with an international bank to transfer funds so they are available to you in the overseas location. Such internships require more advance planning than many domestic ones.

Sometimes, these considerations are dictated by the requirements of the program. In some programs, students participate at in-class seminars during the internship course, which obviously requires them to be in commuting distance to campus. Other programs use online communication for seminars and presentations; therefore the distance away from campus is not a factor.

Virtual/Long Distance Programs

Many programs and internship organizations will allow students to "commute" to work via the Internet. The host organization may be miles or even overseas from the student's location. You will have to check with your program coordinator to see if this is possible and address issues such as contact hours, supervision, and the nature of the projects and duties you will be performing. While this is a very common trend in many business organizations, particularly in the cyber arena, the author advises that most students benefit more from being at an on-site location dealing with people and the organizational environment. Nevertheless, there have been hybrid programs where the intern spent time at the organization's ground site and then worked remotely at another location. The success of these arrangements depends on the type of work being performed, the discipline and skills of the student, and the need for supervision and communication between the student and the field supervisor.

Finding the Site That's Right for You

When you have decided what type of internship you are interested in and where you would ideally like it to be located, your first step in finding an internship site should be to discuss it with the faculty or staff member who is in charge of the internship program for your department or program. That individual will usually have a list of organizations that have previously had interns from your institution. If such a list is available, you should review it carefully. The internship coordinator may also have information on organizations that have expressed an interest in taking interns from your program. Most experienced intern coordinators will always have potential placement sites through past placement records and their networks in state and national professional associations.

The student grapevine or informal information network is another source that you should explore. Discussions with peers who have recently interned often provide information as to the best placement sites, the strengths and weaknesses of certain agencies, and so on. This is encouraged as it gives you a peer review of the intern program.

You might be able to gather information from your college's career services office. Often, this office will have a list of possible internship sites and contact information from all the internship programs on campus. The career services personnel may know of criminal justice internships other than the usual criminal justice organization. For example, an insurance agency that sponsors interns from the business school may need an intern with skills and interest in the computer security area. You may also find references and web sites from your campus career services office with lists of internship placements. At this time there are a number of sites that provide this kind of information for all types of internship placements. You should review a number of sites as it provides a general indication of placement opportunities. Organizations such as The Washington Center (www.twc.edu) enter into agreements with various colleges and universities and provide many internship opportunities with federal agencies in Washington, DC. In this program, students are required to complete fieldwork and attend various seminar programs. Credit hours, however, are awarded by the student's sponsoring college. There are also programs offered by colleges and universities that allow you to enroll and transfer credits earned from an internship back to your college and program of study. Your internship coordinator and academic advisor can advise you of any affiliations your institution may have.

Parents, relatives, and family friends remain a good source for internship leads. Many successful placements have started with a casual conversation at a family or sporting event. However, you cannot allow the relative or family friend to take the lead in the placement process. You need to be your own best advocate.

As discussed in the previous chapter, the Internet is a valuable tool for finding possible internship sites. Many potential internship sites and well-established internship programs maintain Internet sites that offer a wealth of information. Your internship coordinator or faculty advisor may have a list of such sites. Consulting a search engine, such as Google, on government internships will net several federal and state sites with links to many others. You can also visit the web sites of specific government agencies and then search further once you are in a site, using the word *internship*.

Writing a Résumé

In the process of selecting a field site, you may be required to complete an application and/or submit a résumé. This will be used, along with a cover letter and other appropriate materials, in requesting a placement with a particular agency or agencies. Many schools have developed model résumés for this purpose. We recommend preparing your own résumé because it gives you some experience in résumé writing, which you can use in job-seeking situations after graduation. Once you have sent your cover letter and résumé, you may need to contact the agency by telephone to clarify certain points pertaining to the program.

Résumé is a French word meaning "summary." The résumé that you send to an agency or company for placement purposes is a summary of your contact information, background, experience, and qualifications and skills. There are several formats used for writing a résumé; your college placement office may use one that differs from the one we use here. However, human resource managers and placement consultants agree in most instances about the type of information that should be included in a résumé. Figure 3.1 shows a sample résumé.

As presented by Lotyczewski (2011), résumés are designed to accomplish one goal: impress the reader enough to offer you an interview. Thus, a résumé has to be viewed as a marketing tool for your own professional image. A résumé generally has seven areas: Personal Contact Information, Objective or Summary of Qualifications, Educational Background, Work Experience and/or Other Experience, Extracurricular Activities, Interests and Hobbies, and References.

The top portion of the résumé should have your complete address and telephone number. It is also appropriate to include your LinkedIn address for professional networking. If you are living away from home while attending school, you should include your school address because this is where the agency will be apt to contact you. By this time, we assume that you have been warned about changing interesting e-mail addresses such as studone@ or princesslea@ to something more neutral. The same is true for inappropriate recordings (including any music) in your voicemail. As presented by McLeod (n.d.), e-addresses and voicemail recordings are just one of many factors in presenting your professional self.

As cited by Singer (2011), items that are not required on a résumé are age, national origin/citizenship, race, religion, sexual orientation, disabilities, health, marital status, appearance, number of children, type of residence, affiliations, arrest record, and service record. Because of civil action rulings by federal agencies and courts, inquiries in these areas are discriminatory; in other words, they have nothing to do with an initial review of qualifications for the internship, so it is not necessary to include them on your résumé. It is illegal to ask these questions at an interview. However, for law enforcement agencies, these items will often be requested for background investigation purposes for security reasons once a position is tendered.

MARY T. DOUGLAS

PROFESSIONAL OBJECTIVE
  A career in law enforcement and/or fraud investigation.

EDUCATIONAL BACKGROUND
  9/2016–present: Remsen College, Reid, VA
  Major: Bachelor of Science, Criminal Justice
  Degree expected: June 2018
  Related Course Work: Police organization and administration, constitutional issues, community
  policing, report writing and interviewing, computer science, research methods, financial crimes
  investigation, four semesters of Russian
  9/2014–6/2016: Mohawk Junior College, Reid, VA
  Major: Associate Degree of Applied Science, Criminal Justice
  Degree: May 14, 2016

COMPUTER SKILLS
  Microsoft Word, Microsoft Excel, SPSS

AFFILIATIONS
National Society of Leadership and Success   10/2016–present
Association of Certified Fraud Examiners   9/2016–present

AWARDS
College Award for Community Service   2/2017

CRIMINAL JUSTICE EXPERIENCE
  2/2015–6/2016: Security Guard, Sangertown Mall, Reid, VA
  Duties included shoplifter apprehension, routine security checks, and employee and merchandise
  security. Participated in specialized training in suspect apprehension and customer safety.

EMPLOYMENT
  9/2014–2/2015: Part-time employee, PetSmart, Commercial Drive, Reid, VA
  Duties included customer assistance, inventory control, and cashier.
  7/2016–8/2016: Counselor, Black Diamond Summer Camp, Floyd, NY
  Supervised children and adolescents participating in week-long camping sessions.

EXTRACURRICULAR ACTIVITIES
  Criminal Justice Club, Remsen College, Treasurer
  Taught Constitutional Law course to high school students, October 2016
  Coordinator, Criminal Justice Fair, Remsen College, March 2017

REFERENCES AVAILABLE UPON REQUEST

BURRSTONE HOUSE, ROOM 123 • 10 BURRSTONE ROAD • REID, VA 12347
PHONE 315-555-9999 • FAX 315-555-9998 • E-MAIL: MTDOUGLAS@MAIL.COM

FIGURE 3.1 Sample Résumé.

Many career placement offices suggest listing personal qualities or skills related to the position. A quick list here would include skills in oral and written communication, teamwork, and technical proficiencies. If you are sending the résumé to a specific agency, an objective statement would be appropriate. The statement would have some reference to the agency and placement being sought as well as some mention of your specific skills. Here are a few examples:

- To obtain an internship with the (name of unit) where my coursework in criminal justice and investigation will assist in agency objectives.
- To become an intern with the fraud investigations unit where my college coursework related to fraud and economic crime investigation will be applied.

Because your career preparations at present revolve around obtaining an education, the next major portion of the résumé is education. In this area you should include your college, its address, your major or program of study, and your expected date of graduation. If you have attended more than one school during your baccalaureate studies, list them in reverse chronological order, as shown in Figure 3.1. Do not include your high school experience. Because your educational experience may be the only asset that you have in terms of a career in criminal justice, you may wish to elaborate in this area by listing skills you have or courses you have completed that are relevant to the field site. For example, you might want to list certain skills in computer programming, foreign languages, and so on. You also may want to list specific, applicable coursework or educational seminars. Do not list every course you have completed. It is appropriate to list your grade point average if it is above 3.00. If the agency is interested in you, you may be required to provide a college transcript.

Work experience should appear next. Because the résumé is being used for placement in a criminal justice or related organization, it may be useful to create a separate category titled **Criminal Justice/Related Experience**, as shown in Figure 3.1. Many intern candidates have experience directly related to the field of criminal justice—as security guards, police officers at summer resorts, informational technology assistants, or counselors at camps for problem children, for example. If you do not have any related work experience, omit this section and use a section titled Employment Experience. As you can see in the sample résumé, starting and ending dates are presented in reverse chronological order by month and year. Next appear the job title, the place and address of employment, and a brief description of duties.

During the course of their academic career, many students may have joined the student sections of various professional organizations. This is a very important step, as it places the student in contact with members of the profession and the organization's newsletters and training sessions. Organizations that have student memberships include the Association of Certified Fraud Examiners, American Society of Industrial Security International, and many national and state criminal justice associations.

Students sometimes have a tendency to exaggerate the duties they performed. One student who worked as a groundskeeper at a college gave himself the title of "plant control engineer." Another, who had experience as a security guard at a football stadium, termed herself a "security consultant." An extreme example is the student who described his duties as a gas station attendant as: "Supervised the flow of gasoline products from the station to the customer." Be truthful and avoid exaggerated or lofty descriptions.

Extracurricular activities can include all kinds of student activities, such as participation in athletics, professional associations, student groups, and community associations. You should include any leadership positions you have held, such as president or officer of the criminal justice club or student senate, coordinator for Law Day, captain of an athletic team, and so on. This will show that you are a person who gets involved and who may have administrative or leadership potential.

Interests or hobbies generally include activities that are important in your life. They need not appear on your résumé. Under the heading References, many résumés will have an attached sheet listing the names and addresses of persons who have agreed to act as personal references on behalf of the applicant. In all cases, you must contact and obtain permission from the individuals you will list or use as a reference. In most cases, an e-mail message or a verbal agreement by phone will suffice. Obviously, you should select those individuals who can reflect positively on your character or educational skills. Note that references will change over time as you progress in your career.

In Figure 3.2, there is a slightly different format. Here the student used a Qualifications Summary to describe her general competencies. She also listed Additional Seminars and Training to show experiences beyond normal classwork. In this format, the entire Work History is presented, which includes both criminal justice and other work experience.

The résumé formats shown here are appropriate for internship searches and for many initial job searches. For some occupations, there are specific styles highlighting different types of information. Your career services office will have a résumé bank that displays these formats and, no doubt, will sponsor workshops on writing a résumé and review sessions.

Regarding the preparation of a résumé, there are some basic considerations that must be stressed:

1. A résumé must be computer generated, well organized and laid out, and clearly presented, without misspelled words. Keep in mind that the widespread availability of laser printers means that many résumés today look professionally typeset. You want your submission to look better than the others that are being reviewed.

2. The résumé must be updated at crucial stages of your career: completion of a degree program, an award received a promotion, or participation in new activities. Make sure that all information contained in the résumé is accurate, as efforts are often made to verify information presented therein. For example, a student was excluded from consideration for an exceptional opportunity as a result of misrepresenting his academic qualifications on his résumé. The student, who was a candidate for a baccalaureate degree, claimed to have received an associate's degree when in

	30 State Street	Phone: 201-555-1234
	Rockville, NJ 77788	E-mail: cvincent@mail.com
Chris Vincent		
Qualifications Summary	Have worked on progressively challenging assignments throughout college in such areas as accounting, data analysis, network administration, and security. Skilled in several computer software packages. Fluent in Spanish.	
Education	Bandon College, Rockville, NJ Bachelor of Science anticipated: May 2017 Major: Criminal Justice—Economic Crime Investigation Program	
Specialized Coursework	Economic Crime Investigation, Information Security, Accounting (Introductory and Intermediate), Computer Science, Law of Economic Crime	
Computer Skills	Microsoft Excel, Microsoft Access, SPSS, Analyst Notebook-Link Analysis, Lexis.com	
Educational Seminars and Training	Computer Fraud in the Twenty-First Century, New York, NY, 2008 Organized Economic Crime, New York, NY, 2003 Tax Code Revisions, 2003, Parkersburg, NJ, 2007	
Employment	9/2016–present: Bandon College, Rockville, NJ *Network and Computer Lab Monitor* Duties include supervision of all student assistants in the computer lab, responsibility for network administration, student accounts, virus control, and security. 9/2015–8/2016: ACME Tax Preparations, 14 Columbia Drive, Rockville, NJ *Tax Preparation Assistant:* Assisted in the preparation of income tax returns. Interviewed clients, prepared computer entries, and reviewed tax codes for accounting staff. 5/2015–9/2015: Foremost Insurance Company, Parkersburg, NJ *Technology Assistant:* Entered computer data into company data bank and performed routine data inquiries for several departments. Assigned to data analysis based on supervisor recommendations.	
Honors and Affiliations	Bandon College Honors Program Economic Crime Investigation Club	

FIGURE 3.2 Sample Résumé.

actuality he had the number of requisite credits but had not fulfilled all of the requirements for the degree.

3. The length of the résumé will vary depending on your experience and the type of position for which you are applying. As you launch your career, it is unlikely that your résumé will exceed one page. Generally, a résumé should not exceed two pages.

4. Many new formats have interesting designs and make use of color printing. It is recommended that you keep your résumé printed with black ink on white paper, since designs with colors can become blurred during e-mail transmissions. As noted by Lotyczewski (personal communication, 2016), criminal justice organizations are relatively conservative in terms of reviewing new candidates for positions, so creativity is not an important factor.

Cover Letters

When sending your résumé to prospective internship sites, you should include a cover letter. A cover letter is simply your introduction and a review of your qualifications as they relate to the prospective placement. Depending on the placement policies of your program, the internship coordinator may send a standard cover letter with your résumé. However, if you are solely responsible for your field placement, you will have to prepare the letter. In all cases, the letter should be addressed to a specific person. The main guidelines are to be concise, address the letter to a specific person, make sure that the letter is free of grammatical and spelling errors, and, if the agency has had interns before, cite from what source you gained information about the internship opportunity. Cover letter samples are shown in Figures 3.3 and 3.4.

An interesting issue that arises is sending both the cover letter and the résumé by e-mail to a perspective internship organization. What should be included in the transmittal e-mail? There are many variations on this question, but what it comes down to is crafting a short message on why you are sending an e-mail and attaching both the cover letter and your résumé in the same PDF file. The message should state the purpose of your inquiry and a brief review of why you are interested in an internship with the organization. Do not use your entire cover letter as the body of the e-mail message.

The same advice is given for those organizations that use websites for human resource administration including internships. Very often for these websites, you log into the site to file a cover letter and a résumé. Using the portal saves an enormous amount of time, especially if the position requires review by a search committee and/or various layers of managers. One caveat to be aware of when using this medium: make sure that your cover letter reflects the organization to which you are applying. The author participated in a search committee for professor of government and discovered several cover letters addressed to other colleges.

Mary T. Douglas
Burrstone House, Room 123
10 Burrstone Road
Reid, Virginia 12367

October 17, 2017

Mr. Stanley Mason
Chief of Police
Livingston Police Department
25 Dearborn Street
Livingston, MD 24033

Dear Chief Mason:

I am a senior at Remsen College majoring in Criminal Justice and am presently seeking a site for an internship placement for the spring semester. The internship must last for fifteen full-time weeks, for which I will receive fifteen credits. Dr. Leslie Forman of our Criminal Justice Department informed me that you have accepted interns from Remsen College in previous semesters.

I am considering a career in law enforcement and am very interested in an internship with the Livingston Police Department. I have enclosed a résumé and a copy of the *Remsen College Internship Guidebook* for your review. As you will note on my résumé, I have experience in the area of retail security and have participated in a seminar on special tactics. My coursework emphasis is on law enforcement, including courses in computer science, forensics, report writing, and interviewing.

I can be reached by telephone at 315-555-9999 or e-mail at mtdouglas@mail.com. I look forward to hearing from you and will be available for an interview at your convenience. Thank you for your time and attention.

Sincerely,

Mary Douglas

Mary T. Douglas

FIGURE 3.3 Sample Cover Letter.

Follow-Up Calls and E-Mail

If you have not received any response to your application after 2 weeks, call or e-mail the individual to whom you sent it and, in a polite manner, introduce yourself and ask him or her about the status of your request. It is possible that the paperwork was misplaced or that the person was too busy at that time to answer it. In certain agencies, you may be one of several candidates for an internship. In that case, the review and selection process takes longer.

You may also need to call to gather further information. Before you make a telephone call, be sure that you have all the facts about your college or university's internship

Chris Vincent 30
State Street
Rockville, NJ 77788

November 1, 2017

Mr. Gary Rockledge
Prime Data Corporation
235 Beef Steak Lane
Omaha, NE 67566

Dear Mr. Rockledge:

I am a senior majoring in Criminal Justice–Economic Crime Investigation at Bandon College. I am required to complete a fifteen-week, full-time internship during the spring semester for which I will receive 12 credits as a requirement for graduation. I am most interested in fulfilling my internship requirement with your Fraud Management Department.

Enclosed please find my résumé, along with a description of the Bandon College Internship Program. As you can see, I have a substantial background in accounting, computer science, fraud investigations, and data analysis. I have demonstrated competence in the use of Microsoft Excel, Microsoft Access, SPSS, Analyst Notebook-Link Analysis, and LexisNexis. I feel that my abilities and interests are well matched with your organization, and I am eager for the opportunity to develop my skills further within the context of your Fraud Management Department.

I can be reached by telephone (201-555-1234) or e-mail (cvincent@mail.com). I look forward to the opportunity to meet with you and will be available to travel to Omaha at your convenience. Thank you for your willingness to consider me for an internship with your organization.

Very truly yours,

Chris Vincent

Chris Vincent

FIGURE 3.4 Sample Cover Letter.

program, so that you can answer any questions that may arise. The most common questions presented to students are the length and academic requirements of the program. In addition, you should have as much information as possible regarding your potential internship site. Be polite and precise when making the call. For example, you might say something to this effect:

Good morning. My name is Sheila Hogan. I'm a junior at Southwest State University, majoring in criminal justice. I recently sent my résumé to your office regarding a possible internship for next semester. I have a few questions. Is this a good time for you to discuss them with me?

Once you are able to discuss your concerns with the appropriate person, be sure to ask your questions from a prepared list so that you do not stumble through the conversation or forget a crucial point. As you can imagine, comments such as these are unacceptable: "Hey there. This is Chuck Camdiss. I got to do an internship for my school and I heard that you're the person to talk to. If I do one with you, what do I have to do?"

You also need to be aware of the nature and form of any greeting message you leave on voicemail. Abrupt, impolite, or slang-filled messages will not make a good impression on the agency or corporate personnel who are returning your call or trying to contact you.

If you are communicating with a potential internship site by e-mail, you need to treat each message as if it were a written letter going through the mail. You must proofread your message to be sure that there are no words omitted, your grammar is correct, you have used full sentences, and you have no misspellings. Phrases, abbreviations, and lower-casing used in instant messaging are unacceptable. If your e-mail address includes a nickname or slang, you should consider creating an e-mail account with a simpler, more professional address, such as your first initial and last name.

The Internship Interview

The résumé and cover letter are tools to get you through the front door. Once the organization has reviewed your application and résumé and decided to consider you for an internship position, someone will respond and schedule a time for an interview. An internship interview is very important, as it provides an opportunity for you to meet with supervisors in order to give a favorable presentation of yourself that goes beyond the brief and faceless introduction permitted by the résumé. The interview is the place to discuss the various facets of the proposed internship. At this time, issues and questions about both the organization and student responsibilities can be addressed. If the answers are not satisfactory, then you, the organization or both may reject the placement proposal. Be prepared for that possibility and have alternative sites in mind if your first choice does not result in placement. Many students have been not only sorely disappointed but have had their course of study interrupted by failing to prepare for a possible rejection. To avoid such problems, it is advisable to have two or three sites considered as possibilities.

In short, the internship interview should be treated in the same way as an employment interview. The following are some basic items that you should consider before the interview.

Be Prepared and Know Something About the Organization

Through discussions with your faculty advisor and other students, you should try to learn some basic information about the organization. Some things to think about are staff size, area of jurisdiction, and general functions. If possible, you should review current events related to the organization and the immediate area. A good source of information is the

Internet, as most organizations maintain web sites that present the organizational mission, vision, public information releases, and links to various departments and services.

Dress Appropriately

Before you leave for the interview, check your appearance, including the following: combed hair, clean fingernails, shined shoes, and so on. The basic recommendation is for men to wear a tie and jacket and for women to wear a dress or suit. It is advisable to check with the faculty advisor regarding appropriate dress if you have questions. For example, in some criminal justice agencies that work with youths, it is acceptable to wear jeans and a casual shirt or sweater, because the staff is actively engaged with youthful clients in sports, outdoor activities, and arts and crafts. Chewing gum or candy, wearing strong perfume or cologne, or wearing overly dressy or revealing clothing will project a negative image in an interview situation.

Appear Alone at the Interview

Although this may sound silly, there are instances where students brought friends, relatives, or parents to the interview. If someone does accompany you to the interview site, have them wait outside the agency premises.

Plan on Arriving Early

Vehicles break down, traffic gets tied up, trains are late, and unexpected things happen. Build in extra time, even if you have to end up killing time outside the organization because you have arrived early. Unless you are familiar with the potential internship location, obtain the address of where you are to go for the interview. The author had a scheduled lunch meeting at the Mohawk Club and found that the establishment did not serve lunch. The host had failed to include "Country Club" in the e-mail message. Present yourself to the receptionist, secretary, or department head at least five minutes before the appointed time.

Prepare to Answer and Present Relevant Questions

Having reached this point of the internship placement process, you make think that the interview will be easy. Not so. There are many instances in which the internship interview does not go well. In most cases, it is because the student did not prepare for the event beforehand.

At the interview, be alert and be prepared to both answer questions posed by the interviewer and present questions or issues related to your learning goals and placement site considerations. The interview process may be done by one person or a group. In many cases, the résumé will be used as an initial discussion point. Some common questions presented to students are:

- Tell me (us) about yourself.
- Discuss your previous work or college experience.
- Discuss what you know about our agency.
- How can this internship experience contribute to your future goals?
- What do you hope to learn from this internship? What are your goals and objectives for this program?
- Tell me (us) about your academic program of study at college.
- What were your favorite/not so favorite classes?
- What are some major trends in your field of study?
- Why should we let you intern with our agency?
- What are your strengths and weaknesses as they relate to work situations?
- What does your college expect of our organization/personnel?
- Is there any compensation available for the organization/personnel from your college, such as remitted tuition benefits?
- Is there anything in your background that might disqualify you from employment with our agency? (This question is usually presented after the interviewer discusses the general hiring requirements for the agency.)
- In view of our mission, what contributions can you make during your time with us?

The above questions are used for general conversation to engage the candidate and determine his or her interest in the position. According to the Office of Career Services at Utica College (2010), there are other questions that seek to get an idea of the candidate's behavior in ways that he or she might respond to a situation. Questions of this nature might include:

- What are your strengths and weaknesses in a job situation?
- What motivates you?
- Give an example of when you had to deal with interpersonal conflict.
- How do you define teamwork? Can you provide any examples in which you had to lead a team to accomplish a task?
- Can you give examples of how you use time management for your courses and extracurricular activities?
- Relate an unpopular decision you had to make in a job situation.
- How do you resolve conflict with coworkers or supervisors you may not like?

For these behavioral-type questions, it is necessary to have a plan before responding. One that is recommended is thinking first about the question, then describing the action you took, and finally discussing the result of your actions (Office of Career Services at Utica College, 2010).

At some point during the interview, you must be ready to ask questions that relate to the internship or agency. Some questions that you might direct to the interviewer include:

- What duties will I perform?
- What duties have previous interns performed?
- Can you elaborate (on an item covered earlier)?
- I want to improve my skills in the following areas (such as counseling, investigations, technology). Will I be able to do so here?
- Who will be my field supervisor? Will I be able to meet with him or her before I start?
- What hours (or shift) will I be assigned?
- Will there be any potential for employment with your agency after I graduate?
- Are there any particular materials that I should familiarize myself with before beginning my internship (if placement is offered and accepted)?

Many students are apprehensive about going through the interview process. Every interview should be considered good experience for the next one, whether or not you obtain the position. Many human resource specialists agree that it helps to practice before the actual interview and outline responses to the questions presented above. This can be done with a friend or roommate or by using a digital camera. Practicing can help increase your confidence in an interview situation.

When you are actually in the interview, always think before answering questions and answer all questions truthfully. Just as an experienced agency supervisor is aware of exaggeration on a résumé, he or she will be able to sense if you are stretching the truth or using fancy jargon to cover up your ignorance. Do not be afraid to admit that you do not know the answer to a question; instead, say that you do not know much about that topic but are eager and willing to learn. Agency interviewers are especially interested in your future goals, courses taken, and any job-related skills, such as counseling, outdoor leadership, writing, and research.

Upon conclusion of the interview, thank the interviewer for his or her time. A few days later, you should send the person a letter or e-mail thanking him or her for the time spent with you and expressing your continued interest in the agency. A short review of your qualifications is perfectly fine. Above all, make sure that the e-message or note has correct spelling and grammar. A sample of a thank-you letter appears in Figure 3.5.

A recent trend encountered by our students involves interviews by phone or webcam on the Internet. These interviews are done either for convenience because of travel distances or as a first-step review of available candidates. Nevertheless, the same rules apply as if it were a personal interview in terms of being able to answer and present questions. For phone interviews, always use a land-line telephone rather than a cell phone, as there are often problems with wireless reception and voice clarity. Make sure that you are indoors at a location with no annoying factors such as loud roommates, traffic, or barking dogs. Have your résumé in front of you, along with a list of questions you wish to ask.

123 Scales Hall
Hempstead College
Mansfield, NH 13502
June 13, 2016

Mr. James Brown
Chief of Police
Canton Police Department
123 Main Street
Canton, MA 12677

Dear Chief Brown:

Thank you for the opportunity to interview last Friday for a possible internship with the Canton Police Department. It was interesting to learn more about how your department interacts with other units in city government and the many criminal justice agencies in Hampshire County. This opportunity complements my coursework at Hempstead College and future career goals in the criminal justice field. In reviewing our conversation, I forgot to mention that I recently completed an online certificate course on investigative tracking, which might be of some value for your new white-collar crime unit.

If you have any additional questions, please do not hesitate to contact me. I look forward to hearing from you regarding this opportunity.

Sincerely,

Katherine Raymond

FIGURE 3.5 Sample Thank-You Letter.

Above all, be ready for the interview when the phone call is expected to begin. You can count on being automatically disqualified if you are not available or forget to call in on time. If the interview is to be conducted via webcam, make sure the background is neutral. There should not be any silly pictures or beer signs in the background. As with a face-to-face interview, dress professionally.

Background Screening

Most internship programs have a process of screening students in order to determine if they will be allowed to intern. This step dictates whether an intern will proceed with a placement. The screening may include academic standing, completion of program course requirements, background knowledge related to the internship area, and personal responsibility. Background knowledge refers to the completed coursework that makes you knowledgeable in the general area of the agency being considered. Faculty may evaluate you in terms of your sense of responsibility and ethical commitments, based on what they know of you in an academic and/or social setting (e.g., as a member of a criminal justice club). This background screening helps faculty determine if you are prepared to participate in an internship.

After going through the program's screening process, submitting your résumé and cover letter, and completing the internship interview, you may have to agree to a background investigation. There was a time when both public and private-sector employers could ask almost any question of a prospective employee, regardless of whether it was job related. Because of civil action and antidiscrimination legislation and court rulings, however, employers now may ask only questions that are relevant to the position. However, greater leeway is allowed for law enforcement and other positions that require background investigations for trustworthiness, criminal history, personal habits, and the ability to handle stressful situations. Some agencies may even use polygraph tests or drug tests before allowing you to begin your internship. The following information may be requested in a background investigation for an internship placement.

- **Employment history**. In addition to the information provided on your résumé and during the interview, the agency may seek information by contacting present and former employers, including those from part-time positions. The information you have provided will be checked to ascertain honesty and reliability.
- **Previous residence**. Some agencies may want to check on living habits and financial responsibility with former landlords and neighbors. They may also want to know previous residences in order to contact local police data banks regarding warrants that do not appear on state and national criminal history computers.
- **Arrest and conviction history**. Some agencies require pre-employment (or pre-internship) fingerprinting to obtain an accurate criminal history. A person with a felony conviction is barred from virtually all law enforcement or government positions requiring a security clearance. Some individuals are arrested for felony offenses, but plead guilty to misdemeanor charges. Conviction on a misdemeanor offense, while not an automatic bar to employment is reviewed for the type of offense, the circumstances of the arrest, and the age of the candidate when the offense occurred. In our experience, students with misdemeanor convictions may be barred from internships based on departmental policies. For example, a student convicted of driving while intoxicated was rejected by several area police departments but accepted by a department in an adjacent state. That agency offered him an internship because the offense occurred during his sophomore year and was considered part of the growing up experience. Similarly, a shoplifting incident that occurred early in high school may be forgiven but would be reviewed critically if it occurred the summer before entering college.
- **Academic record**. Some internship placement sites request writing samples and transcripts, particularly in situations in which research or computer skills are an integral part of the internship work experience. Grade point average is often a factor in the selection process.

- **Alcohol and other drug use**. You and your former employers, professors, and/or references may be asked about your alcohol and other drug use as part of your interview or background investigation. In addition, you may be asked to undergo a drug test as part of the screening process.
- **Academic and disciplinary record**. One office that today receives many inquiries by potential employers is the dean of students or campus judicial officer. The intent here is to find out if you have been the subject of any major disciplinary issues during your college attendance related to academic dishonesty, crimes, or violations of college policies.

If you have any questions or concerns about a possible background investigation, it is advised you discuss the matter with your faculty advisor or internship coordinator. In addition, as a criminal justice student, you should think now about your living habits in terms of unethical or criminal behaviors. Some students are still surprised when rejected for internship placements based on college-related problems, such as academic dishonesty, substance use/abuse, vandalism in the residence halls, gambling debts, lewd conduct, cyber behavior (see Chapter 2), and poor academic performance. Above all, do not lie or suddenly have moments of forgetfulness. Serious issues regarding personal character and criminal history have a way of becoming known to the internship placement agency even without computer or fingerprint data checks. In one recent instance, an intern candidate was dismissed from his placement after failing to report that he had been charged with smoking marijuana in a car behind a school, after the arresting officer, who was from another agency, saw him at the courthouse with his field supervisor while he was doing intern-related tasks.

The Issue of Pay

The issue of pay for interns became dominant in recent years, especially after the start of the 2008 recession, which began with the collapse of the home mortgage market and several major international banks (Huhman, 2011; Perlin, 2012). With thousands of college graduates looking for work, some employers began using unpaid interns to augment and replace regular positions. The concept of "internship" became a rite of passage for those seeking to gain full-time employment with a particular company or to gain experience in a particular field even though the internship had no relationship with an academic institution or a degree program.

In April 2010, the Department of Labor issued Fact Sheet 71 regarding internships and whether participants had to be paid a minimum wage under the Fair Labor Standards Act (FLSA). The FLSA regulates all areas of employment including the definition of the work week and federal minimum wage requirements. The Department of Labor issued the following six criteria that must be applied when making a determination as to whether the person should be paid:

- The internship, even though it includes actual operation of the facilities of the employer, is similar to training that would be given in an educational environment.
- The internship experience is for the benefit of the intern.
- The intern does not displace regular employees but works under close supervision of existing staff.
- The employer that provides the training derives no immediate advantage from the activities of the intern, and on occasion its operations may actually be impeded.
- The intern is not necessarily entitled to a job at the conclusion of the internship.
- The employer and the intern understand that the intern is not entitled to wages for the time spent in the internship.

According to the fact sheet, if all the factors are met then an "employment relationship" does not exist under the FLSA and the intern does not have to be paid. Reviewing the issue from a legal perspective, Gilbertson and Eilts (2011) report that the Department of Labor does not recognize an "employment relationship" for those internship placements that are part of a student educational program and mainly benefit the student. At the start of this controversy, the Department of Labor regulations did not apply to not-for-profit agencies.

As noted by Huhman (2011), item 4 in the six-part test provides the most interesting issue because employers do in fact derive some advantage from the activities of the intern (if not, why bother even accepting students?). These criteria also impact related civil actions, such as sexual harassment and discrimination complaints, which could be barred for student interns since an "employment relationship" may not exist. Certain states, such as Oregon, have extended these rights to those employees classified as interns.

In 2012, Ross Perlin wrote a book titled *Intern Nation: How to Earn Nothing and Learn Little in the Brave New Economy,* which outlined the explosion of internship programs, particularly those for students who had graduated and were without jobs. He argued that most internships, especially those in the private sector, were basically free labor and that all interns should be paid a minimum wage. The book cited current practices of not paying interns by such organizations as Disney, the United States Congress, the White House, and scores of American corporations. It sparked debate in internship circles on the issues and concerns related to paid internships and provided the impetus for a number of groups that advocate for paid internships. Some observers, such a Perlin, feel that all interns should receive payment and benefits for their work. Others, such as Huhman (2011), find that the experience, if properly created and mentored, will have greater future payoffs in terms of job placement and career development. She posits that in most cases, interns not being paid should be limited to no more than 20 hours a week.

Soon after the publication of *Intern Nation,* a number of former interns initiated lawsuits against their former employers. In one pre-trial settlement, a *Saturday Night Live* intern class action lawsuit was settled for $6.4 million before trial, of which approximately 18 percent went to attorneys involved in the action (Patten, 2013).

The most noted was a lawsuit filed by several interns against Fox Searchlight Pictures for not being compensated for their work on the financially successful movie *Black Swan*. In addition, one plaintiff moved to include all interns working for Fox between 2008 and 2010. In 2012, a federal judge ruled that the company violated federal minimum wage and overtime statutes according to the Federal Fair Law Standards Act and New York State Labor Law. In November 2013, this ruling, as well as a similar case filed against the Hearst Corporation, was granted an appeal by the Federal Appeals Court in New York.

On July 2, 2015, the United States Court of Appeals for the Second Circuit issued a decision that vacated the District Courts rulings (Glatt et al. v. Fox Searchlight Pictures, Inc. et. al., 2014). The Court, instead, created the following set of factors that should be weighed to determine if an intern were entitled to compensation:

1. The extent to which the intern and the employer clearly understand that there is no expectation of compensation. Any promise of compensation, express or implied, suggests that the intern is an employee—and vice versa.
2. The extent to which the internship provides training that would be similar to that which would be given in an education environment, including clinical and other hands-on training provided by educational institutions.
3. The extent to which the internship is tied to the intern's formal education program by integrated coursework or the receipt of academic credit.
4. The extent to which the internship accommodates the intern's academic commitments by corresponding to the academic calendar.
5. The extent to which the internship's duration is limited to the period in which the internship provides the intern with beneficial learning.
6. The extent to which the intern's work complements rather than displaces the work of paid employees while providing significant educational benefits to the intern.
7. The extent to which the intern and the employer understand that the internship is conducted with entitlement to a paid job at the conclusion of the internship.

As noted by the Court, the above factors are non-exhaustive, and other evidence could be included in appropriate cases.

To date, there continues to be careful monitoring of recent legal activity. These cases and the backlash against unpaid internships prompted many private-sector companies to reevaluate their programs. Many colleges and universities are rethinking whether internships, especially those unpaid, ought to be required or done on a voluntary basis. Another situation with potential impact on internships occurred on May 18, 2016, when the Department of Labor announced new overtime rule changes in the workplace by raising the salaried overtime benchmark from $23,660 to $47, 476 for executive, administrative, and professional workers who work more than 40 hours per week. Observers find that this change will have an impact on administrative assistants, research analysts, and managers in a wide range of occupations designated the "Prada Economy." This term is based on a 2006 movie, *The Devil Wears Prada*, which portrayed an overworked administrative assistant in a fashion magazine publishing house (Scheiber, 2016). The new regulations, in effect December 1, 2016, will force companies to review how business is conducted during the work week and perhaps impact the number of interns and recent graduates (Burns, 2016).

Liability and Insurance

You should be aware of your college or university's liability and insurance policies regarding internships. An internship in the criminal justice area presents risks of injury to the student. The most common risk faced by student interns is personal injury while performing internship-related duties, especially those that arise from a motor vehicle accident. Both the agency and the student must be safety conscious. Because faculty supervisors are not present, the duty of care rests with the field supervisor, who must make decisions on whether the student can observe or participate in an activity. At the same time, the student must make similar decisions. In addition, some guidelines should be agreed upon before the internship begins. For example, for law enforcement intern placements, it is recommended that students either stay in the patrol car or remain at a safe location if the field supervisor has to respond to a "shots fired" or "officer down" call. In probation department internships, students should not be on their own conducting home visits in rough neighborhoods or assigned to an isolated section of the office if dealing with a dangerous felon.

It is important for the intern to realize the inherent risk in criminal justice internships. Some of our students have confronted dangerous individuals, been involved in patrol car accidents, and been a part of unexpected, unsettling, or frightening situations. You may be asked to sign a consent form informing you of inherent danger and releasing the agency from liability. While these forms do not bar future legal action or recovery completely, especially if negligence is involved, they are useful for ensuring that the parties understand the risks involved in the placement. Students must be allowed to reject a potentially high-risk assignment without academic or disciplinary penalty.

A question that is frequently posed by students and agencies is what happens if the student, agency, and school are sued for an alleged act of misfeasance, malfeasance, or nonfeasance during the internship. Specific examples here might include false arrest or detention, libel, slander, defamation of character, invasion of privacy, or wrongful entry. According to Harry Buciffero, an expert in nonprofit insurance risk management (personal communication, June 1, 2016), if an incident were to occur, there is the possibility of litigation or claims by or against the student, the school, or the host entity. Insurance issues may not always be clear because a claim could represent both general liability, which includes bodily injury or property damage, and professional liability for actions taken or not taken by the person(s) involved in the claim. Thus, there are no certain answers to these questions because every case will have different circumstances. Singer (2011) points out that the question to be answered will be the nature of the relationship between the intern and employer/internship site.

At this time, there are no known major civil or criminal cases that involve criminal justice student interns. Nevertheless, campus and agency placement coordinators should review this possibility with appropriate counsel and insurance agents. Insurance carriers do offer professional liability policies directed to off-campus learning activities. Some colleges offer insurance for students specific to internship placements.

In terms of academic programs dealing with this issue, there are no set national policies or practices in place. Some colleges and universities assume all liability and insurance claims for their students. Others will assume liability except for health care costs and hospitalization and require the student to have health insurance. In other programs, the college and university requires the host agency to assume all damages related to the field experience.

Other colleges require that student interns purchase their own insurance policies prior to an internship placement for the duration of the placement. You should investigate what insurance coverage is expected of you as an intern prior to the commencement of the internship, for your own protection as well as for the benefit of your host organization. Appropriate insurance coverage may open the door to internship opportunities not otherwise available.

Based on the above discussion, it is always recommended that students be required to have medical insurance in the event of accident or illness. One student was sent to the hospital for observation after the patrol car she was riding in collided with another vehicle. This simple ride and evaluation at the emergency room came to $2200. Based on the chaotic state of health care, some students thought they had insurance coverage based on their parents' coverage or through the school. In many cases, this proved unfounded because of age requirements, suspensions in coverage after employment terminations, and various other reasons.

Conclusion

It is the responsibility of the criminal justice faculty and the internship coordinator to approve only those agencies that have high standards of professional performance and that are willing to work with you and your faculty advisor to provide a worthwhile and educational program. In turn, you, the student, have a responsibility to present yourself in the best light: from a complete professional résumé and cover letter to your appearance and performance during the internship interview. It is important that you understand the academic and placement requirements of the program. Working together, you, your faculty advisor, and the agency personnel can ensure the most appropriate internship placement for you. This chapter also outlined the major issues facing interns in terms of pay, liability, and insurance.

■ ■ ■ ━━━

Thinking About Your Internship Placement

1. Develop a "me file." Include your transcripts, copies of your best term papers, names and addresses of all former residences and employers, and current references.
2. Prepare a résumé and cover letter, and keep them updated.
3. List the factors that you should consider in selecting an internship site, in the order of importance to you.
4. Develop a list of possible internship sites from a variety of sources, including your internship advisor, previous interns, and the Internet.
5. Develop questions that you would ask in an internship interview.
6. Develop and be prepared to answer a list of questions that might be directed to you at an internship interview. Include questions that address your motivation, work ethic, leadership qualities, and technical skills.
7. Review the liability and health insurance requirements with your internship coordinator or faculty supervisor.

━━━ ■ ■ ■

Professional Concerns

Setting Goals and Identifying Educational Objectives

4

The four types of goals important in shaping an internship experience are knowledge acquisition, performance assessment, personal growth, and professional development. After defining goals, one must set specific and measurable learning objectives to help achieve those goals and allow assessment of progress. While it is important to define goals early in an internship experience, you should remain flexible. That is, the student should be prepared to modify goals as he or she becomes more familiar with the workings of the agency. New goals may be added during the experience. The process of setting goals and assessing progress will help the student develop professionally once employed in a criminal justice agency.

The purpose of this chapter is to help you determine specific goals and define objectives to help you work toward attaining them. In addition, it offers you a methodology with which to assess your progress during the internship. After reviewing this chapter the reader should be able to set a minimum of two learning goals for each of the above defined areas.

Introduction

Once you have chosen a field site, you can decide what learning goals to set for yourself. A learning goal is an end you will strive to accomplish through your participation in an internship. It will have the potential to change your behavior in particular situations, your understanding of issues, or your performance in certain skill areas.

Why is this important? Learning goals should reflect the overall goals for your degree program. According to Peat and Moriarty (2009), the goals for many programs involve the following:

- Application of theory to practice.
- Communication skills.
- Writing skills.
- Information about the work of criminal justice and related fields.
- Critical thinking in terms of dealing with criminal justice problems.

From these general goals, specific learning goals are developed in all courses, including the internship. For internship courses, there are some obvious goals that are at play here, which might include: (1) learn about the actual practice of the criminal justice field and the functions of your position and others at your field site, (2) attempt to apply what you have learned in the classroom to the real world, and (3) gain experience and contacts that will aid in the search for employment. While these are goals you should keep in mind, they are too broad to be the only goals of your internship.

From a practical standpoint, you may be asked during an interview what you hope to gain from your internship experience. On the other hand, during your internship, you will be bombarded by a variety of experiences. Thus, if you do not identify specific goals, and a method for attaining them, you may find that you cannot articulate specifically what you gained from your experience. Setting specific goals may also help you to expand beyond the usual boundaries of a placement to give you a truly unique and rewarding experience. Your goals will help you to negotiate the specific tasks or experiences you may have. For example, a student interning at a juvenile detention facility set a goal to run a specific unit toward the end of her internship. She was initially told that such a goal was unrealistic, as the agency had never entrusted an intern with such administrative responsibility. Just prior to the end of her internship she was given the opportunity to meet this goal. Had she not identified her goal, it would never have been realized.

Many students often find it difficult to determine specific goals for their internship experience. They may not have any experience with goal setting beyond New Year's resolutions and may not have thought much about their interpersonal skills. This is compounded by the fact that they do not know much about their internship site or what they may be doing during their time there. You should keep in mind that goals are an iterative process; that is, it may take several revisions before you end up with the right goals for your internship. You should brainstorm possibilities with your fellow students, faculty, former interns, and friends and family. Faculty, former interns, and professionals in the field will be able to point you in the direction of the knowledge and skills that you will need to develop to make the transition from student to professional worker. The people who know you best may be able to provide some insights into how you interact with others.

In searching for an internship, you have had to set goals and objectives in an informal manner. Your goal has been to seek the best possible internship for you in the specific area of the criminal justice system. The steps you took to achieve this goal are your objectives. For illustrative purposes, this goal and its objective could be formalized in the manner outlined in the next section.

Goal

To get hired as an intern in an agency or organization where I can gain the knowledge and skills that I will need to seek employment in this or other like agencies/organizations.

Learning objectives to achieve this goal:

1. Review internship opportunities with intern advisor.
2. Assess these opportunities based on comments from faculty and former interns.
3. Review social media sites such as Facebook, Twitter, and LinkedIn to identify possible internship opportunities and to gather intelligence on them.
4. Prepare résumé and perform mock interviews.

Understanding the process is the first hurdle, but how do you set goals for an experience that is still unclear to you? Students get hung up on picking the best goals and objectives at the outset. This is not a test, and there are no right or wrong answers. The best approach is to brainstorm ideas based on what you want to gain from your internship experience. You should be realistic, but do not limit yourself by making predetermined assumptions about what an agency may or may not allow you to do.

Setting Realistic Goals

In setting realistic goals, you should consider the following for your internship:

1. The amount of time you will spend at the internship site.
2. The duties that the agency will and will not allow you to perform.
3. The skills and competence levels you possess.
4. The actual location of the site in terms of distance from campus or home.
5. Your knowledge and understanding of the workings of the criminal justice system in theory and practice.
6. Your personality (particularly your strengths and weaknesses).
7. The overall size and mission of the agency.
8. State and national legal guidelines and statutes.

The time students spend at an internship site may vary from a few days a week to a full-time commitment for a semester or during a summer session. You must decide upon goals toward which you can make considerable progress or that can be achieved during the time you will spend at the site.

The duties assigned to you are influenced by your time commitment, your skill level, the success the agency has had with previous interns, the staff complement, and the agency's formal and informal policies regarding interns. While these factors may limit the activities you are asked to perform, they should not entirely limit the goals you set. Many agency supervisors will reconsider your assigned duties once they become aware of your abilities. This is especially true if you are able to perform assigned tasks at the same level as the agency staff or if you are able to perform duties that agency staff cannot.

If you can demonstrate that you have acquired skills that will be of use in the agency, you may be allowed to become more involved. For example, if you have had counseling courses or experience in working with people in this capacity, you will be more apt to be allowed to work with clients in a probation department. If you have had some experience in legal research, you may be asked to do similar work in a law firm or district attorney's office. Computer skills are a major asset in any environment. Your goal in these cases might be to refine or expand your expertise on a specific topic such as social engineering or malware.

The courses you have completed, your level of understanding of the actual workings of the criminal justice system, and previous work or internship experience will be considered by the agency in assigning duties. If you have taken only general survey courses, then your goals may be focused on developing an understanding of specific areas related to the criminal justice system and gaining valuable field experience. If, on the other hand, you understand the agency's functions in general and you possess specific knowledge or skills that you want to develop further in a practical setting, you should set goals that approximate the duties of particular staff members in the organization.

You should take into consideration your own personality and ability to relate to others. Goals may be set to develop individual strengths or to improve weaknesses. For example, if you think that you lack self-confidence, you can set specific objectives to bolster it.

Very often, student interns decide upon goals that are not legally possible. For example, one student wanted to conduct an interview with either an abused or neglected child, which would be against the department's policies and state laws. The goal had to be re-crafted, whereby he would shadow and observe his field supervisor conducting such an interview.

We now turn to types of goals, and what goals to set. The above considerations should be kept in mind throughout this process.

Types of Goals

As discussed at the start of this chapter, you should set goals in four specific areas: knowledge acquisition, performance assessment, personal growth, and professional development.

Knowledge Acquisition

Knowledge acquisition is the type of goal that helps you to develop knowledge in areas in which you have either taken no courses or topics about which you wish to learn more. With the assistance of your faculty advisor and field supervisor, you should develop a reading list of books, journal articles, and agency materials relevant to your internship placement (e.g., for a probation department placement, readings in pretrial diversion; for a cybersecurity unit analytical reports on malware). Any knowledge acquisition goal will also help you to become a self-directed learner as you assess areas in which you are deficient and work to improve your knowledge in those areas through readings and discussions with faculty and professionals.

The following are examples of knowledge-acquisition goals:

- I would like to learn more about the laws pertaining to child abuse cases and the court proceedings surrounding them.
- I would like to gain a better understanding of how law enforcement utilizes the latest advances in digital forensics to solve crimes.
- I want to learn more about the issues related to sex offender registration programs.
- I want to learn about the threats of computer hackers on an agency's critical infrastructure.
- I would like to gain a better understanding of the impact of data breaches of protected health information on medical identity theft.

Throughout your program of study, you have been introduced to various theories and concepts related to criminal justice, criminology, financial fraud investigations, and cybercrime. It would be very appropriate for you to apply these to work at your internship site and/or to specific problems that you are working on as assigned by your faculty or field advisor. These questions can be woven into knowledge acquisition goals. For example, what are the theories or concepts behind a certain program dealing with youth gangs or defendants agreeing to be placed into a drug court rehabilitation program? What drives certain people to become computer network hackers or committing financial crimes?

As you have learned, many public policies and programs are based on certain theories as to why people commit crimes or what can be done for crime prevention. The application of theories and concepts at most internship sites is a very appealing academic endeavor.

Performance Assessment

Performance-assessment goals will fall into two categories: demonstrating understanding of the everyday workings and processes of the agency, and demonstrating proficiencies in particular skills.

In order to develop an understanding of the agency, you must evaluate the situation, identify causal relationships, and observe patterns. For example, a student intern in a probation department who is assigned a small caseload might set the following goal: "To develop an understanding of the agencies and services available for referral in the community and to be able to make referrals." To attain this goal, the intern would first read a city- or county-wide Web directory of agencies. He or she would then talk to probation officers to discern to what agencies they have referred clients satisfactorily. The next step would be to visit the organizations to gain firsthand information. In addition, talking with probationers who have been referred to the agencies would provide information on benefits to the individual. Finally, the intern would make referrals and evaluate the benefits to the client.

As another example, a student who is interning in a law enforcement agency might set this goal: "To develop an understanding of the process of interviewing a crime scene witness and be able to conduct an interview." The process of attaining this goal would include tasks such as researching the legal issues pertaining to witness interviews and then discussing them with a supervisor, discussing the interpersonal and social aspects of interviewing witnesses with the supervisor, assessing the pertinent background information of several cases, observing professionals in the field, interviewing witnesses, and being critiqued by the supervisor.

Goals can vary. A student interning with a computer security firm set a goal of developing skills in the area of penetration testing. He was taught how to seek out vulnerabilities in a client's computer system and to probe those vulnerabilities to gain access to what was thought to be secure data. After observing several of these planned attacks, he was allowed to participate in an operation under close supervision.

Skill goals are set either to improve existing skills or to develop new ones. You should assess the skills necessary to perform the particular jobs in the agency you have chosen. Based on these and your assigned duties, you should develop a list of skills you would like to develop or improve during your internship. The following examples clarify this.

A student working in a district attorney's office, for a judge, or in a public defender's office might set a goal of developing or improving legal research skills. A student in a law enforcement agency working with the investigative unit might have as a goal the development or improvement of fingerprinting skills. Similarly, a student working for a youth department might want to develop his or her skills at assessing the best placement sites for clients.

Many students have no way of gauging how their current skill set can be an asset to the internship agency and are therefore at a loss about how they might contribute to the mission of the organization. Skills developed in courses such as accounting, computer science, investigative methods, and counseling could provide a new perspective. As a recent graduate, you may have been exposed to new Internet research methods, counseling techniques, and software such as crime mapping. You may have a deep understanding of how things work as a result of your daily activities. For example, you may be an expert in the use of social media, something that many of those at your internship might not use or have only had limited experience with. Your understanding of how people use social media could make a contribution to cases where suspects may be tracked through their use of these media.

You should not be discouraged if you are not allowed to use the specified skills at the beginning of the internship. Many agencies insist on a trial period before allowing an intern to function as a staff member. It is best if you are allowed to practice the skill under supervision and then have your proficiency evaluated. If this process is repeated several times, you will have an opportunity to develop the skills you desire.

Personal Growth

An internship experience offers you a tremendous opportunity to grow and develop as a person. You should inventory your personal assets to determine your strengths and weaknesses. Discussions with friends, family, and faculty may help you define these. While the other types of goals are developed to fit the agency assignment you have chosen, personal-growth goals are applicable to all settings. As one student wrote, "I am eager to learn more and to be exposed to varying situations with different types of people." The following are examples of the goals you might set:

1. To become more open-minded and reduce stereotyping of people who are different from me.
2. To be more assertive and to initiate interactions with those who tend to intimidate me.
3. To overcome a lack of self-confidence in establishing interpersonal relationships.
4. To overcome the feeling that my opinions are inferior to those of others.
5. To become more self-disciplined and organized and get to work or appointments on time.
6. To communicate messages more clearly and accurately.
7. To accept helpful feedback from others less defensively.
8. To respond calmly when others communicate criticisms or hostility toward me.
9. To become more self-directed.
10. To start managing time in terms of completing tasks and finishing assignments.

Professional Development

Most students choose an internship site because they have identified a potential career. Articulating specific career goals will aid you in testing out your aspirations. The goals can be specific (e.g., you want to pursue a career as a law enforcement probation officer, fraud investigator, cybersecurity analyst). They also may be general (e.g., you want to work in an agency that provides direct services to clients). Professional goals may be set for short- and/or long-range time periods. For example, your goal may be to work in a legal agency to ascertain whether you want to go to law school.

Unlike the other types of goals, you will probably have one major professional goal. However, you may work in a setting that allows you to interact with a variety of agencies in the criminal justice system as well as ones that are tangential to it. In this situation, you will be able to interact with a wide range of practitioners who may be willing to introduce you to their agencies and their world of work. For example, a student interning at a nonprofit organization was given the task of identifying potential members of a public/private partnership focused on identity theft. The organizations involved included law enforcement agencies, the district attorney's office, banks, victim assistance groups, and large retail companies. At the end of his internship, there was an opening in a corporate security department of one of the member banks, and he was hired. He said he never would have considered working in such a setting if he had not been introduced to it through his internship.

You will hear the term "professional development" mentioned in a slightly different context at your internship site. Most organizations require their employees to attend a certain number of professional development seminars or training sessions each year to remain current in their field. Certain professionals, such as lawyers, accountants, and psychologists, are required to attain a set number of continuing education credits each year to maintain their professional license. These sessions are focused on new knowledge acquisition, improving or developing new skills, and interpersonal growth. In many ways, your internship is the beginning of a life-long professional development journey, and learning to set goals and learning objectives is a vital part of this process.

Developing Learning Objectives for Your Goals

Once you have formulated your goals, the next step is to set specific learning objectives to define how you intend to accomplish those goals. In setting objectives, you should work with both faculty and field supervisors to ensure that the objectives are realistic, attainable, and measurable. Once the learning objectives are agreed upon, your field supervisor can shape your internship experience, based on the tasks you need to complete as you work toward your goals. Your objectives are essential not only in determining your responsibilities at the internship site but also as a mechanism to assess your overall performance and as a basis for discussion during periodic supervisory meetings.

Some examples of objectives set to reach different types of goals will help clarify this process. A personal growth goal stated earlier was to overcome a lack of self-confidence in establishing new interpersonal relationships. While this is an important goal statement, no indication of how it will be achieved is included. What is necessary is a specific plan including tasks, situations that promote learning, and a means of assessment—in other words, objectives. In this particular case, the following objectives, or learning tasks, may be set:

1. I will be meeting with several new people in my internship setting. After these meetings, I will assess how I felt, why I felt that way, and how I thought others perceived me.
2. I will spend time discussing these situations with my advisor and field supervisor. The field supervisor may be able to tell me how others in the agency perceived me.
3. I will continue this process with any new relationship I develop during my internship.
4. I will keep a log in which I will write down my impressions throughout the semester.

Learning tasks for a skill development goal might follow the format in this example. One student intern working in a district attorney's office wanted to develop his legal research skills further. He set the following learning objectives:

1. I will begin legal research on an assigned case being undertaken by my field supervisor.
2. I will compare my research with his or hers, discussing areas in which I need to improve.

3. I will request the opportunity to do legal research on my own and have it critiqued by my supervisor.
4. I will continue to do as much legal research as possible for the remainder of my internship.

Knowledge acquisition goals require different tasks. This is illustrated by the following example. An intern wanted to learn more about suicide, as she was working in a setting where juveniles attempted to take their own lives. She set these learning objectives:

1. I will review class notes on the subject.
2. I will choose a list of readings, compiled with the help of my faculty and agency supervisors.
3. I will meet with the staff psychologist to learn more about juveniles and suicide.

In general, learning objectives for knowledge-acquisition goals should include the following:

1. Become aware and informed about the topic.
2. Analyze, synthesize, and generalize the readings and discussions.
3. Take action or think about how you might act in specific situations (Permaul, 1981).

Once you have written your goals and objectives, you need to share them with both your faculty and agency supervisors. It is crucial that your agency supervisor knows what your goals are for your internship. He or she should know whether they are realistic for that particular site. It is also important to have your supervisor sign off on them, that is, agree that your goals are reasonable and attainable.

Methodology for Assessing Progress

As you develop into a self-directed learner, you should assume the major responsibility for assessing your progress in performing your learning objectives and, therefore, in attaining your goals. This will help you to determine whether your goals and learning tasks are realistic and attainable in your internship setting. While the exact assessment methodology will depend on the goal and its objectives, the following techniques may be helpful.

Written Analysis

This can take the form of notes, a log, or a written memorandum to your faculty supervisor. Placing your thoughts on paper will force you to think through the experience and give you a historical perspective over the course of the internship (Chapter 6 discusses written documentation in detail).

Periodic Feedback from Others

You should discuss your progress in regular meetings with your faculty advisor and field supervisor, or in seminars with peers who are doing or have done internships. Based on the feedback, you may want to change your learning objectives or add new goals.

Assessing your goals should be an ongoing process throughout your internship. In formulating your goals before you begin your internship, you will assess what you know, can do, or are; what you need to know, be able to do, or be; and what you want to know, do, or be. During your internship, it is important to take stock periodically of where you are in terms of your goals. If you find you have accomplished several of them, it is time to determine others, so that the remainder of your internship will be worthwhile. If you are having trouble reaching your goals and find that your efforts to do so have stalled, you should discuss them with both your agency and faculty supervisors to decide what you can do to accomplish them or if you need to make modifications to them. It may be that your supervisor will allow you to take on added responsibility so that you can attain your goals. Assessing your goals as you complete your internship is a crucial element of career development. You may find that you are in exactly the right line of work for you or that you need to explore other areas.

Conclusion

The four types of goals important in shaping your internship experience are knowledge acquisition, performance assessment, personal growth, and professional development. After defining your goals, you must set specific and measurable learning objectives to help you achieve those goals and allow you to assess your progress. These should have some relationship with the general learning goals of your program of study.

While it is important to define goals early in your internship experience, you should remain flexible. That is, you should be prepared to modify your goals as you become more familiar with the workings of your agency. You may also want to add new goals during your experience. Setting goals and assessing your progress will be important parts of your professional development during this experience (Chapter 13, "Assessing Your Experience," deals directly with evaluation of your progress in achieving your goals). This process will help you to develop professionally once you are employed in a criminal justice agency.

■ ■ ■ ▬▬▬▬▬▬▬▬▬▬▬▬▬▬▬▬▬▬▬▬▬▬▬▬▬▬▬▬▬▬▬▬

Planning Your Internship

1. What are the main student learning goals for your program of study?
2. Based on your internship expectations, list specific goals in these areas:
   a. Knowledge acquisition.
   b. Performance assessment.
   c. Personal growth.
   d. Professional development.
3. State at least two learning objectives for each of the goals presented in Item 1. These are necessary so that you can assess your progress.
4. Under knowledge acquisition, include one goal that deals with a theory or concept that impacts the operations of your organization or work unit.
5. Review your goals and objectives with your faculty and internship supervisors to ensure that they are appropriate and realistic. Can they be accomplished in the semester within which you are interning?
6. At around the mid-point into your internship, review your goals and objectives. To what extent are they being accomplished? Did you set new goals and objectives during the course?

▬▬▬▬▬▬▬▬▬▬▬▬▬▬▬▬▬▬▬▬▬▬▬▬▬▬▬▬▬▬▬ ■ ■ ■

5

Your Role as an Intern

Interns begin in an observer role and then progress to a role that includes some limited participation in the activities of the agency along with continued observation. Eventually the intern becomes a participant-observer. Whether an intern moves to the more responsible role of participant-observer depends on several factors, including student skills, the needs of the agency, the level of agency staffing, and the number of hours per week as well as the number of weeks for the placement. The role changes as the intern progresses through a series of stages. The issues that arise at each stage are different and must be dealt with as they occur. As an intern becomes more involved in the actual operations of the agency, he or she should take care to examine the experience objectively. Seeking the support of supervisors and peers is helpful.

After reading this chapter, the student should list the main stages of being an intern and some of the issues that he or she may face at each stage.

Introduction

On the first day of your internship, you will find yourself in a totally new situation. You will be learning a new job, the physical layout of the building, getting to know the staff, and learning about the structure of the agency. Although, compared with an employee, less will be expected of you and fewer demands will be made of you by the agency, you must be able to do two things at once: perform some duties as an involved member of the agency while maintaining the ability to examine, process, and analyze your experience objectively as a student. As an intern, you should never become solely a participant. Remember, you are there to learn.

While in the position of observer, you may be able to move around the agency freely to learn about the entire operation. It is likely that you will be able to observe situations that outsiders cannot, will have access to confidential materials, and will have a legitimate reason to ask questions.

Experiential Stages

Faculty supervisors of interns have observed that the role of the intern changes as he or she progresses through a series of stages. These stages include initial entry, a probationary period, a stage as a productive worker, and termination. In the business world, the stages an employee goes through are known as the socialization process. They include anticipatory socialization, accommodation, and role management (Gibson, Ivancevich, & Donnelly, 1997). The stages you are likely to experience are discussed in detail here to help you better understand the experience and allow you to anticipate the changes that will occur.

Anticipatory Socialization

Anticipatory socialization takes place before you begin your internship. "The first stage involves all those activities the individual undertakes prior to entering the organization. . . . The primary purpose of these activities is to acquire information about the new organization" (Gibson et al., 1997, p. 36). As you go through the process of procuring your internship, you will be learning as much as you can about the internship site. You will also form expectations about the organization and your role there. Some of your knowledge may come from the organization's web site or from others who have interned at the site or who are or have been employed there. Some may come from your faculty supervisor and from coursework you have completed. You need to be prepared, however, for the likelihood that not all of your expectations will be met.

Initial Entry

The entry period can last from a few days to a few weeks, depending on the intern orientation program and the amount of time you are spending at the agency per week. Interns generally have two initial feelings: they are excited about the internship and apprehensive about the unknown. Typical questions students raise are "Will the staff accept me?" and "Will I be able to perform the duties and tasks asked of me?"

You will be treated as a visitor at the initial entry stage. The agency supervisor will generally want you to become acquainted with the staff members and their duties, as well as the organizational structure and functions of the agency. You may be given material to read about the agency. Many students complain that they spend the first few days of their internship reading manuals, case files, and policies and procedures. Some agencies have developed manuals specifically designed to acquaint new interns, while others rely upon a less formal introduction. Some well-developed internship programs offer a structured orientation program designed to facilitate the initial entry. This orientation process, whether it is just reading or other activities, provides a critical foundation for the next phase of the internship.

The most important aspect of this stage is that you will see the organization or unit through the eyes of an outsider, whether a client or an interested citizen. The role of observer begins the minute you enter the front door. Care should be taken to record your first impressions, both positive and negative.

You will be what is called a "known observer." Your supervisor will introduce you as a student doing an internship. The staff may have several reactions to you at this point, ranging from a warm welcome to ignoring you. Their responses will depend on past experiences with interns, their understanding of the intern role, and/or whether they consider you to be a threat or potential annoyance.

While some of the staff may not openly greet you and may give you the impression that they see you as a marginal person or an intruder, you should not take it personally. Time will probably change their attitude, especially if you become a contributing member for the organization. You are, however, bound to react to the way you are received by the personnel with whom you will work. The examples here show how differently students felt at the beginning of their internships.

One student found that he was readily accepted by the staff because many of them had been interns.

Several of the probation officers in the department have been required to complete practicum or internships themselves. Because of this, I believe they have a better understanding of my purpose within the office. This is a benefit to interns like me because the members of the department realize that I am not there to report on their actions. Personnel who have completed internships also can better comprehend how an intern feels and what some of his concerns may be.

A formal internship program may offer students a comfortable beginning.

It was wonderful that all of the interns got to spend the first week together. Though the sessions were sometimes overwhelming, and sometimes boring, we were all in it together, which made it more comfortable for all of us. We all became friends very quickly, almost like a trauma bond. There was so much information to take in, we really had to rely on each other to fill in the gaps. We ate together during our breaks, and we are looking forward to getting our specific assignments. Since we will be working in teams, it is really nice to have this opportunity to get acquainted with each other and with our supervising attorneys.

A student in a police agency was almost immediately treated as an unimportant observer.

[S]ometimes I feel I'm in the way or I'm just another person the deputy has to worry about or tag along in the patrol car. I felt that way when I first started and I also feel it is true in one way or another to at least one or two deputies in this department. Also,

when I go to the scene of some incident, I am made to feel by others that I am not part of this agency.

This student had to deal with the problems of marginality and intrusion. His early perception of not belonging in sensitive and confidential interactions with clients or of being in the way when a staff member was carrying out his duties led to feelings of intrusion. This is not uncommon in internships. The feelings become less of a concern to interns as they become more involved in the workings of the organization and begin to be contributing members of it.

With marginality, it is the staff member or members who feel that the intern is not able to contribute much. When the intern becomes aware of such feelings, he or she may feel like he or she is in the way or as if he or she is a burden. Feelings of marginality are most apt to be fostered in an agency that has not had an intern before or one that has had a bad experience with an intern. Some staff members may never change their views, possibly because they feel threatened by an intern's education level or resent having to work with a student. Feelings of marginality are often alleviated as the student takes on greater responsibilities. The important thing is not to let these few people affect your views of yourself or to outweigh the opinion others have of you.

Another student saw her problems as emanating from her own perceptions and thoughts.

One disadvantage of my role as an intern has been at times I have a feeling of isolation—a feeling that I don't really belong. A lot of this problem lies within myself and my way of thinking. I feel it has taken a while to open up and be myself. It is not that people here make me feel uncomfortable. I allow myself to feel this way. It's taking me time to adjust to a new environment, new ideas, new people, and the working world. This is no longer my home or college environment. It is a big step for me—it is down to serious business. I have had a lot of anxiety and apprehension about it.

Probationary Period

The next stage of experience is a probationary period, during which you will not be considered an outsider or visitor. Your supervisor will begin to allow you to observe situations as if you were a regular worker. Direct contact with clients, co-workers, or other criminal justice agencies may begin. Attendance at a variety of professional meetings may now be open to you.

During this period, your supervisor may begin to assign tasks to you and will watch your performance carefully. A supervisor who develops confidence and trust in your performance will likely be willing to assign you more demanding tasks. It is therefore critical that you complete any task assigned, no matter how small or seemingly unimportant, to the best of your ability and in a timely fashion. You should remember that a certain amount of drudgery comes with every job. This was very apparent at a homeland security training center where hundreds of class registrations and attendance forms had to be manually scanned and then sent to headquarters. The job was completed in due time with the student's recommendation that iPads be purchased for completion of this mundane task. A good rule of thumb is to observe what other workers in the agency do. If your workload reflects the same percentage of copying, filing, and data entry as other workers, then there is no cause for alarm. However, if you find you need to wear sunglasses to protect your eyes from the constant lights of the copy machine, discuss the matter with your supervisor and your faculty advisor.

Another common problem is having nothing to do, especially after completing assigned tasks. If this occurs, then do not just sit there, but speak up and ask if there are other items that need to be undertaken either with your immediate unit or perhaps another department. Perhaps your field supervisor has to be away. Go to another co-worker and see if he or she is in need of assistance. As discussed in one career site, be sure to schedule frequent meetings with your field supervisor to lay out a schedule of what needs to be done (Wetfeet, 2013). The primary purpose of the internship is for you to learn.

Interns are generally exposed to a whole array of new situations during the probationary period. At this stage in the internship, you may feel overwhelmed and confused. The gap between the theoretical operation of the criminal justice system and the everyday workings of the agency will become evident. That in itself is confusing, but you also may begin to question your ability to perform the tasks the agency personnel perform. Do not expect to perform as well as experienced staff members. As one student wrote:

> As an intern, I am not expected to know all the facets of the program and sometimes I have the feeling that I should know them and expect too much out of myself. I have to be more understanding of myself and my role as a participant-observer. I need patience with myself in the learning process. It will take me time to absorb everything.

This period offers you an excellent opportunity to ask questions. No one expects you to know everything about the organization, its clients, and the role it plays in the criminal justice system. Most people will be happy to answer your questions and, in fact, this is one way of demonstrating an interest in the agency and what the staff is doing. Many agency supervisors have commented that they really appreciate students' questions, especially if they have been routinely performing the same tasks. They claim that it affords them an opportunity to reevaluate their performance and to look at familiar situations in a new way. Above all, ask questions if you need guidance in completing tasks or if you feel you are getting over your head in terms of assignments and your skills sets.

One student summed up the probationary period in the following way.

> A few of those advantages are being able to read confidential material; you can get an overall view of how people work and how the Department for Youth works; you're

allowed to do certain tasks but nothing that you can't handle that could get you into serious trouble. It gives you the freedom to move around the office and meet a lot of people. My supervisor has been very open with me and I'm sure this will continue. He feels that I'm not a threat to him, which makes me feel good. The others in the office for the most part have been helpful and friendly.

Another advantage of the probationary period is that interns are apt to become more accepted in the agency. One student's acceptance was aided by a journal article he had read and shared.

As I noted, this past week I have accomplished a lot along the lines of becoming accepted as an intern. There was an article in last month's Law and Order *magazine about internships. Many of the officers read it and I think it helped them accept me as a "part" of the department and understand what I am trying to accomplish. I am sure I will stumble on other problems with my status as participant-observer, but I think I am over the hardest part.*

Many problems can arise during the internship's probationary stage. While they are common to the internship experience, you will not necessarily experience all or any of them. One problem is mistrust of you by some personnel. Some staff members may think of you as a spy—someone who will report to a superior about them. In response, they may be very careful about what they say around you. Time may help alleviate this problem, as coworkers realize that you are not repeating everything you hear or running to a supervisor with reports about them. Two interns commented on their problems with mistrust.

I feel that fellow workers think that they must work harder when I'm around. I've noticed that it puts more pressure on them to look busy and not waste time when I'm around. When this happens, I get the feeling that they wish I was not around. I don't blame them for this, because I've been in that type of situation before. Not too many people like being watched by an outsider. The people in the office want all of us interns to think that they are doing a good job and are busy all the time. I think that this problem may last for some time until they trust me. I realize that it does take time to trust one another. I'm also careful not to say anything negative about anyone else for the same reasons they have. I think both myself and the other employees have our guard up and all are careful of what we do and say.

As a participant-observer working for the Department of Youth, I have faced some problems as an intern. I've gotten the feeling that other people in the office are careful of what they say in fear that I may repeat what they have said. This has happened a few times already and I can tell they are uneasy at times. An example of this is when one member of the office says something negative about another person, they try to make sure that I don't hear. I have noticed that they don't really trust me yet as a fellow worker. I hope that with time this problem will correct itself and employees will look at me as one of them.

You may find that your age poses problems for you as well. The majority of the interns in undergraduate programs have been in their early twenties. They are generally younger than the staff and either younger than the clients or very close in age to them. The disadvantages of this are revealed in the following student's comment.

I also think that my age plays a role as a disadvantage. Just because a person is and looks younger than many people you come in contact with, they think less of you. I have noticed this a few times when I've gone to the community programs. My supervisor introduces me to someone and they think I'm just an intern, and thus I really don't get the respect that I should. Sometimes I get the feeling that strangers don't care and don't have the time to talk with me because I'm an intern. This problem does not happen all the time, but I see this as a problem that will continue throughout my internship.

On the other hand, age can be an advantage when working with younger clients. They may be able to relate to you better because you are closer to their age, and they may not see you as just another authority figure.

In carrying out your duties, you may find that others within and without the agency do not consider you an official staff member. An intern described one such experience in the following manner.

A disadvantage of being a participant-observer is that you lack clout and credibility. For example, my supervisor asked me to call a witness to inform him that he was to be subpoenaed to appear in court. A few minutes after making the call, the man called back and asked for my supervisor. He wanted to verify the call; he did not believe that I was working for the district attorney's office. Apparently, my voice was strange to him and he did not understand that I was interning with the DA's office; otherwise he would not have called to verify.

There is little you can do about a problem such as this, unless you interact with the client or agency on a regular basis.

One problem you may encounter is that one faction or clique within your agency will try to draw you into their allegiance. This may be tempting if you are feeling that you do not belong and are looking for support. We caution you, however, not to become aligned with any one group. What may appear to be a safe crew of people who offer you acceptance and support may turn out to be a limiting and confining group from which escape is difficult, if not impossible. Such affiliation can restrict your ability to experience the full range of opportunities available. You should make every effort to remain neutral in intra-agency conflicts.

Sometimes certain aspects of an intern's personality and interpersonal style can be problematic at an internship site. If you find this is the case for you, you may want to consider an additional personal-growth goal for your internship. The following comment exemplifies a student who had a problem with his personal style.

> *One of my major problems in this department is my personality or personal style. I am a rather aggressive and straightforward person and this sometimes gets me into trouble. I generally speak my feelings and often people get upset. It is going to be hard, but I will have to try to be less direct in what I say. As it is stated in our readings, I should be nonthreatening and attempt to be supportive.*

This student might add as a personal-growth goal "striving to be more tactful and sensitive in dealing with others." A passive and/or introverted student may want to set a goal to take a more active role at the internship site and to make an effort to interact more effectively with others, so that he or she will not be seen as disinterested, unwilling to become involved, or interning only for the credit hours.

One further difficulty that you may face is losing sight of your role as an intern. As you move toward the third stage—productive worker—you will participate more and may forget that you should continue to be an observer. "Going native," as it is sometimes called, can seriously hamper your ability to learn more about the agency and yourself. One intern summed up this dilemma as follows.

> *While at present there are no serious problems or dilemmas that I am facing in my internship, there is one small problem that I do feel is worth mentioning. This problem has to do with the delicate balance between a participant-observer and a full-time staff member. While I do believe the only way to gain a full understanding of the operations of any office is to become involved in the day-to-day activities of that office, I also believe to become so immersed in the operations of the organization as to become a substitute for a full-time staff member will defeat the purpose of me being here, which is to learn. Although at this point in my internship I do not perceive this as a problem, I do think there is the possibility of a future conflict. However, I think being cognitive of the potential conflict should, in itself, prevent any serious problems.*

Accommodation

The accommodation stage of the socialization process encompasses both the initial entry and probationary stages discussed above. According to Gibson et al. (1997), there are four main activities in the accommodation stage: developing interpersonal relationships with other employees, learning what is expected of you, determining your role in the organization, and assessing how well you are performing. As is evident from the student statements, at this stage, gaining acceptance of fellow workers and confidence in your ability to be successful in your internship is paramount.

Productive Worker and Role Management

By the time you have reached the productive worker stage, you will be expected to perform certain tasks and duties as an agency staff member with little or no direct supervision. Because you will have demonstrated your abilities and competencies to your supervisor, he or she will trust you to handle your assignments professionally. As an intern, you may progress rapidly through the first two stages (initial entry and probationary) and find yourself confronted with the difficult challenges of the third stage before you are ready. On the other hand, you may never reach this stage. The amount of time you spend at the agency each week and your performance in the first two stages are the two major factors in determining how soon you will reach the productive worker stage (if at all). Some agency policies prohibit interns from undertaking the duties associated with this stage.

The expectation of the role management stage is that you will experience conflict, between the demands of your work (or internship) life and home life and between your work group and others in the organization. It is unlikely that, as an intern, you will reach this stage. If you do, it is essential that you maintain your perspective (Gibson et al., 1997).

During these stages, your perceptions of the agency may change. Your first observations were made as an outsider; now you will see things as an insider. You will probably see some discrepancies between the goals and objectives of the agency and its practices. The problems and limitations of the criminal justice system may also become evident. What is most important is that you do not lose your observer perspective. It affords you the opportunity to raise questions, define problems, and search for possible resolutions. In order to maintain your perspective, you should discuss your experiences and feelings with your faculty supervisor and fellow interns, as well as read relevant literature and visit other agencies.

Termination

The termination process involves your separation from staff and clients. It is a time to reflect on your experience, assess yourself, and look to the next stage of your career. If you deal with clients, you should give them some warning that you are leaving and let them know that their cases will be transferred to another staff member. Consult with your supervisor about the appropriate time to do so and about how the transition will occur.

Your clients may react in a variety of ways, from being totally indifferent to being angry and hostile. The rapport you have built with your clients, the benefits they have received from the relationship, and their degree of dependence on you will all contribute to their responses.

While termination with the staff is likely to be easier, there are a few things to keep in mind. First, if you have been handling the cases of specific staff members, you should inform them of the status of the cases. Second, any unfinished projects or reports should be documented in such a way that others can complete them.

You should use this period to assess your experience (see Chapter 13 for assessing the agency and yourself). You may have mixed feelings during this stage. You may feel that you are just beginning to function well in the agency and have so much more to learn, or you may be relieved that a difficult course is coming to an end. Be prepared to experience a variety of feelings during this time. The end of your internship may have a deeper meaning for you, especially if your internship comes at the end of your college career. You may find yourself needing to cope with feelings of sadness about the end of your internship, anxiety about where you might go next, and/or elation about a job well done.

Many interns are ready to seek employment at the end of their internship. Whether or not this is true in your case, you should take this opportunity to explore career options with your agency and others and to request letters of recommendation. See Chapter 14 for a detailed discussion of this topic.

What If?

Having worked with many students over the years, there have been a few occasions in which things did not work out. Sometimes there is a major issue going on at the agency that has nothing to do with the student—for example, a reorganization or a major layoff— and all new workers (and interns) are not welcomed with great enthusiasm by staff members. In other cases, the student commits a major error with a field supervisor or a client and is immediately "demoted" to doing lesser duties or is shunned by colleagues. In one particular case, a student was ill but did not call the agency supervisor. He did not know that the schedule had been changed where he was to give a report on staffing to senior administrators that very afternoon. "I knew I had committed a serious error and found that things had changed for me with the department," he reported. "I was told that I had really screwed up and it took some time for my supervisor to have some confidence in me." If this occurs you need to contact your faculty supervisor and have a heart-to-heart discussion about whether this placement should continue. Such a discussion will also involve the field supervisor, and no doubt will be difficult, but it needs to take place. There is no need for you to be completely miserable for the internship and perhaps not get any academic value for the rest of the experience. In many cases, the matter can be resolved and the placement can continue. If not, perhaps an alternative assignment may be in order.

Conclusion

Your role as an intern will change as you progress through a series of stages. The issues and problems that arise at each stage are different and must be dealt with as they occur. Knowing that these are experiences faced by most interns will help you to understand and anticipate the changes. As you become more involved in the actual operations of the agency, you should take care to maintain the ability to examine your experience objectively. Seek the support of your supervisors and peers in this regard.

■ ■ ■ ──

Your Role as an Intern

1. How did you prepare yourself for this internship? In going through anticipatory socialization, did you actively pursue information? From what sources? With whom did you discuss your internship? What did you find out that you had not expected?
2. Describe how you felt during the initial entry and probationary periods. How did you deal with uncertainty and conflict?
3. As you make the transition to productive worker, what changes do you anticipate?
4. What will you have to consider as you approach the termination of your internship?
5. Discuss with your advisor the possible obstacles you might face at the various experiential stages of the internship.

── ■ ■ ■

6

Being a Participant-Observer

An intern assumes the role of a participant-observer, who is someone who works in and studies a particular setting as well as the people and events within that setting. For most students, this is a new role, requiring different skills than those employed in the classroom. This chapter discusses some standard methodologies for describing, analyzing, and assessing the experience. These methods will help you to gain the most from an internship experience as well as assist in written assignments associated with the course. As interns/participant-observers become immersed in the setting, the line between student-researcher and -worker in the agency can become blurred. The intern must remember that he or she is a student who is there to learn firsthand about the field of criminal justice.

After reading this chapter, the student should be able to discuss how he or she will function as a participant-observer during the internship experience. Additionally, the student will be able to review the main steps for conducting both structured and unstructured interviews during the internship experience.

Participant Observation

Participant observation is the most appropriate methodology for documenting your internship experience. Frankfort-Nachmias and Nachmias (2000, pp. 257–8) discuss the use of this method as follows:

> *The method of data collection most closely associated with contemporary field research is participant observation, whereby the investigator attempts to attain some kind of membership in or close attachment to the group that he or she wishes to study. In doing so, the participant observer attempts to adopt the perspectives of the people in the situation being observed. . . . Direct participation in the activities of the observed often entails learning the language, habits, work patterns, leisure activities, and other aspects.*

You may not realize it, but when you engage in any social interaction, you are acting as a participant-observer. Refining your skills and systemizing your approach are essential to becoming an accomplished participant-observer.

From your research methods courses, recall that the researcher must first gain access to an agency or organization. The hurdle of initial entry (one that most participant-observers face) is generally resolved for you through your internship interview and placement.

Many researchers who perform field observations face the issue of what role they should take in the setting. Again, this issue is partially resolved for you, especially if the agency has had previous interns. Here you will have a defined role in the organization: an intern. Although this may mean different things to people inside and outside the organization, it still gives you a certain level of legitimacy in the organization. As an intern, you may be viewed by workers and clients of the agency with acceptance, indifference, suspicion, and (in some cases) hostility. You should not take this personally; rather, you should attempt to understand why your presence evokes different reactions from different people.

After establishing your role, determine what you want to observe in-depth and distinguish what is important from what is trivial. Your attention may be focused by particular interests and goals you have, by assignments from your course requirements, or by the tasks you perform at the agency. If you are required to write a final paper or complete a final project, the topic you choose may determine areas you want to explore. Once you have decided what you want to concentrate on, the next step is to gather the information you will need.

Data Collection

Participant-observers attempt to collect a wide variety of data with regard to an issue or event rather than rely on only one piece of evidence or a set of statistical data.

> It is important to remember that observation, as a method of data collection, uses many techniques. . . . It can take place in natural settings, which enable studying phenomena, such as learning, as they occur in real-life situations (e.g., the classroom or the playground) or in the controlled experimental settings found in the laboratory. The choice of a procedure is guided by the requirements of the research. While the use of observation is determined by the state of knowledge about a general problem, the procedures used may be quite flexible.
>
> Frankfort-Nachmias and Nachmias (2000, p. 191)

It is very important before you begin your internship that you develop a methodology for recording your observations so that you can carefully record your initial impressions. Your first impressions are important because they are formed when you are still an outsider and can see the agency from the viewpoint of a client or the general public.

The first data you collect will be through direct observation. During the first few days of your internship you do not need to be focused on any particular topic; that is, you should record your impressions without regard to any particular issue or area. As you become a participant-observer and become more familiar with the setting and the people in it, you should begin to define specific areas that you want to document based on your goals and the academic assignments.

Your first direct observations might include the following:

1. A careful description of the physical environment, including such items as the amount of space allocated to the agency, layout of the rooms, colors used in decorating, items on the walls, and placement of the furniture.
2. An assessment of the staff in the agency, including the number of males and females and their positions, age distribution, racial composition, how different people dress, how status is exhibited, how space is allocated, types of positions in the agency, and who interacts with whom.
3. An assessment of the clients/public dealt with, including gender, age, racial composition, and socioeconomic status; how the staff relates to the clients/public; and attitudes and impressions clients may have during initial contact with the agency.
4. Your first impressions of the agency and the interactions you have with the staff, clients, and the public.
5. A review of the types of assignments and tasks that you are asked to perform.

The following is an example of one student's early direct observations of her agency.

The first floor of the police department has a lobby, a records room, a switchboard control room, a booking room, a firing range, and a briefing room. The lobby is very large and dimly lighted. The lobby seems very cold and official in its appearance. An admittance window sits at one end of the lobby. Each person who wishes to enter the department further must be checked in by the receptionist. She must buzz the two doors on either side of the room to admit people. This window cuts the rest of the department away from the public who enter the lobby. This system is excellent for security reasons, but it does tend to put a wall between the officers and the public.

As you become more familiar with the setting, your observations should become more perceptive. You should begin to understand the workings of the agencies through ideas that others have shared with you, concepts you have read about or learned in a classroom environment, and even through hunches. Such reflection adds meaning to your experience. As your internship progresses, your initial ideas should be further developed or rejected, based on the collection of additional data.

Once you have decided what your focus will be in gathering information, you should apply a more refined approach to collecting data. Interviewing key staff members and clients in your agency may give you an in-depth understanding of specific issues or problems. While you may use other methodologies to ascertain the information you require, nothing delves into the individual's perceptions, attitudes, and thoughts better than an interview.

Interviews are used by interns to collect information for particular assignments during your internship (e.g., the legal basis of the agency, budget matters, the final project) or to help them further understand an issue at hand. The number of people to be interviewed and the degree of structure in the questioning format are dependent on the information required. The following is a recommended step-by-step process for developing and administering a good interview.

Determine the Area of Interest

Identify a particular area of interest about which you want to gather firsthand data. The topic should be well defined so that you do not find yourself with only broad, ambiguous material at the conclusion of your interview. A common error made by interns is choosing an area that would require either a life's dedication or a team of researchers to complete. For example, one student, interning in a probation department, wanted to study alternative programs to adjudication. This was an enormous undertaking. After he narrowed his topic to a study of how the participants in a diversion program felt about the effectiveness of the program and the counseling they received, he was able to interview several of the program participants and the staff to gather the information he needed. Another wanted to review ways to combat the increase of ransomware, by which a computer is seized by a hacker and payment must be made to unlock the computer for data access. This is an emerging crime trend, and experts are still unsure of how to deal with this problem.

The Structured Interview/Creating Standard Questions

Once you have determined the topic of interest, the next step is to develop a series of standard probes. This ensures that you query each person in a similar way. This is not to say that you should merely read the first question, wait for a response, and then proceed to the second. Rather, the set of standard questions should be used as a checklist to ensure that you cover all the topics. Interviews can be free flowing and cover the same questions in different orders.

The types of questions you choose will have a bearing on the data you collect. Because you want to gather as much information as possible from the interviewee's perspective, you should ask open-ended questions rather than closed ones. For example, "You feel that you're getting something out of being in the program, don't you?" may solicit a narrow or expected response. If you asked, "Some people get something out of being here and others don't seem to; how about you?" the interviewee may respond with personal feelings, attitudes, and opinions on the program, without feeling that you are looking for a particular answer.

In many cases, you will want to start with general questions and move to more specific ones. In order to clarify points or delve deeper into what the individual is saying, you may want to ask him or her for specific examples. As a follow-up to the earlier question about the program, you might ask, "Can you give me an example of a situation when you felt you got something out of the program?" or "Why do you think you feel positively about this situation?"

Good interviewing skills are learned through experience. For help in developing your questions, consult texts, review course materials on interviewing, and/or go over your questions with people who routinely conduct interviews. Once you have decided on the format of the interview, practice with friends or relatives before your first actual interview.

Decide Who You Will Interview

The people you choose to interview will be determined by the data you need. Consultation with your agency supervisor first is paramount for choosing clients and/or staff members who may be willing to cooperate. In many cases, your agency supervisor may be the best person to start this interviewing process. In other situations, he or she may give you some advice on whom to approach or may even set up the interview for you.

Take your clues from the supervisor. Do not simply go into the workplace and start asking interview questions without this guidance! In one situation, a student stopped police personnel in the hallway to ask them questions about ethics (see Chapter 8) and was given the automatic brush-off. His supervisor was not too happy about this initiative either, as coworkers had no idea what was going on!

In approaching the selected individuals, you should:

1. explain the purpose of the interview,
2. explain why you have selected them, and
3. be sure they realize that you are asking them to volunteer to be interviewed and that there will be no repercussions if they do not wish to participate.

This last point is very important because many clients, especially those who are in a vulnerable position, will volunteer in order to appear cooperative or because they fear some type of negative treatment. Others might think that they will be given special treatment if they participate. You should deal with these issues directly before you allow someone to volunteer.

It is essential that you discuss confidentiality with those you wish to interview before beginning. Assure the individual that anything that is said will remain confidential and that, in reporting the content of the interview, names will not be used. See Chapter 8 for ethical guidelines.

Record the Interview

In recent years, questions have been asked about student interns recording interviews through digital devices such as cell phones or small cameras. At this time, the author would generally advise against using any device, simply because criminal justice agencies are fairly conservative. Usually, the use of a cell phone to record a scene for most practitioners indicates that the recording will be used for a future complaint against the agency or be broadcasted on YouTube. As discussed before, there are serious issues of privacy and confidentiality that always need to be addressed in dealing with clients. This may change in the future as more criminal justice practitioners, such as police, will be using body cameras on their uniforms or jackets or in courtrooms to record transactions. But for the time being, do not take out a cellphone and suddenly start to ask questions.

On the other hand, there are those occasions during which a digital recording might be in order and agreed to by the field supervisor. For example, there may be an emergency situation which you are asked to record on your phone. In these cases, some discussions need to take place in terms of the future use of the recording, as it may become an item of legal evidence. As in most cases in an agency, the final say rests with the discretion of the agency field supervisor and the situation at hand.

Write Up the Interview

After each interview, you should carefully document the responses, including responses relevant to your research area, verbatim statements that you may want to include in your report, and a list of new questions and issues derived from the interview. Even if you have recorded the session and taken notes, you should do this as soon as possible so that your recall is fresh as you transcribe and organize your information. You may be certain that you will remember everything you were thinking about during the interview, but the best way to ensure that is to write it up immediately.

Informants, at least in the context of an internship, are people who take interns under their wing and share with them their personal views of the agency, staff, and clients. They are a valuable resource for the participant-observer. Regardless of their motivation or objectivity, they can offer a view of the setting, the people, and the events that occur in the setting (any of which may not be obvious to the observer). One student found this to be true as she gathered information for her final paper.

> I received very useful information from Harry in regard to my topic. I also was given some other sources of information that I can use. The only problem that I discovered from Harry is that the drug sweep that occurred is not in any way documented. There are no records kept of any of the plans or procedures of the raid. It seems that having documentation of these incidents just wouldn't be practical and it is additional work that there is no manpower to do or hours to cover. Therefore, once again, much of the information about the sweep process is from verbal sources.

The insight gained from such encounters may lead to new areas of study and to a greater understanding of who is involved and why things happen.

With valuable information that can not be obtained in any other way, you need to be cautious and objective. For example, one intern was drawn into a particular subgroup in the agency because of his relationship with an informant. He was clearly identified with that group and found it difficult to interact with other staff as a result. Remaining neutral in office politics is important if one is going to function as an independent participant-observer. Moreover, situations are not always as they appear at first glance. Try to remain objective and open to other explanations for particular situations and behaviors. The following journal entry indicates one intern's acute awareness of the need for neutrality and objectivity.

I have been taken into many people's confidences around here. I know so much gossip about everyone it's hard to even think straight when someone starts to tell me more, like who they don't like. I feel like I'm getting so wrapped up in all this back-stabbing. I can't stand it. Before it goes any farther, I am trying to just gain people's confidence without having to join in on the gossip. I have never seen so many people that didn't like one another. The thing that surprises me the most, I think, is the fact that so many men gossip. I thought women were the ones that gossiped. Not true here. That is probably due to one of two things: either the fact that there are so many men working in one place all together and it is more noticeable, or everyone simply hates one another and their personalities completely conflict.

The Unstructured Interview

Another method to gain information is through the unstructured interview. As discussed by Maxfield and Babbie (2008), an unstructured interview is a conversation that deals with a specific set of topic goals that the interviewer wishes to learn about. This is a very good method since you are in the organizational environment for a relatively long period of time and you can meet with various people throughout the internship. For example, learning about the budget process may not occur in one scheduled appointment. It would require a number of "sessions" over the course of a period of time with the interviewee in order to gain a good working knowledge about the budget and the budget-making process. In most cases, undergraduate students would not have any experience about this kind of topic. Official documents can help you become more familiar with the client population and assist you in doing research. For example, reading several cases (provided you have permission to access them) will acquaint you with basic demographic and background information on the clients in your agency. A more detailed analysis of specific areas of interest may yield information that will allow you to corroborate previously gathered data. For example, one intern wanted to study the effectiveness of an intensive supervision program (ISP) at her field site, a probation department. The director of the program stated that the ISP was 90 percent effective, but a careful analysis of client files from the previous two years indicated that the program was effective with only 50 percent of the clients. Using the same method, another student was able to develop a profile of juveniles who had been tried as adults.

Before you go into official files (digital or paper), be sure to obtain permission from your field supervisor and find out the "rules of engagement" in terms of preparing your reports. For example, a closed criminal case may be reported with few prohibitions. However, a new piece of software that is under development or testing may be entirely off-limits for any external reports including those to your faculty supervisor. Remember, the main thing here is to do no harm to either your agency or those whom you are working with.

Another area for review would be organizational web sites and related professional associations that have a wide range of information related to your organization and its workings. For example, a student dealing with alternatives to incarceration for juvenile offenders was drawn to official reports and reviews completed by the state bar association and the state professional association for juvenile probation and law enforcement officers.

Data Recording

Besides deciding what you want to observe and what method to use in collecting data, you will need to determine how you will record your observations. There are several methods used to document field experiences, including a daily calendar, diary, log, journal, or a field notebook. While some of these terms are used interchangeably, the major differences are in the detail and type of information recorded. For example, a daily calendar usually includes descriptive information (e.g., appointments, events or situations, meetings, and tasks completed). While a calendar allows one to quickly ascertain daily activities, it leaves out the essence of the experience. Without further documentation, the details may be forgotten. A diary usually includes the information entered into a calendar as well as a more personal recording of the experience. Feelings, thoughts, and beliefs are included, but not in any systematic way.

Logs, journals, or field notebooks are used by participant-observers to document their experiences carefully and systematically. Along with the descriptive and personal material included in the first two forms, these recording formats include a focus on particular issues or phenomena. Situations and events are studied, and efforts are made to explain them, based on hunches, inferences, and hypotheses arrived at through careful observation. In some cases, researchers record their field interviews and their assessment of documents in their field notebooks. The following example was drawn from a student's field notebook.

> *Our second activity of the evening was a missing person's report. The missing person was a twelve-year-old boy who had been missing from his family since 9 A.M. The boy*

had been suspended from school that morning and his sister had heard from friends that he was seen on the school playground in the afternoon. Officer Smith wrote all of this information on a small note pad that he carried. He did not copy the information directly from the complainant onto one of the offense/incident report forms as most of the other officers would have done. He did not write a report right away on the incident. He used his discretion as an officer in his decision to search for the boy rather than spend half an hour to forty-five minutes in one spot writing the report and then handing it in to headquarters. We had a good description of the boy, who was wearing red sweat pants, a black jacket, and a blue cap. The family also showed us a picture of the boy. I believe that Officer Smith made the right decision to look for the boy instead of filing the routine paperwork, which would not help to find the boy. Officer Smith said that he would file the report if he could not locate the boy within a couple of hours. We located the boy about an hour later, several blocks away. I believe that Officer Smith used his discretion properly in this instance. I believe that the officers need to be given more discretion for the taking of reports. The department has become very strict with reports, ordering the officers to take reports on almost every call that they respond to. I believe that it is important for the police officers to have discretion because they are dealing with individuals and unique situations.

This student recorded a description of the incident and her personal feelings about it, focusing on the issue of officer discretion in dealing with situations while on patrol. If she were to choose to write a paper about officer discretion, she would be careful to record other incidents showing the need for such discretion.

Recording good field notes on a regular basis takes a great deal of discipline. This is especially true after a long day at the agency. The accuracy of the notes will be greatly affected by even a few days' delay in recording them. It is suggested that the notes be written or digitally recorded after work rather than on site (which might affect people's responses). Because your notes may contain confidential and sensitive material, you should not bring them to the agency. One intern left her written field notes at the agency by mistake. The next day, several of the staff behaved decidedly cool to her. This was rather perplexing to her, as she had developed a good rapport with them in the 2 months of her internship. Later in the day, her agency supervisor returned her notebook, containing her impressions of the staff and the workings of the agency; it had been read by some of the staff. While the student was able to minimize the damage with most of the staff and her supervisor, there were some people who never spoke to her again.

Besides damaging relationships, this student could have caused problems for some of the staff and clients by revealing sensitive material. To protect the identity of those you are observing, it is important that you do not use actual names. In addition, you should not write about ongoing cases in a manner that will reveal confidential material that might affect the outcome of the case if that material becomes known.

Most researchers write their notes in complete, grammatically correct sentences. Shorthand or short phrases tend to lose some of their meaning when reread weeks later.

Try to use specific words and phrases whenever possible. Street jargon and racial or sexist slurs are to be avoided unless they are part of a direct quote or you are documenting the behavior of certain individuals.

One Final Word of Caution

As interns/participant-observers become immersed in the setting, the line between student-researcher and -worker in the agency becomes blurred. You will have to remind yourself that you are a student who is there to learn about the field of criminal justice firsthand. Your ability to record your observations objectively will be greatly impaired if you are not able to stand back and view the people, events, and situations as a participant-observer.

■ ■ ■ ▬▬▬▬▬▬▬▬▬▬▬▬▬▬▬▬▬▬▬▬▬▬▬▬▬▬▬▬

Thinking About Your Internship

1. Discuss how you will keep field notes.
2. Use your field notes to describe the environment at your internship site. Consider colors, furniture, arrangement, noise level, employee dress, activity level, and anything else that contributes to the daily environment.
3. Using your field notes, describe the people with whom you are working, both personnel and clients.
4. Using your field notes and referring to Chapter 5, chart your progress through the probationary and productive worker stages.
5. Using your field notes and referring to Chapter 5, identify specific issues and problems you face at each stage.
6. Develop an interview following the procedures outlined in this chapter on a topic assigned by your instructor.
7. Develop a profile of a specific client group using the agency files.

▬▬▬▬▬▬▬▬▬▬▬▬▬▬▬▬▬▬▬▬▬▬▬ ■ ■ ■

7

Intern Supervision

Interns are supervised both by a professor (faculty supervisor) and a staff member at the internship site (agency supervisor). These supervisors should be concerned foremost with the professional and personal development of the student. Thus, it is essential for the intern to understand the supervisory process and to be able to determine the extent and type of supervision needed from three sources: the faculty supervisor, the agency supervisor, and coworkers. It is very important to have smooth and effective communication between intern and faculty and agency supervisors. In field situations, it is important that interns receive and transmit information and understand what is going on. During an internship, agency supervisors who are good communicators use a technique that is often referred to as coaching. A good coach will not only direct an intern, but will explain the legal, ethical, and operational ramifications of what is occurring. At the end of this chapter, you will be asked a series of questions on your views of supervision and how you have handled supervision from your previous academic or work experiences.

Definition of Supervision

If supervision is not merely about having an authority figure watch over others to make sure that they perform tasks properly, then what is it? Supervision is a process in which two people (e.g., student and supervisor or student and coworker) work together for the primary purpose of enhancing the professional and personal development of the person being supervised. Therefore, the major objective is learning, with the performance of tasks viewed as a means to an end. Nevertheless, it is important to note that the organization has work to be done, and your supervisor is accountable for the quality of that work, including your job performance. The goals and objectives that you have set (see Chapter 4) may provide the parameters necessary for productive and appropriate supervision as defined in this chapter.

Your relationship with your supervisor should be one of interdependence rather than dependence. While you and your supervisor may begin as master and apprentice, your relationship should move toward two people participating in a learning process. There will be mutuality in the relationship because, while you will receive a great deal of feedback, you will also contribute your input.

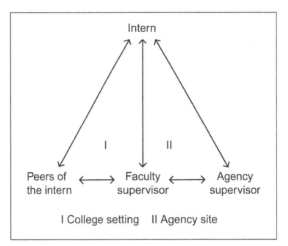

FIGURE 7.1 Student-Centered Model of Supervision.

Figure 7.1 illustrates the student-centered model of supervision that is found in most internships. The student must coordinate his or her interactions with the faculty supervisor, agency supervisor, and peers. This model is student-centered because the amount of supervisory interaction depends on how much the student seeks it.

Faculty Supervisor

Your internship experience will be supervised by a professor or internship coordinator whose role will include several responsibilities. He or she will act as a liaison between the college and the agency, especially during the placement and evaluation periods, setting the requirements for the internship course and monitoring your experience. The faculty supervisor will help shape your internship by giving you a series of readings and academic assignments and by requesting the organization to allow you to observe, and participate in certain tasks at the field site. He or she should also be available to discuss sensitive issues or interpersonal problems that arise at your internship site, and, above all, be accessible if an emergency arises.

Both the internship coordinator and your faculty supervisor will want to help you have the best possible experience. The first step in this process is to discuss your interests and career plans so that the coordinator can help you find an appropriate internship. Preparing a goals and objectives statement such as that presented in Chapter 4 is one of many ways to explore potential placements. This is especially important if the coordinator seeks to match students with potential placement sites. If you are required to find your own site, before striking out on your own, you should spend some time discussing the options that can offer you the type of experience you desire.

Your faculty supervisor, who often is not the program's internship coordinator, will monitor your progress directly during the internship through methods such as individual and conference telephone calls, the grading of academic work during the semester, e-mails, and agency visits. For the former, while you may think he or she is checking up on you, the main purpose is to be sure you are having a worthwhile experience. Visits, e-mails, and phone calls made by the faculty supervisor early in the internship often help resolve problems quickly. They also serve to clarify the purpose of the internship for placement sites that have not had interns previously from your school, or for agency supervisors who have had no experience supervising students. As an example of how a professor can improve your experience, consider the following. Most probation departments are unwilling to allow interns to write pre-sentence investigation reports. However, when a professor intervenes and suggests that the student and a probation officer do the same report separately and then compare and critique them, the agency supervisor usually agrees.

In rare cases, you and your professor may agree that a particular internship site is not appropriate. Early visits and phone calls can determine this and make it feasible to procure another site for the student. For example, one student was placed in a state attorney general's office, where he found that recent political changes had left the office in chaos and without adequate staff to provide an appropriate internship experience. After a brief period of doing little more than answering the phone and reading old files, the frustrated intern contacted the faculty supervisor. The faculty supervisor called and subsequently visited the internship supervisor at the site. It was evident that the agency was not in a state to offer the intern the supervision and guidance necessary. The student (to his relief) was placed elsewhere. In another case, the agency, a not-for-profit child assistance program, was closed by the state for financial fraud and the student arrived to see a sign reading "Closed by Order of the State." Again, a new placement was arranged.

In a broad sense, your faculty supervisor will shape your internship experience. Through course assignments, you will be required to observe specific aspects of your placement environment. Your written communications will help the professor monitor your internship. Your openness and willingness to discuss problems, shortcomings, and feelings will help him or her better understand your experience. This, in turn, will put the faculty supervisor in a position to help you work through and resolve personal and professional issues. A common misconception among students is that if they write about or discuss their difficulties and weaknesses, they will not get a good evaluation or grade. The paradox is that the less you talk about these issues, the more the professor will question how much you are actually gaining from your internship. No one expects that you will not have problems in what is probably your first professional experience. Neither does anyone expect that you will not have concerns about your ability to perform new tasks. The mark of maturity is that you have the insight to identify these problems and make an effort to work on them. Remember, a major goal of any internship is to grow, both professionally and personally.

There are some issues you may encounter that should be discussed with your faculty supervisor before approaching anyone at the site. Most of these are in the realm of ethics.

Once you are accepted by an agency, you are allowed to view the internal workings of the system. Some of the observations may reveal ethically questionable activities, such as the provision of free food or services or computer use policies. Others may reveal methods that are in direct conflict with what you may have learned in class, such as a questionable search-and-seizure situation. In such cases, it is advisable to call your faculty supervisor and discuss the matter. Your professor can counsel you on how to proceed with the matter or may choose to handle it personally. You want to avoid being labeled a squealer, so you should not report the matter directly to your agency supervisor before talking with your professor. Such a label would hamper your role as participant-observer for the remainder of your internship.

Your faculty supervisor can help you balance your experience or bring it into perspective. You may be confronted with cynicism, stress (both psychological and physical), violent crime, child abuse, deplorable home conditions, and/or indifference by agency workers. For example, someone working in a police department may see the body of a person who has been violently murdered. Many police officers have, by necessity, developed a callous outward appearance toward such atrocities. Because of their attitude, you may not feel comfortable discussing your feelings with them. Your faculty supervisor, being removed from the situation yet at the same time familiar with it, may be the best one with whom to discuss your reaction.

Above all, it is important to be in frequent communication with your faculty supervisor either by e-mail or phone. If you have questions about course assignments, simply ask. If there is an emergency, or you have fallen ill or were hurt at the internship site, you or the agency must call your faculty supervisor. One of the first clues that things are not going well is a student who fails to check in or complete assignments according to a defined schedule. While assignment lateness may have a negative impact on your final grade, most faculty supervisors are concerned about the success of the placement and the student's well-being. In a few instances, students have fallen off the radar screen generally for personal reasons that often have nothing to do with the placement. There may be a family matter or personal health reason for this situation. When this occurs, the faculty supervisor will contact not only the field site, but maybe family and friends to locate the student. In rare instances, the student intern may be summoned back to campus as a first step for termination of the experience based on unprofessional behavior.

Field Supervisor

Your field supervisor is extremely important to your internship because he or she is at the site and, as a mentor, can provide you with many experiences and opportunities that cannot be found in a classroom. In the initial meeting, you and your field supervisor should discuss the expectations and goals you each have for the internship. This discussion should also cover the routine you will follow: your hours, the rules and regulations of the agency, appropriate dress, the schedule for supervision, work areas, and your role in the agency. During this time, the schedule for major projects and any formal training should be discussed. It is important that you share copies of course outlines, evaluation procedures, and any other school information related to the internship program.

Your supervisor, who may be the head of the department or a designee, will expect you to conduct yourself in a professional manner and follow the prescribed codes of conduct for agency employees. You will be asked to become familiar with the rules and regulations that govern employee behavior, partially through reading internal documents regarding guidelines for interns. Very often, these formal guidelines do not exist for student interns and so you will have to ask. After the orientation period, most experienced intern supervisors phase in increasingly more difficult tasks as the intern demonstrates competence. As discussed in Chapter 5, the first phase begins with simple assignments and then continues on with more complex tasks. The parameters for this process are set by the organization's mission and your goals. Eventually, most student interns become productive workers under the guidance of the field supervisor.

The supervision schedule you set up with your designated supervisor will depend on whether you work with him or her on a daily basis. If you work with your supervisor daily, the tendency is to discuss issues, problems, and questions as they arise. This type of supervision has some shortcomings, however. You may find that after rethinking an issue, reading about it, and/or discussing it with a fellow intern or agency employee, you have new ideas or questions that you would like to discuss with your supervisor. Without a scheduled session, this may be difficult to fit into a daily routine.

It is important, therefore, to consider two types of meetings. Weekly sessions can be arranged to discuss the events of the week, your progress toward your goals, experiences that you would like to have in the future, and your development as a professional. A mid-internship meeting can be held to assess your performance and experiences to date and to structure the remaining time. (Of course, issues and concerns arising from your observations and experiences can be discussed at these meetings as well.)

Your relationship with your field supervisor will be similar to the relationship between you and your faculty supervisor. The most important thing to remember is that you should not be reluctant to discuss problems, shortcomings, and successes. This is the only way you can derive maximum benefit from the experience. It is wise, however, to be measured and thoughtful regarding what information you choose to share with your supervisor. You should exclude revelations of irrelevant personal information, as inappropriate self-disclosures can result in a negative evaluation. The information you let out is out to stay and cannot be taken back; always exercise self-restraint and good judgment in deciding what to share. It is important to maintain an open relationship with your field supervisor, however, because the intern, the supervisor, and the agency all lose when the intern stops communicating his or her concerns.

This raises the question of why organizations like to participate in intern programs. For the most part, many organizations are recruiting future college graduates or for the profession. Many supervisors enjoy working with students as it helps them to continue as a teacher and to evaluate the workings of their own organization or department through questions presented by the student during the semester. The author enjoyed these encounters with students, and it also allows any field supervisor to keep abreast of new trends that are occurring in the academic environment.

While many intern-supervisor relationships are successful, it is possible that you will find yours is not. A supervisor may not have time to meet with an intern because of work-related situations such as major projects, personnel shortages, or unexpected crises. In some situations, the student and the supervisor have a clash of personalities. If your agency supervision is inadequate, find out why and, if necessary, ask that the responsibility for your supervision be transferred to someone else. Your faculty supervisor will be able to help you keep your perspective, sort out the problem with the agency, and expedite any necessary change.

On a final note, students who are in virtual placements, or in situations where the supervisor is in another city, must go out of their way to stay connected. It is important to have regularly scheduled phone or online interchanges in order to gauge the progress of assigned projects and completion of learning goals.

Peer Support

Other agency staff also can provide a valuable perspective to your internship. Those who started as interns themselves will understand what you are experiencing. Employees who have not held their positions for very long also may have some of the same feelings and experiences that you do. These coworkers can offer you the viewpoint of one who has recently been through that initial transition. Discussing particular situations, clients, and so on with several agency employees can provide you with a variety of reactions and methods of handling cases or incidents. As there is generally no single correct way of handling a particular situation, you must synthesize the differing viewpoints and decide which is the best method for you.

Other student interns who are having an experience similar to yours can be a valuable resource. When faced with a new situation, many people wonder whether what they are feeling is shared by others or is unique to them. Common perceptions include feeling overwhelmed, anxious, inadequate, and unprepared for the experience. While a faculty or agency supervisor can appreciate your situation and offer support during this period, your student peers are likely to be having similar reactions at the same time. Discovering that you are not alone and learning how others are coping with these issues can aid you in working through this period. Quite recently, three interns assigned to a forensics center found that they had a number of things in common and soon established an informal working/support group to deal with various issues and tasks that arose during the semester.

Many programs have gone to an online format, which allows for discussion threads among student interns. An exchange of feelings and experiences through online chat-rooms or formal discussion threads will also help you broaden your perspective. Not all probation departments, district attorney's offices, crime and cyber research laboratories, and police agencies function in the same way. For example, if you are in an urban police department, you can discuss your experiences with someone placed in a rural or suburban setting. Areas to compare might be managerial style, interpersonal interactions, inter- and intra-agency relationships, and the different methodologies used in completing a task. This information may be useful to you in determining the type of setting in which you would like to work.

Because any interchange that you have with a fellow student will require you to comment on his or her situation, you will begin to develop some supervisory skills. Understanding your needs and goals for supervision will aid you in helping others. When discussing other students' problems and issues, listen carefully to what they say and try to help them as best you can. Try to refrain from giving advice based solely on your personal experience. It is important to remember that other students' situations will not be the same as yours and that they are dealing with different personalities in their internship settings. Therefore, simply saying, "This worked for me, why don't you try it?" may not be appropriate. Rather, you could discuss why it worked for you and what the similarities and differences would be if the other person were to do the same thing.

In talking with your peers, you may find that there are situations with which they cannot help you or vice versa. In such cases, it may be suggested that someone else be consulted (probably the faculty supervisor). The following example illustrates this point. Student A e-mailed Student B to discuss a problem she was having. It centered on behavior she had observed that was ethically questionable. The student observed officers in the department in which she was placed disappearing for long periods of time. She became aware that the officers were meeting outside the department to play poker during work hours. This practice left the student covering the department without supervision for long periods during the day. She was not sure whether she should bother the faculty supervisor with the details and did not feel comfortable talking to her agency supervisor for fear of being labeled a squealer. After talking together about the issue, Student B strongly encouraged Student A to talk to their professor. Student B explained that, in this case, the professor was the best person to assess the seriousness of the situation and to determine how it should be handled. Student A finally called the professor and was able to resolve the dilemma satisfactorily. At the end of the semester, Student A stated that had it not been for the support and encouragement of Student B, she would not have discussed the matter with her faculty supervisor.

Peer support can be sought in a formal setting or through informal methods. In large organizations that take anywhere from five to fifty students per term, seminars involving all the students allow time for peer discussion and support. As previously mentioned, if the professor has set up an online course, you will have discussion threads or chatrooms available for this purpose. Informally, as illustrated in the example above, you can call or arrange to meet with a fellow student when an immediate need arises. Interns have set up their own discussion groups to stay in touch using a variety of free collaboration tools readily available on the Internet such as Google Groups and LinkedIn.

Conclusion

Communication between you and your faculty and agency supervisors is very important. In field situations, it is important that you all receive and transmit information and understand what is going on. During an internship, agency supervisors who are good communicators use a technique that is often referred to as coaching. A good coach will not only direct you, but will explain the legal, ethical, and operational ramifications of what is going on.

Thus, supervision must be viewed as a means of development, both professional and personal. The ability to seek supervision and benefit from it is a skill that you will use again and again in your career. The three sources you have available to you during your internship—faculty supervisor, agency supervisor, and your peers—can each contribute to your growth in different ways. However, the key to your development is your ability to understand the supervisory process and to seek out answers to your questions and peer support on a regular basis.

■ ■ ■ ━━━

Thinking About Your Internship

1. What experiences have you had with supervision in previous work or school situations?
2. What do you want to gain from supervision during your internship?
3. If you are currently an intern, describe the supervision you are receiving from your field supervisor.
4. How can you use supervision to grow professionally and personally?
5. From what type of supervision do you learn best?
6. How do you feel about authority figures?
7. How do you react to constructive feedback, both positive and negative?
8. How well can you give feedback to others?

━━━ ■ ■ ■

8

Ethics in Practice: Guidelines

Criminal justice interns may see people being treated unjustly or unfairly, or fellow agency workers and supervisors involving themselves in unethical or illegal activities. Once one begins to compromise values and ethics, it becomes a slippery slope from which recovery may be difficult, if not impossible. An intern may not be in a position to change things, but examining occurrences can help an intern clarify and rethink his or her position. Interns are not immune to ethical dilemmas. While some issues are clear-cut, others are much more difficult to discern. The criminal justice system should exemplify justice and make justice its end. Individuals should be treated fairly and justly in its administration. To do otherwise makes a mockery of the system. The administration of justice can only be improved through high ethical standards and personnel who are willing to abide by them. At the end of this chapter you will be asked to review a number of questions on ethics that will deal with ethical issues both before and during your internship.

Introduction

The abstract issue of ethics is dealt with in most criminal justice programs either through a specific course on ethics, the application of ethical issues in topic courses, or a combination of the two. Within the classroom, it is usually easy to determine the right course of action when presented with a case situation. However, when interns are confronted with real-life situations in the field, human, organizational, and practical factors tend to cloud the issue, raising doubts as to the proper course of action. It is important to distinguish between your personal ethics and your emerging professional ethics. Regardless of your personal ethical positions, you will need to meet the demands that will be placed on you as a result of ethical standards in the profession you desire to join. Most professions set ethical standards for their members that serve as guidelines for decision making and boundaries for professional behavior. Violation of these may result in the loss of the right to practice (e.g., a lawyer being disbarred or a psychologist losing his or her license).

As a professional, you will be confronted with ethical and moral dilemmas requiring you to choose between compelling alternatives. For example, you may be faced with a decision between something that you believe may be harmful to your client and an action that violates the policies of your organization. Another common dilemma occurs when you observe something that you believe is either unethical or illegal among your colleagues. Should you report the incident to your supervisor or keep quiet in order to maintain good relations with your fellow workers? As discussed by Jordan et al. (2007), students sometimes face these real-life situations as they complete internship programs.

Learning about and practicing the ethical standards of a profession is an important objective in your internship. Being confronted with moral dilemmas in practice is part of your development as a caring professional interested in the application of justice in our system.

Codes of Ethics

A code of ethics provides broad ethical statements to guide employees in their professional lives. Most agencies and organizations have codes of ethics that are unique to them. They express the organization's philosophy and guide the behavior and decision making of the people in the organization. Andrew Olson of the Center for Study of Ethics in the Professions at Illinois Institute of Technology writes:

> Codes of ethics are to be reflections of the morally permissible standards of conduct which members of a group make binding upon themselves. These standards of conduct often reach beyond or delve deeper into societal morality in order to give guidance to people within a group on issues that are specific to the group. Often, codes of ethics prioritize commonly conflicting principles, which underlie the standards of conduct within an organization, either by explicitly weighting the principles or implicitly ordering the principles in order to give guidance on how one is to act as a morally responsible agent of the group when situations require an element of compromise between principles.
>
> Olson (2008)

It is evident from current events, dealing with such issues as police brutality and use of force, corporate fraud, illegal computer use, and political corruption, that employees in every venue are faced with ethical dilemmas, some of which are complex and sensitive. Codes of conduct or ethics have become essential, as all organizations realize that they have a responsibility to their employees, customers or clients, communities, shareholders, and suppliers. When you begin your internship, you should ask for a copy of the code of ethics so that you know your internship site's expectations in terms of ethical standards. A police department code of ethics might include an ethical behavior statement such as this one from the International Association of Chiefs of Police: "On my honor, I will never betray my badge, my integrity, my character, or the public trust. I will always have the courage to hold myself and others accountable for our actions. I will always uphold the constitution of my community and the agency I serve" (International Association of Chiefs of Police, 2004).

One tenet of the Association of Certified Fraud Examiners (2004) Code of Ethics is: "A Certified Fraud Examiner shall, at all times, exhibit the highest level of integrity in the performance of all professional assignments, and will accept only assignments for which there is reasonable expectation that the assignment will be completed with professional competence." Similarly, Lockheed Martin's Code of Ethics and Business Conduct includes statements such as: "Lockheed Martin holds each director, executive, leader, employee, and agent accountable for upholding our Vision, our Values, and our Code. In so doing, we ensure that Lockheed Martin's business will be conducted consistent with the high ethical standards that we demand from each other, and that others have the right to demand from us" (Lockheed Martin, 2006). Codes of ethics are as diverse as the organizations or agencies for which they are written.

You may find that you will be required to study and/or receive training on your site's code of ethics. You may also be required to sign a code-of-conduct statement that indicates you are aware of and/or have received training on the code. Violations of the code of ethics or conduct can result in disciplinary action, which may include termination.

Ethical Standards for the Emerging Professional

To help you avoid the pitfalls that many interns have encountered, several ethical standards are discussed in this section. These, of course, are not intended to supplant your internship site's code of ethics.

Corruption and Misconduct

Corruption and misconduct are persistent problems in both the private and public sectors. Corruption is the misuse of one's official role to obtain personal gain. It includes criminal behavior such as accepting a bribe. Misconduct relates to various kinds of behaviors prohibited by the agency, such as failing to respond to an emergency call or being rude to a complainant. Over the years, several students became involved in corrupt activity or misconduct. Some of the most blatant examples follow.

> *On his way home from the agency, a sheriff's intern was issued a summons for speeding by the state police. He attempted to fix the ticket by having his field supervisor call the state police station commander requesting that the ticket be voided. The intern's field supervisor terminated his internship immediately.*

As an intern, you have an obligation not to engage in illegal activity. The intern above jeopardized not only his internship, but also his future, by attempting to subvert the justice system.

A suspect was being transported to the station house when he became unruly. After he spit through the protective screen, the field supervisor and the student took him out of the car and beat him up.

John Fuller writes in his article, "Street Cop Ethics": "Don't be provoked into an unnecessary use of force incident. Meet force with force and don't get hurt, but don't go over the line and engage in an obviously brutal response. When the resistance stops, the force should stop. Beating a drunk into the sidewalk because he insulted your mother is police brutality, plain and simple" (Fuller, 2001). While the student in the above incident clearly should not have participated in an excessive use of force, there is another ethical dilemma inherent in the situation. Even if he had not participated, he would have observed a misuse of power and would be under obligation to report it. Admittedly, this is a difficult thing for an intern to do. In cases such as this, it is best to go to your faculty supervisor for guidance and advice.

After being arrested, a prisoner confessed that much of the merchandise in the vehicle was not his. Members of the squad, including the intern, helped themselves to various items and took them home.

In this case, the intern clearly engaged in illegal activity. While you will feel peer pressure in your role as intern, you must maintain your ethical standards and make every effort to remove yourself from any situation that makes you feel uncomfortable.

While working a late tour, an intern and his supervising officer decided to sleep for a couple of hours.

As noted by O'Connor, "Sleeping on duty, of course, is just an extreme example of goldbricking, the avoidance of work or performing only the amount minimally necessary to satisfy superiors. Goldbricking can take many forms: from ignoring or passing on calls for service to someone else; overlooking suspicious behavior; or engaging in personal business while on duty" (O'Connor, 2005). If you are faced with a situation involving sleeping on duty, it is best to discuss it with your faculty supervisor as soon as possible.

During a lunch break an intern with an urban police department requested access to a computer with Internet capability. While using the computer, the intern sent e-mails to several of his friends and accessed pornography sites. The intern's field supervisor terminated his internship immediately after computer logs started showing hits on the porn sites.

Regarding this matter, Lockheed Martin's Code of Ethics and Business Conduct states:

Proper use of company and customer property, electronic communications systems, information resources, material facilities, and equipment is your responsibility. . . .

While these assets are intended to be used for the conduct of Lockheed Martin's business, it is recognized that occasional personal use by employees may occur without adversely affecting the interests of the company. Personal use of company assets must always be in accordance with corporate and company policy—consult your supervisor for appropriate guidance and permission.

Lockheed Martin (2006)

Following your agency's acceptable-use policy for technology is critical. Certainly, accessing pornographic web sites would not be acceptable use. If you are unsure about using Internet access for personal e-mail, social media, or Web surfing, ask your field supervisor. In addition, we caution against conducting excessive personal business (e-mail, phone calls, booking airline travel, and the like) while you are at your internship site.

While these are clear examples of corruption or misconduct committed by interns with or without direct knowledge of their field supervisors, other situations with which you may be faced will fall into an ethical gray area. Such situations may include

1. Acceptance of meals at a discount or without payment;
2. Receipt of merchandise from merchants at discount rates;
3. Admission to sporting and entertainment events without charge;
4. Use or the threatened use of force;
5. Acceptance of gifts;
6. Use of confidential information for private gain or to impress peers;
7. Access to mail, e-mail, copiers, computers, and other services for personal use.

You may find that the department or agency does not have clear policies about such conduct. In many of these gray-area situations, you will have to make your own judgments, based on your value system. That is not to say that making such a judgment will be easy. It may be tempting to let the peer pressure of agency employees override your value system. The classic example is what is called the "coffee-and-doughnut syndrome." While interning with a police department, you may have decided that you would never accept free coffee or doughnuts from the coffee shop, but once there with three or four officers, you may have trouble maintaining your stance. It is then important to "ask yourself why the guy is offering the freebies. Could it be that he wants you (or the officers you are with) to give his place more attention than you give the other businesses on your post? Think about it—is he entitled to extra-special attention for the price of a burger and coffee?" (Fuller, 2001).

Concerns have been expressed by students in dealing with real or perceived powers given to them by the agency. For example, at some intern sites, students have been given peace officer powers of arrest. In many cases, based on the nature of the interaction or transaction, a client or practitioner assumes that the intern he or she is dealing with is an official agent of the agency. In all cases, you have to remember that you are a student learning to be a professional, something that is not always easy, and you will make mistakes as well as difficult decisions. You may want to discuss such situations with your peers and/or faculty supervisor.

Working at Your Competence Level

Early in your internship experience, you may feel overwhelmed with the responsibility of your position and wonder if you can adequately perform your assigned tasks. You may at first be reluctant to ask questions, either because you think you should already know the answer or because you do not know whom to ask. If the issue or problem is minor, being hesitant to ask will not make it worse. However, if the welfare of an individual client or agency employee is a concern, you have an obligation to overcome your reluctance and seek help. Failure to do so may be detrimental or fatal; the consequences of such behavior should never be underestimated.

As you become a more skilled intern, you may perform many of the same duties as employees in your agency. While your competence in handling routine issues may not be questioned, you may encounter cases or situations about which you are unsure. Consultation with others in the agency, especially your supervisor, is very important before making a decision. You may not be aware of some of the factors that should be considered in assessing a situation. Some of these may include informal agency policies, undocumented background information on the individual in question, or policies of other criminal justice agencies that must be consulted. Whether or not your initial inclination is the one that is followed, it never hurts to confer with a fellow employee or supervisor (whether during your internship or after a professional position has been procured).

At some time during your internship, a task may be assigned to you and subsequently transferred to another employee. You may be upset if this occurs and see it as unwillingness on the part of your supervisor to let you handle interesting tasks. If this happens, however, it will probably be because the task requires special attention or services and your supervisor does not feel that you are skilled enough to handle them. In at least one situation, the intern's attitude toward such a transfer improved after it was explained that the supervisor did not assign the client to any employee who had been there for less than 2 years.

The balance between accepting a challenging task and the realization that you have exceeded your competency in a given area is one with which all growing professionals grapple. You want to assume the challenge, knowing that if you do well it will help your confidence and improve your abilities. At the same time, you must be concerned with the less desirable effects that could occur, including consequences to others.

Maintaining Confidentiality and Privacy

Confidentiality is perhaps the most important issue in any criminal justice internship. As an intern, you must learn the confidentiality limits set by the law, your organization, and your field supervisor. You have a responsibility to your agency not to discuss privileged information outside the organization. For example, if, as a police intern, you are working with an officer on an important lead, your discussion of it with friends may compromise the case. If you are working with a client, there may be certain things that your supervisor has told you must be reported, either because of the law or agency policy (e.g., an admission of guilt). There also may be some things that your supervisor wants reported because they are not within your ability to handle (e.g., a contemplated suicide).

The issue of confidentiality becomes important when there is a major crime in a community. Several student interns assigned to a district attorney's office quickly learned this after a major assault-murder took place under the guise of religious counseling. Other issues may not be so clear-cut. For example, if someone is hinting at committing a crime or talking about escaping from a correctional facility, you must determine the potential for carrying out the act, the seriousness of the act, your responsibility to the agency and society, your competence in handling the situation, and the effect that revealing the information will have on your relationship with the individual. This is a very difficult assessment to make. You may want to seek assistance from your agency or faculty supervisor.

Another issue that arises with confidentiality is "need to know." This recently came up at a meeting with cybersecurity student interns working on various projects. What it means is that you do not have to know everything that is going on in the unit unless it has a direct impact on your work. It also means that you are not to go prying into other employee or intern projects unless invited to do so. This becomes important as one aspect of confidentiality in the workplace.

Interns in positions that involve counseling sometimes make the unrealistic promise of unqualified confidentiality in order to establish the proper climate for a good relationship. In fact, this can destroy the relationship if the intern finds he or she must break the confidentiality because of a legal issue or agency policy. Mandated reporting of child abuse or neglect is a good example. If a client discloses information regarding the abuse or neglect of a child, the law requires most agency personnel to report it. Failure to do so would violate the law as well as agency policy. If a client has not been advised that such reporting is mandated, feelings of betrayal and anger may result, and the relationship that the intern has invested in building may be forever destroyed. Setting limits on confidentiality before you are faced with such a situation puts the individual on notice that, in certain areas, you will not be able to withhold disclosures.

It is recommended that you prepare a short statement on confidentiality. This will help you to clarify your obligations, as well as give you a ready fallback reply when you are faced with such a situation in the field. For example, when counseling or interviewing clients, you should let them know that you cannot promise them absolute confidentiality. Rather, you could say "everything you share with me will remain confidential unless you tell me about doing bodily harm to yourself or another and/or you discuss committing illegal acts. In those cases, I may have to discuss what you reveal to me with my supervisor."

Determining how much to share with colleagues and supervisors is another problem faced by interns. If you are working with a client on someone else's caseload for the duration of your internship, are you obligated to report everything disclosed by the client to that employee? How much of your discussions do you have to report to your supervisor? These are questions that should be discussed with other employees and the supervisor before you begin working with clients.

The confidentiality requirements concerning the information learned in a business setting may not be as clear-cut as in the public sector. You may be asked to sign a nondisclosure form before beginning work. This document states that the signer will not disclose any proprietary information to anyone outside the organization or, in some cases, outside the group in which they are working. In some cases, your faculty supervisor may also have to sign a nondisclosure statement in order to review the work products you complete at the site. The following is a very specific statement from the United States Postal Inspection Service (2012):

> *The student must also understand that he or she will not publish, nor reveal to any other person, including the University or any current or former employee or contractor of the University, any classified, restricted, or administratively controlled information of which he or she may have knowledge because of the participation in the internship program, or any other information transmitted to the student in confidence in the course of his or her participation in the internship program with the agency. Further, the student must surrender to responsible agency officials all classified, restricted, or administratively controlled documents and material which he or she has been charged with or possessed during the internship program. The student may not retain possession, custody, or control of any documents or material containing classified, restricted, or administratively [sic] controlled information following completion of the internship program.*

At all internship sites, you should treat all information to which you have access as confidential, unless you know it has been publicly disclosed. Information relating to fraud operations and the results of the fraud operations should not be disclosed. You may gain knowledge of the organization's key clients. While some corporations use such information for marketing purposes and, therefore, publicly disclose it, there are many situations in which the client list is not disclosed for security purposes. In your work, you may learn about thresholds for investigation and prosecution that are set as a result of limited resources. If these thresholds were revealed and the information given to the wrong people, criminals would know which fraud cases are pursued. They could then exploit the agency's vulnerabilities and fly under the radar.

While confidentiality is concerned with the assurances of not divulging information shared with you in a trusted relationship unless consent is given or required by law, privacy focuses more on the rights of the individual to control private information that may be disseminated about them. For example, if a victim reveals information to you in your role as intern and a trusted agent of the organization, you are required to keep that information confidential and discuss it only with staff who have a need to know. On the other hand, if you read a victim's file, you have an obligation to keep that information private. There is no reason why you should share that information outside of the organization, as it could cause harm for the person. You need to be especially vigilant if you are interning in a locality where you live and know people who also may know the victim, including yourself or family members.

Proper handling and security of an individual's private information, or information not known publicly, is critical to maintaining the person's rights. It is the responsibility of the organization to comply with laws and regulations. Personal identifier information such as date of birth, Social Security number, address, financial accounts, and protected health care information—such as diseases, medication, and unique health care identifier—may be accessible to you in the individual's files. This information, either online or in paper format, must be handled according to the protocols and security requirements of your organization. The mishandling of such information can cause harm to the individual through identity theft or medical identity theft and to the reputation and credibility of the organization. These breaches can take many forms, such as leaving sensitive files on computer screens while taking a break, leaving files on a desk and leaving for the day, or taking files out of the office and not maintaining control of them. What do you do as an intern if you observe breaches of these policies? You should first mention it to your faculty advisor and seek his or her guidance on how to handle the situation.

Regarding the subject of privacy, you need to know that, as an intern or employee using an organization's technology equipment (computers, phones, network), you have no right to privacy in a private setting and a limited degree of privacy in a governmental setting. What you write and say (e.g., voicemail) is open to your employer to review, especially if there are use policies and you have signed one. Your e-mails may be read and your Internet activity monitored.

Maintaining Appropriate Interpersonal Relationships

You should maintain professional relationships with clients and staff in the agency at all times. You may be tempted to become friends with some of the individuals serviced by your agency in order to improve your relationship with them. This can lead to situations that require you to compromise your standards in order to continue the friendship. One very competent intern, working at a summer camp for emotionally disturbed and delinquent youths, allowed herself to be talked into taking two youths to the local town after curfew. While there was an unresolved question as to whether any alcohol had been consumed by the minors, the fact that the two youths were missing with the intern after curfew was a very serious matter. The intern did not think what she did was out of line until she was asked to leave the camp the next day. She was not allowed to complete her internship there. By becoming too friendly with the kids, she lost sight of her responsibility to the camp, the youths, her college internship program, and herself as an intern and emerging professional.

While it seems obvious that sexual relationships with clients are unethical, it does happen on occasion. In one case, an intern became romantically and sexually involved with a person at a youth detention facility and jeopardized both career and reputation, the youth's record at the facility, the facility's reputation, and the college's internship program in terms of being able to place another intern at that site. Once the relationship began, it quickly went out of control and caused the intern to lose objectivity, professional standards, good judgment, and moral and ethical sense. The two plotted about times that they could rendezvous, which necessitated deceit and lying. Once they were caught, the intern faced censure by the state and was placed on a list preventing employment with children or juveniles for 7 years. Academically, the intern's grade (and, therefore, grade point average) dropped considerably, and the intern was stripped of a prestigious award. While we all may find ourselves, at some point in our lives, in questionable situations because we are caught up in emotions that cloud our judgment, it is imperative that you do not allow this to happen with a client in the criminal justice system. To do so will damage your reputation and have severe consequences.

Romantic and/or sexual relationships with the agency staff are also ethically unsound. Major corporate and political figures have suffered complete downfalls when their romantic and sexual relationships were reported in the national media and social media networks. As the entire nation watched, the unethical behavior of the president of the United States and a White House intern was detailed before a grand jury and the national media in 1998. While this case is extreme, it should stand as an example of the dangerous and far-reaching consequences of inappropriate relationships during an internship. As with any romantic relationship, your objectivity is lessened and the potential for problems with that individual and others in the office increases.

Unfortunately, it is not uncommon for interns to be approached by staff members. This is not confined to male staff and female interns. A young male intern in a public defender's office found himself being approached by a female staff member on a regular basis. Although he found her attractive, he politely declined her offers, and she eventually began dating a young professional from another related agency. While there are many ways of handling such advances, one creative intern told a staff member (on the third attempt) that the university prohibits her from becoming involved with fellow staff members on internship assignments and that such involvement had to be reported to her professor. The employee backed off.

This inevitably leads into the topic of sexual harassment. Sexual harassment occurs when

1. A supervisor demands sexual consideration in exchange for a job benefit;
2. A coworker makes unwelcome sexual advances on another worker in the form of pressure for dates, stalking, love letters, or phone calls; or
3. The activities or behaviors by one or more employees create a hostile work environment that might include pranks, jokes, or comments of a sexual nature, or allowing sexually explicit posters and magazines to be kept in general work areas.

It might also include unwelcome brushing against the body or inquiries into one's sexual activities or past experiences.

Both public- and private-sector agencies have been forced to address sexual harassment complaints because of the high cost of civil judgments and settlements, negative media coverage, overall disruption in the work environment, and individual human costs. Sexual harassment is a violation of Title VII of the federal Civil Rights Act of 1964 and various state human rights laws. Companies and individual supervisors have been held liable with regard to sexual harassment complaints by failing to take timely action. Most state laws today also include prohibitions against retaliation for someone who makes a sexual harassment complaint.

From a legal standpoint, there are questions as to whether interns are indeed employees who may make complaints about harassment and discrimination. If you have concerns regarding issues of this nature, you should contact your faculty supervisor immediately for advice. One intern found herself in the midst of a love triangle that resulted in official reprimands for the employees involved. Two coworkers at a residential treatment facility for juveniles had been involved in a long-term relationship in violation of agency policy. When the intern arrived, the male staff member began paying excessive attention to her, which in turn caused his girlfriend to become jealous. The girlfriend then engaged other staff members, as well as residents, in making remarks and behaving aggressively toward the intern. Despite the fact that the two staff members continued to deny the nature of their relationship, it did not take long for the intern to figure out the source of the problem. Although the agency administration and the faculty supervisor attempted to mediate, the intern could not remain at that site because the environment had become too hostile. The staff members were officially reprimanded, and the intern was placed at an alternative site. Because she wisely used the resources available to her, she lost no time and achieved a positive internship experience.

Disclosing Knowing a Person of Interest Outside the Organization

If you intern in your hometown area, you may know individuals who come in contact with the organization in a negative manner. The individual may be a high school acquaintance, a college friend, a relative, or someone you have interacted with in some other capacity. These are difficult situations, especially if the person is a defendant or target of an investigation. In all situations in which you may have direct dealings with them in your official capacity as an intern, you should disclose the relationship to your field supervisor to avoid any potential perceived conflict and any concern that you showed this person preferential treatment. Depending on the situation, your supervisor may assign you to another case or be able to counsel you on handling a situation in which you have some history with the person.

Questions to Consider

If you are wavering in a situation, or wondering what is the right thing to do, think about these questions:

1. Are my actions legal?
2. Am I being fair and honest?
3. Will my action stand the test of time?
4. How will I feel about myself afterward?
5. How will it look in the newspaper or on electronic news media?
6. Will I sleep soundly tonight?
7. What would I tell my child to do?
8. How would I feel if my family, friends, and neighbors knew what I was doing? (Lockheed Martin, 2006)

Of course, knowing when you should ask these questions is important as well. Lockheed Martin's Code of Ethics and Business Conduct suggests the following as warning signs.

You're on Thin Ethical Ice When You Hear . . .
Well, maybe just this once. . . . No one will ever know . . . .
It doesn't matter how it gets done as long as it gets done.
Everyone does it.
Shred that document.
We can hide it.
No one will get hurt.
What's in it for me?
This will destroy the competition.
We didn't have this conversation.

Lockheed Martin (2006)

It is important that you are aware of your agency or organization's ethical standards and the indications of possible ethical transgressions. Asking and answering questions such as those noted above, as well as consulting with fellow interns and your supervisors, will help you to maintain your integrity and have a successful experience.

Ethics in the Age of Transparency

The bounds of confidentiality, appropriate conduct, and interpersonal relationships extend to blogging and social network web sites. There have been numerous accounts of employees being fired as a result of information they have revealed in their personal blogs or in their Myspace or Facebook pages. In some cases, employees damaged relationships by discussing their colleagues and supervisors. Others have revealed confidential information and trade secrets. There have been instances of employees posting photographs or information that placed them in compromising positions. Social media exchanges among jurors in courtroom proceedings is such a problem that many courts have confiscated digital devices during trials or have monitored social media pages when the jury is out of the courtroom after business hours (Urbina, 2014).

As a result of the age of transparency in which we all operate, many organizations have instituted policies outlining rules for blogging and use of social media. In general, these policies direct employees to accept responsibility for what they write, to maintain confidentiality as outlined in the organization's code of conduct, to be respectful, and to avoid obscenity, dishonesty, and personal attacks. The policies also apply to blogs that are sanctioned by the organization and thus direct employees to add value, follow the law, respect copyright, and discuss with their manager any topics about which they are uncertain before posting their comments ("Policies compared," 2005).

As an intern, it is your responsibility to be cognizant of your organization's policies concerning online posting, just as you must be aware of codes of conduct, e-mail, and Internet policies. However, because your internship will be a step toward eventual career employment, you must be even more cautious of what you communicate in your personal blog, Facebook page, or similar outlet. You must remind yourself, particularly after a stressful day, that anything you post is public and enduring. You do not want something that you write out of frustration or anger to be a nemesis for you as you continue on your career path.

Examining Your Value System

Your understanding of your own values and the ability to be tolerant of the values of others will affect your attitude and behavior toward clients, agency employees, and the public. If you see those who come in contact with the criminal justice system as lowlifes, scum, or dirtballs, then you will not be effective in your work. You may not like what they have done, or you may not accept their lifestyles or values, but that does not excuse you from carrying out your duties in a professional manner.

Sometimes interns who perceive themselves as liberal and tolerant of others are surprised to discover that they are biased, prejudiced, and do not want to treat fairly all those with whom they come in contact. While this can be a disturbing thing to learn about oneself, it may be one of the most significant experiences you will have. If faced with this revelation, you may be able to change your attitudes toward those who hold different values. If you cannot tolerate differing views, you will quickly become cynical and lose a degree of effectiveness.

Sharing feelings with other workers, field supervisors, fellow interns, and your faculty supervisor can help you through this difficult period. One word of caution is necessary. Do not let others prejudice your thinking; make your own assessment of others. Just as you have to decide whether to accept that free cup of coffee and doughnut when you are with a group of employees from the agency, you also have to decide whether to adopt cynical and hardened attitudes toward alleged criminals or clients. To do so may mean compromising your own ethical standards in order to be accepted as "one of the crowd" in the agency. This will be a difficult assessment for you to make. You should continually remind yourself that you are in a professional position and adopt the attitude appropriate for that position. You, as a member of the criminal justice system, must treat all persons fairly and equitably.

Justice and Fairness

As a practitioner in a major social institution—the justice system—you will be confronted with ethical issues dealing with justice, fairness, and punishment. As a student of criminal justice or criminology, you probably have formed values in these areas based on classroom experience, academic readings, newspaper articles, and discussions with others. As with your personal values, your conceptions of the criminal justice system will be exposed to the realities of the administration of justice.

Initially, you may feel that what you learned in the classroom has no relevance to the real world. One student was outraged by the extent of plea bargaining (even for major crimes) that she observed while working for a district attorney. Another intern saw two police officers rough up a suspect and perform an illegal search and seizure. He wanted to tell the suspect his rights but kept quiet because he wanted to be accepted by the police. Both students were troubled by their experiences. For the first time, they realized that the administration of justice is not always fair and just. Bargain justice and street justice are commonly observed by interns, frequently raising ethical and moral dilemmas. How should you handle them? What is your responsibility here?

While there are no clear-cut answers, the following guidelines may be helpful. First, you should not interfere at the moment a situation occurs. In some cases, your perception of the situation may not be accurate, and your intrusion may be resented or may worsen a potentially dangerous situation. An example of the latter occurred with an intern in a youth department. The intern and her supervisor were interviewing a juvenile delinquent who suddenly became very angry and threatened bodily harm. The supervisor was able to diffuse the situation by calmly talking to the youth. The intern said that she thought they should have gotten really tough with the youth. After the fact, she realized that had she reacted to him that way, he probably would have actually tried to hurt them.

If you are faced with an unethical or illegal situation that is troubling you, we recommend that you first discuss it with your faculty supervisor. Your professor can act as a sounding board and offer you suggestions for handling the problem. Then you will have to decide, with his or her help, whether you want to discuss the incident with the employee involved or perhaps the agency supervisor. In either case, there is a risk involved because of your status in the agency. Staff members may not appreciate an intern, who may have a lot of book knowledge but little experience in the field, criticizing their performance. They generally like it even less when such behavior is reported to their supervisors. However, some comments made by interns to employees or supervisors on events they have witnessed have been received very well. Many employees solicit comments from interns in order to help them evaluate their performance. They feel that after doing the job for many years, they may be overlooking things or may not be aware of new laws or methods. Supervisors have also appreciated the comments of interns about employees who have acted in an unprofessional or illegal manner. When asked by his supervisor what he had done that day, one intern inadvertently commented that he and the civilian officer (non-sworn) with whom he was working stopped a car on an interstate highway for speeding. The supervisor, who was the police chief, called the officer in and gave him a final warning. The civilian officer had assumed he had the powers of a police officer and had repeatedly acted as such. Rather than being ostracized for revealing this information, the intern gained further acceptance in the agency.

Criminal Justice Interns' Observations of Misconduct

Jordan et al. (2007, pp. 298–9) conducted a survey of students who had completed their criminal justice internships to ascertain their observations of misconduct and the reporting patterns of their experiences. The authors wanted to learn how commonly student interns in criminal justice agencies observed or suspected misconduct by agency employees; whether interns communicated these observations to others; and whether students are prepared through instruction to cope with these troubling situations.

Even though the study was exploratory and has several limitations, which are addressed by the authors, it does provide a window into the ethical situations confronted by interns. The study results include:

- A significant number of interns representing four universities noted that they observed some form of misconduct. These areas included "illegal behavior, violation of legal procedures, violation of departmental policy, disrespect (lack of courtesy), unprofessional behavior toward citizens, unprofessional comments or behavior in a private setting, biased investigation or enforcement activity, and officer telling you not to pass on something you heard or observed" (Jordan et al., 2007, p. 303).
- "More than half the respondents (55%) reported observing at least one instance of misconduct suspected or believed to be unethical." More than 23 percent of the former interns believed that the behavior fell into one of the more serious categories: "illegal conduct, conduct violating legal procedures, and biased activity" (Jordan et al., 2007, p. 303).
- 74 students of the 125 students who responded to the survey observed some form of misconduct. However, only 55 reported it or talked to anyone about their observations.

It is very possible that you will be faced with one or more ethical situations in your internship experience. Thinking about these situations ahead of time, and discussing them with your faculty supervisor and fellow interns, will help you handle these events and learn from them.

What Gets Interns into Trouble

After reviewing this chapter with a number of students, the following question emerged, "Aside from the blatant examples presented in the chapter, what gets interns into trouble during their internship?" It is a fair question, and the following points come to mind in no particular ranking:

1. Being repeatedly late for work or not completing assignments. In the former instance, this often occurs when the student is working outside their level of competency, does not ask questions about the assignment, or simply does not do the assignment. In all instances, it is important to ask for further assistance and clarification when you are given an assignment, or by simply saying, "I do not know how to do that" rather than just not performing the task.
2. Addressing the head of the organization by their first name in public and without permission (one case that comes to mind involved the county district attorney).
3. Inappropriate dress or wearing clothes dirty or torn.
4. Constant use of the smart phone during the internship work hours.
5. Lack of personal hygiene related to bathing and use of deodorant.
6. Falling asleep at one's desk or during court sessions.
7. Failing to complete academic assignments or attend class meetings according to the required schedule.
8. As mentioned previously, going on to social media sites that have nothing to do with assignments or tasks during work hours.

Conclusion

As an intern, you may see such things as people being treated unjustly or unfairly, or the involvement of fellow agency workers and supervisors in unethical or illegal activities. While these may be realities in the administration of justice, you should not condone or accept them. Once you begin to compromise your values and ethics, it becomes a slippery slope from which recovery may be difficult, if not impossible. You may not be in a position to change things as an intern, but examining occurrences can help you to clarify and rethink your own position. In your role as an intern, you will not be immune to ethical dilemmas. While some issues are clear-cut, others are much more difficult to discern. Experience with these situations is part of your development as a professional. A listing of other issues that have resulted in interns getting into trouble at the placement site is also presented.

■ ■ ■ ▬▬▬▬▬▬▬▬▬▬▬▬▬▬▬▬▬▬▬▬▬▬▬▬▬▬▬▬▬▬▬▬▬

Thinking About Your Internship

Discuss the following with faculty, students who have interned, practitioners, and, if appropriate, agency personnel at your internship site.

1. In your efforts to establish good rapport with your peers, were you ever placed in situations that compromised your values? How did you resolve them?
2. Do you think you have been influenced because of the official power of your position?

For interns in the field, address the following:

1. Have you ever been tempted to use your internship position for personal gain which would be viewed as dishonest or lacking integrity?
2. What ethical standards are present at your agency?
3. What ethical issues have you been confronted with thus far in your internship experience? How did you handle them? Would you act differently if you were to be confronted with them again?
4. Given the emergence of technology in the workplace, what are the potential issues and concerns that you may face? Consider the following: use of e-mail, blogs, and social networking web sites; acceptable computer use; Internet access; and access to secure files and databases.
5. What are the codes of conduct or ethical standards for employees at your internship site? What issues do they raise that you had not considered? What issues do you think are not raised that should be?

▬▬▬▬▬▬▬▬▬▬▬▬▬▬▬▬▬▬▬▬▬▬▬▬▬▬▬▬▬▬▬▬ ■ ■ ■

PART III

The Role of the Organization

9

Organizational Characteristics: Formal and Informal Structures

It is important for student interns to have an organizational perspective in order to examine how a criminal justice agency or private-sector company operates. In analyzing the formal and informal structures of an agency—the official and unofficial relationships and channels that affect the environment and how things are accomplished—the intern will see how the structure of the agency has an effect on the behavior of organizational members and agency clients. This chapter applies Weber's classic characteristics of a bureaucracy (Thibault et.al., 2014, pp. 79–80) to illustrate the dynamic forces that occur in both the formal and informal structures. This chapter also presents some current organizational trends affecting the workplace and an overview of human resource administration issues as they relate to recruitment and selection, training, and collective bargaining. More importantly, the success or failure of your internship will depend on how well you adjust to the organizational demands of your field site.

The Formal Structure

An organization is a collection of people formed to achieve a number of goals (Jones, 2007). For this discussion, criminal justice organizations are created by the state to execute, interpret, or legislate the law and provide public safety services to citizens. In the private sector, companies are duly created under various federal and state laws and regulations to create or provide goods and services and make a profit. There are also organizations designated as not-for-profit (e.g., probably your college) that operate under specific state and federal laws to provide a service.

The characteristics of the formal organization are of great importance to you because they contribute to and guide the daily operations of the organization in which you are placed. These characteristics were first conceptualized by German sociologist Max Weber, who wrote on the nature of bureaucracy and its role in industrialized societies in Western Europe in the nineteenth century.

Formal organizational structure refers to the totality of defined hierarchy or chain of command, rules, and codes of conduct that apply to agency operations and work relationships among employees. Organizational theory postulates basic premises on how organizations work and how participants interact with each other and the external environment. Despite its negative connotation today, the term "bureaucracy" refers to a specific form of social organization for administrative purposes (Hall, 1999). Bureaucracy is the most prominent form of organization for criminal justice and most private-sector agencies in the United States.

It is important to note that Weber was conceptualizing what he referred to as an "ideal type" of organizational arrangement, which exists only in theory. Each of Weber's characteristics is presented here and explained through the use of a hypothetical organization: the Flanders County District Attorney's Office. Do not make any immediate identification with any particular district attorney office, as Flanders County is based on our observations of a number of criminal justice offices around the United States.

Welcome to Flanders County

Flanders County is located in an area of 120 square miles and has a population of 300,000. The county seat is located in the city of Flanders, which is the only city in the county and has a population of 100,000. The district attorney's office occupies the entire third floor of the county office building.

The general objective of the Flanders County District Attorney's Office is to prosecute all criminal matters in the county. This objective is achieved by

1. bringing all criminal matters to trial in the proper court;
2. reviewing felony arrests through the grand jury process and securing indictments against suspected persons deemed likely to have committed offenses;
3. initiating criminal investigations through the grand jury process;
4. extraditing criminals who committed crimes in Flanders County and fled to another county, state, or country; and
5. applying and executing electronic surveillance devices for criminal investigations with the cooperation of county police agencies.

Having presented this background, we now proceed to illustrate the Weberian characteristics present in this organization.

Hierarchy of Authority

According to Weber, offices and positions are arranged in a hierarchical fashion so that each office or position is under the control and supervision of a higher order. This characteristic is clearly indicated in the organizational chart in Figure 9.1. This is to ensure and define levels of subordination among individuals, units, offices, and departments.

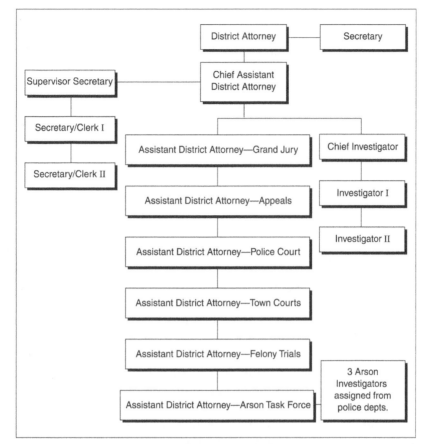

FIGURE 9.1 Flanders County District Attorney's Office Organizational Chart.

At the head of the organization is the district attorney. Directly below the district attorney is the chief assistant district attorney. Below the chief assistant district attorney are the assistant district attorneys. Organizationally, the six assistant district attorneys report to the chief assistant district attorney, who, in turn, reports to the district attorney. The chief assistant district attorney is responsible for assigning the investigative and secretarial staff to the assistant district attorneys as needed. This type of hierarchical organization is typical of criminal justice agencies. Obviously, larger agencies will have more levels and smaller agencies will have fewer levels.

Division of Labor

Specific activities may be assigned to certain individuals according to expertise, training, education, and competence. For example, in Flanders County, the district attorney and the chief assistant district attorney have overall managerial duties in the agency, while specific areas of the prosecution work are assigned to the assistant district attorneys and the investigative staff. The areas delineated in the organizational chart are grand jury, appeals, police court, town courts, and felony trials; one assistant is specifically assigned to manage and prosecute cases involving arson, through the Arson Task Force. Thus, the assistant district attorneys develop expertise in their assigned areas. While each one must keep abreast of new legal developments, they rely on each other for specifics; for example, if the police court assistant district attorney wants to know the latest state Supreme Court rulings regarding search and seizure, he or she discusses it with his or her colleague assigned to appeals.

Career Orientation

In most criminal justice organizations, there is a system of promotion for career advancement. According to Weber, promotions to higher levels in the hierarchy are based on seniority, skill in performing the job, and achievement. These attributes are judged by superiors who are qualified to make such decisions. Career orientation also includes protection against arbitrary dismissal through civil service law or organizational policies related to tenure. If done correctly, career orientation management can help to foster loyalty to the organization.

This Weberian aspect is evident in the Flanders County District Attorney's Office. Each employee can move to the top of the hierarchy through conscientious work. There is, however, a dichotomy in career mobility between the attorneys and the rest of the office staff. First, assistant district attorneys are appointed by the district attorney in consultation with the chief assistant. Appointment is based on law school grades, letters of recommendation, and previous experience in criminal work or law enforcement. Technically, salary increments and promotion for the assistants are based on achievement and successful performance of assigned duties.

For the clerical staff, promotion from one grade level to a higher level is based on civil service examinations and recommendations by the clerical supervisor and the chief assistant district attorney. Investigators are also appointed and promoted by civil service examination and their supervisor's recommendation.

The position of district attorney completely deviates from Weberian norms. The Flanders County District Attorney is elected to a four-year term of office. The candidate may or may not have had previous experience as an assistant district attorney, but information conveyed in an election campaign usually must show that he or she has some experience in criminal matters. This deviation is true for many criminal justice agency heads (such as sheriffs, police chiefs, public safety commissioners, and agency directors) that are elected or appointed by political officials, while their subordinates are appointed and promoted through civil service procedures. Therefore, the heads of many criminal justice agencies have arrived there through the political process rather than through merit.

Rules and Regulations

All public, and most private, organizations have rules and regulations that form the daily operational guidelines of the agency and establish the rights and duties for each position. These are often referred to as agency policies and are listed in a handbook, an operations manual, a duty book, or a set of standard operating procedures. Laws and regulations outside the agency—such as the state penal law, criminal procedure code, or administrative regulations by state or federal agencies—also provide guidelines for criminal justice agencies.

The primary rulebooks for the Flanders County District Attorney's Office are the state criminal procedure code and the penal law. These should be on the desk of every assistant district attorney and investigator, and they are consulted repeatedly. There is also a handbook of rules and procedures for the office that reiterates the criminal procedure code. This handbook includes the more important elements of the state code, such as time requirements for handling cases, schedules for rural courts, and proper methods for filling out various forms. Handbooks for other criminal justice agencies may list rules regarding hours of work, break times, seniority hierarchies for use when a supervisor is away, and dress codes for the office staff.

In addition to the legal codes and office handbook, there are other rules and regulations that affect the daily operations of the office. These include the union contract covering clerical workers, operating memoranda from the various courts with which the office has dealings, and a myriad of lesser law codes to which the staff must refer (e.g., family court acts, domestic relations acts, environmental conservation acts). These should be presented to you as part of your orientation at the internship site.

Efficiency and Effectiveness

According to Weber, efficiency and effectiveness in an organization are guaranteed if the organization subscribes to the tenets of hierarchy of authority, division of labor, career orientation, and rules and regulations. There is some confusion about the usage of the terms "effectiveness" and "efficiency." Hall (1999) writes that "effectiveness" is the degree to which an organization realizes its goals, while "efficiency" relates to the amount of resources used to produce a unit of output. Hall points out that many organizations are efficient without being effective, and others are effective, but hardly efficient. Consider the following situation. If you were to review the annual report filed by the Flanders County District Attorney's Office, you might assume the organization was effective. Convictions for all classes of offenses increased by 25 percent over last year. However, budgetary expenditures increased by 55 percent, which was not viewed as efficient by many legislators. Too often, effectiveness and efficiency are erroneously equated.

Impersonal Orientation

In the Weberian scheme, the working atmosphere should be one of impersonality. This is especially important in a district attorney's office because there are many cases that can evoke a bias. Although assistant district attorneys may have little respect for child molesters, rapists, and other sexual offenders, there must be some level of objectivity so that these offenders can receive justice. This is especially important for the appeal process, in which a crucial error can overturn the entire conviction.

Communication

For Weber, the management of communication is based on written documents that move through the hierarchical chain of command. In the Flanders County District Attorney's Office, communication moves formally from the district attorney to the chief assistant district attorney, to be directed to the intended office and/or person. Accordingly, any communication from an assistant district attorney to the district attorney must go through the chief assistant in the form of a memorandum or letter. The chain of command process becomes cumbersome as each piece of communication must pass through the chief assistant district attorney, yet it is necessary in a hierarchical system.

These, then, are the main facets of what is commonly referred to as a formal organizational structure. However, this is only a model; it is Weber's conception of how things should be. Not surprisingly, the Weberian model has been criticized as impersonal, dysfunctional, and unrealistic because it ignores the human factor.

The Informal Structure

During your internship, you may find that your organization or unit does not operate strictly according to a formal organizational structure. Organizational theorists refer to this phenomenon as the informal organizational structure. The informal organization, in many cases, addresses the criticisms and shortcomings of the formal system. This structure develops through individual and group relationships, and as Thibault et al. (2014) point out, the informal structure tends to humanize the formal organization. The informal structure is often important for the individual in a bureaucracy because it provides a sense of identity and, at times, personal and job security within the formal parameters of the organization.

As you will see in the comparison of the informal and formal structures of the Flanders County District Attorney's Office, the informal structure can dictate, influence, and, at times, stall official policies and dealings with clients. It will become apparent that the informal structure has a great influence on communication among the members of the organization and outsiders.

Hierarchy of Authority

On paper, the Flanders County District Attorney's Office is supposed to operate according to the organizational chart in Figure 9.1. This formal structure, however, can present problems as each level of the hierarchy produces a block for doing daily tasks. By the term "block" we mean that any part of the organizational structure can influence or change the outcome of a process occurring between a subordinate and a superordinate. Organizational communication best illustrates this concept. For example, in the Flanders County District Attorney's Office, when an assistant district attorney needs to use an office vehicle, he or she is supposed to file Form DX001 with the chief assistant district attorney. Very often, the chief assistant is unavailable, so it is common practice for assistant district attorneys to tell the secretary that a car is needed and Form DX001 will be entered into the system later. Investigators are also required to follow this process, but their forms are to be approved by the chief investigator and then the chief assistant district attorney. In reality, the investigators follow the same practice as the assistant district attorneys. Form DX001, which is supposed to guide the flow of communication between levels, has become a nuisance.

At your field site you will soon find that in order for work to be accelerated, all members rely on the informal hierarchical system. The informal hierarchy in any criminal justice agency can be based on a number of things, including expertise and seniority, ethnicity, blood relationships, mutual interests, comparative upbringings, and any combination of these variables. The informal structure of the Flanders County District Attorney's Office is shown in Figure 9.2.

The golfers constitute an important group in the office. Composed of the district attorney and certain assistants, and referred to by other staff as the henchmen, this group has a dominant role in formulating agency policies. Because of their mutual interest in golf, many staff members feel that decisions are often made on the fairways or at the nineteenth hole. Another distinct group consists of the go-getters, who are assistant district attorneys and an investigator with no more than 5 years on the job. The go-getters are known for working and playing hard in and out of the office. Disdaining golf, this group frequently socializes at certain nightspots and engages in racquetball or tennis. They see their term at the Flanders County District Attorney's Office as a stepping-stone to future law-related jobs, such as federal prosecutors, judgeships, and elected offices.

The Arson Task Force forms another clique. Consisting of one assistant district attorney and his investigators, most staff feel that this group is decidedly off in another world. It is not uncommon for the task force to disappear for days at a time to work at an arson scene. Because of the dirty and hazardous tasks involved in arson investigation, most staff members wear jeans and sport shirts instead of the customary business dress.

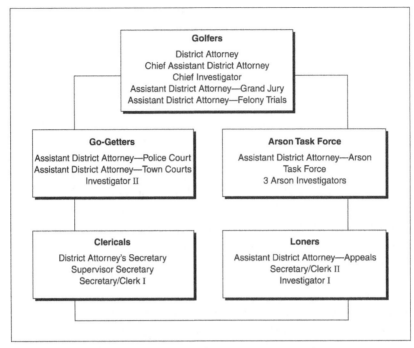

FIGURE 9.2 Flanders County District Attorney's Office Informal Organizational Chart.

The clerical staff generally interact and socialize among themselves and tend to view their jobs as just a job. Finally, there are some staff members who do not belong to any group. Although diligent and intelligent workers, these people are generally viewed as loners, both on and off the job.

In the informal organization, rivalries often occur as various groups compete for rewards, resources, or power within the organization. In the Flanders County District Attorney's Office, there is a sharp rivalry between the golfers and the go-getters. Generally, the go-getters view the golfers as married to the district attorney, always receiving favors and promotions because of their close ties. The golfers, on the other hand, view the go-getters as a bunch of kids just out of law school who have yet to earn their stripes in the legal business. Outwardly, there is a cordial professional atmosphere among all groups. However, the facade between the golfers and go-getters dissipates at staff meetings, office-wide social gatherings, and even in opinions regarding the conduct of important cases. For example, at one staff meeting, the go-getters sat together while the golfers sat on either side of the district attorney. The meeting concerned the conduct of a recent murder case prosecuted by a golfer, in which the defendant was acquitted primarily because of a faulty search warrant. The go-getters were vehement in their criticism of the mistake. The golfers tended to defend their colleague's actions. Because of this kind of attitude, the chief assistant district attorney is careful not to assign certain individuals to work together on major cases.

Division of Labor

In many organizations, the division of labor is not clearly defined, and job titles and descriptions do not coincide with the organizational chart. As an intern, you may find that certain personnel in your agency perform a wide variety of duties not included in their job descriptions. Some of those job descriptions may be vague, indicating that either the organization does not know what that position should encompass or that there is really no need for the position in the first place.

At the Flanders County District Attorney's Office, the position of secretary to the district attorney provides a good example of this issue. As with many secretarial positions of this nature, the secretary often performs a number of tasks for the employer that could never fit into a job description but have become expected duties. Imagine if a civil service announcement included the following:

1. Plans all office parties.
2. Frequently does not tell the exact truth as to the whereabouts of the boss.
3. Edits speeches that the district attorney gives at public events.
4. Knows the whereabouts of every file in the office.
5. Unofficially reviews every budgetary expenditure and tells district attorney if a voucher does not appear to be correct.
6. Informs boss immediately if an interesting item is heard either in the office or through the political grapevine.

Although these are not officially noted in the job description, they become integral duties.

One frequently mentioned criticism of division of labor is that keeping a person at one specific job produces boredom. Boredom in any criminal justice job is easy to explain if you keep in mind one variable: routine. Eventually, an assistant district attorney assigned to police court will become bored as the same types of cases appear repeatedly. Many police officers assigned solely to road or foot patrol express feelings of boredom because they are dealing either with the same kinds of incidents repeatedly or they are working in a zone in which there is little activity.

As an intern, no matter what agency you are assigned to, you will quickly discover that there are periods of downtime. You will also find that some jobs are tedious but very important. For example, an intern assigned to a district attorney's office spent a week listening to conversations taped from an eavesdropping device. Her task was to pinpoint those conversations regarding a drug ring in which the defendant was a participant. Another intern with a police department had to sift through the training records of the entire department for the past five years in order to prove in a civil lawsuit that everyone had completed mandated use-of-force training.

Formal managerial solutions to counter boredom include enlarging the person's job description, transferring the person to another position, or promoting the person to a higher level in the organizational hierarchy. Informally, many workers enlarge their own job descriptions to make their daily work more interesting. One example involves a police dispatcher who took on the task of public relations officer and dealt with the media personnel when they called for news items. Eventually, everyone in the station house, including the district commander, thought that the dispatcher was the official public relations contact because the job was performed so well.

Career Orientation

Achievement and seniority are the main avenues for upward mobility in any organization. However, the informal structure very often has an impact on the future of one's career. The Flanders County District Attorney's Office illustrates a point in this respect. Quite recently, Jill Smith was promoted to chief assistant district attorney, much to the chagrin of the entire office. When the former chief retired, most people assumed that Joseph Walsh would assume the position. Surprisingly, Walsh was not promoted. Most of the assistant district attorneys concluded that Smith was rewarded for actively campaigning for the district attorney in the last election. Although he had the most seniority and was deemed most competent by the staff, Walsh had not been active in the campaign.

In this case, political activity was an important factor for promotion. This is not surprising because all criminal justice organizations are politically active, both internally and externally. Many agency heads, such as sheriffs, district attorneys, and judges, are elected and appointed based on political affiliation in their community or jurisdiction.

Rules and Regulations

Criminal justice agencies are confronted with the dilemma of enforcing state statutes while at the same time following rules and policies for the conduct of business. Very often these internal organizational policies and rules mirror state statutes, such as with arrest procedures. There are a number of formal laws, rules, and policies about which agency personnel must be aware and to which they must conform.

Often, the vast array of statutes and rules become so complex that the agency staff does not adhere strictly to all the laws of the state or the policies of the organization. In all agencies related to law enforcement, prosecution, or corrections, there is the variable of discretion, which can dictate how laws will be enforced, depending on the situation at hand. A police officer's decision to arrest someone, a prosecutor's decision to prosecute an offender or plea bargain a case, or a probation officer's decision to revoke a client's term of probation are based on the informal norms of the organization.

You will also find that organizational policies and rules are not always followed. All too often, formal policies and rules become dysfunctional when they provide obstacles for adjusting to new situations. You may have heard this during course registration: "The course is officially closed but speak to the instructor and maybe she will let you into the course." It is at this juncture that informal processes may take over, supplanting or bypassing the formal system. In Flanders County, the workday for the district attorney's office is 9:00 A.M. to 5:00 P.M. Most assistant district attorneys, however, are more likely to work from 7:00 A.M. to 10:00 P.M. because of night court or preparation for a trial. Because of these long hours, most of the assistant district attorneys and investigators think nothing of leaving early on Friday afternoons. To an unknowing observer, this might seem inappropriate.

However, the informal system can be equally dysfunctional. For instance, on Fridays, many agency employees take a two-hour lunch to shop and do other personal errands. Practices of this nature abound in many organizations and do nothing for productivity. Very often, employees who do not conform to these established norms are subject to ridicule and harassment. One young investigator recalled that, when he first started the job, he tried to schedule a drug raid with a number of police departments for Friday afternoon. The chief investigator made it known that Monday would be a better day. The young investigator persisted and finally was told that, if he did not like Monday, he might not have his job for long. The raid was rescheduled.

Efficiency and Effectiveness

On paper, the Flanders County District Attorney reports that his office is both effective and efficient in achieving the agency's goals. However, even a quick glance at the goals shows that they are quite broad, making them ambiguous and easily manipulated.

Impersonal Orientation

While courtroom proceedings appear to be impersonal, this is hardly the case in out-of-court contacts. Being formal and objective is hardly the stance taken at Flanders County and in most criminal justice agencies. The casual manner in which criminal justice professionals such as prosecutors, defense attorneys, and judges conduct business during procedures such as plea bargaining may be shocking at first. For instance:

> Prosecutor: "Now John, you know this guy is a turkey. Hell, he just got out of the can last week for the same thing."

> Defense Attorney: "I know, but in this case the cops really messed up. They busted him because the store owner said that the holdup man was wearing a red jacket. There were fifty people in that mall with red jackets on."

> Prosecutor: "Yeah, yeah, yeah, and everyone was carrying a Glock. No deal."

On-the-job humor also adds to impersonality in many criminal justice agencies. It helps to lighten the real pain and anguish of seeing death, lying, cheating, chicanery, and people at their worst.

Communication

The hierarchical communication chain of command, as we have seen, cannot meet all the demands placed upon an organization and its personnel. Going through channels may be seen as important, but there are other variables to be considered. The informal communication chain of command plays an important role in an organization in that messages are channeled and decoded based on friendship, the clique network, and the status of the individual or office issuing or receiving the message.

The Flanders County District Attorney's Office provides an example of a routine directive that was interpreted in several ways and, therefore, not followed as intended. The chief assistant district attorney issued a memorandum stating, "As you know, we are public servants and must project a professional image at all times. All male office personnel are required to wear a shirt and tie during the summer months." The memorandum was not countersigned by the district attorney, resulting in diverse interpretations of a rule that was not seen as official policy. Many of the golfers disregarded it because they felt they were professionals, not office personnel. The go-getters not only ignored it, but added numerous caricatures to the paper and used it to decorate the men's room. The Arson Task Force members wrote a counter-memorandum requesting a dispensation because it is unsafe to wear a tie under fire-scene turnout gear. They continued to wear their jeans and sport shirts. As you can see, the communication process is complex in any organization, no matter how routine the communiqué. Personalities, egos, and misunderstandings must all be taken into consideration.

Private-Sector Settings

The discussion on bureaucracy in the Flanders County District Attorney's Office has equal application to students who are interning with private corporations or not-for-profit organizations, which will be labeled for this discussion as "the private sector." While Weber's principles often appear in discussions on public administration and bureaucracy, they are also applicable to private organizations. Private-sector bureaucracies are really no different from those found in the public sector; the big difference is that the private-sector organizations are interested in profits, or for non-profits, raising money from fundraising or obtaining government grants to fund operations.

The Formal Structure

Again with Weber's principles as a base, we will apply the same organizational concepts found in the Flanders County District Attorney's Office to the Fraud Unit of Northwest Frontier Bank Corporation, a fictitious company.

> *Northwest Frontier Bank is a large financial services holding company with assets of more than $50 billion. The company provides full-service commercial banking in*

more than 1200 offices in 10 states, offering such services as investment management, mortgage banking, insurance, and brokerage services. In recent times, the company has adopted a centralized–decentralized scheme of management. Bank offices in various regions are managed locally in such areas as account management, lending, and advertising. Corporate headquarters, which is located in a large city in the north-west United States, has control of information technology and operations, training, product development, fraud control, and any other areas that affect the company as a whole. The chief executive officer and executive staff are selected by the Board of Directors, who, in turn, are elected by shareholders.

The Hierarchy of Authority and the Division of Labor

The bank's organizational chart reflects the typical hierarchical model and the division of labor found in many major corporations. The Fraud Unit's organizational chart is shown in Figure 9.3. This unit is located at corporate headquarters and is composed of 20 employees. Its main mission is to detect and identify fraud that affects the company's assets and security systems in such areas as credit cards, computers, communications, and interstate and international operations. Employees do not have official law enforcement powers. Prosecution is conducted by federal and state prosecutors based on the information obtained by the unit.

At times, the division of labor can become quite complicated. Each regional branch can deal with physical security systems and seemingly minor local incidents (e.g., a bank teller who steals money during transactions or false credit cards being used for unauthorized ATM transactions). However, a local incident may have greater implications. Thus, local branch managers are required to report every fraud or investigation being conducted in conjunction with local or state police to the Fraud Unit.

Career Orientation

The Fraud Unit is somewhat unique within the bank's career ladder structure. While most bank executives are college graduates who started from the ground up in a branch office, some of the Fraud Unit personnel are former federal or state investigations agents who retired after 20–25 years of service. In recent years, college graduates with accounting and computer skills have been hired. For the former law enforcement officers, the Fraud Unit is the next step in their careers; for the recently graduated, it is the first step in their professional lives.

Rules and Regulations

Northwest Frontier Bank must abide by various federal laws, such as the United States Banking Act and the Gramm-Leach-Bliley Act. In each state, operations are governed by specific state statutes that are overseen by state banking commissions.

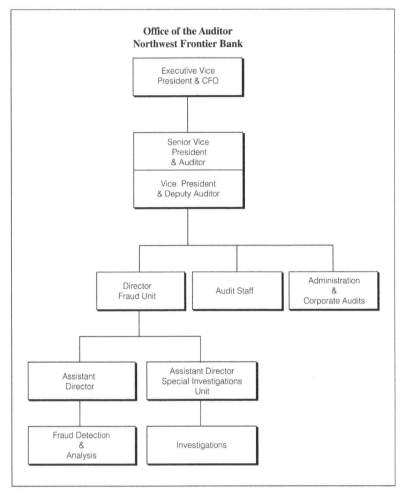

FIGURE 9.3 Northwest Frontier Bank Corporation Fraud Unit Organizational Chart.

For the Fraud Unit, the company's operating policies are contained in the main reference manual, which presents procedures for virtually every kind of transaction. Employees also deal with the Federal Criminal Code and the penal and criminal procedure codes for every state in which offices are located. Procedures for responding to fraud appear in a general manual of operations because the unit is relatively new and each case has its own unique characteristics.

Efficiency and Effectiveness

As with the Flanders County District Attorney's Office, the Fraud Unit of Northwest Frontier Bank can be characterized as efficient in responding to fraud complaints by customers and auditors. All fraud complaints that are known to the unit are investigated in a timely manner. A staff member can be dispatched to any location in a matter of hours. The unit has set up guidelines on how each incident should be handled and in what time period.

The effectiveness of the unit is based on several factors. Certainly, with increased resources, the Fraud Unit could further reduce the amount of fraud. The decision usually comes down to an equation of whether the costs of security will result in sufficient savings to the corporation. Unfortunately, as far as the Fraud Unit is concerned, the corporate leadership believes that a certain level of fraud is just the cost of doing business. In an ideal world, the true sign of effectiveness would be zero losses. As a measure of effectiveness, the unit's annual report notes that the many cases investigated resulted in the prosecution and conviction of various individuals, returning several million dollars in restitution to the company.

Impersonal Orientation

The Fraud Unit deals with a variety of economic crimes, committed both by employees and individuals outside the company. The common denominator for many of the crimes is greed. While staff members do not usually take things personally in dealing with cases, it can be difficult to remain impersonal when individuals under scrutiny are known to the investigators.

Communication

The chain of command for communication in the company-wide structure is usually based on a hierarchical model. While the head of the Fraud Unit has considerable input into the overall security plan, the corporate leadership determines the amount of resources for and communicates the level of effort expected of the Fraud Unit.

Internally, the Fraud Unit's personnel operate outside the normal hierarchical communications model based on the need to act quickly and efficiently. Reports on incidents are filed with the director, and he or she, in consultation with the Vice President for Operations, decides who, in corporate headquarters or in the various regional offices, will receive copies or notification.

The Informal Structure

Two major cliques have evolved within the Fraud Unit: cops and non-cops. The non-cops, college graduates without law enforcement experience, often feel like outsiders when the cops start recounting cases and real police action. The difference becomes apparent when the cops can simply call former colleagues and ask a favor in order to gain information, while the non-cops must explain who they are and go through bureaucratic channels. The real defining factor here is age. The cops are 45–55 years of age while the non-cops are in their twenties.

As a whole, the unit tries to remain outside the mainstream of company politics, which, at times, can be quite vicious. It seems that a company attitude of "How could you let this happen?" has evolved when it comes to fraud perpetrated by employees. Many times, such incidents come to the attention of the unit and other company officials through routine audit procedures. In one case, a branch bank manager was embezzling money every third Friday and covering it up through correction credits on the bank's computer. Although he was arrested and convicted, another executive used the incident as a lobbying effort for a promotion, stating that his colleague, the regional manager, should have known what was going on.

Members of the unit do not generally keep strict hours according to the company policy of an 8:30 A.M. to 5:00 P.M. workday. Because of the large geographic area that needs to be covered and the many overnight trips that accompany investigations, this is not possible. Investigators tend to mirror the informal norm at corporate headquarters, where executives often arrive by 7:00 A.M. and do not leave before 6:00 P.M. Clerical and other support staff tend to follow the official workday hours. According to one vice president, it is tough to find time just to think about things once the phones start ringing and the day is tied up in meetings or presentations.

Different Structures

The organizational structures presented in this section are very traditional, but the concepts still apply to a majority of public and private sector organizations. There are a number of trends, particularly in research and software development companies, whereby the organizational structure is "flattened" to reduce the number of management levels and "silos" between departments and to increase communication and teamwork and productivity. As discussed by Morgan (2014), the traditional hierarchy model discussed earlier in this chapter is not conducive to innovation and communication, and the bureaucracy is often "sluggish" in responding to new challenges. The traditional models have also been turned upside down with the wide range of communications that are now available.

Interns working in newer organizational environments are surprised to learn that there are often no set work hours, that they are part of a team, and have some say as to projects they are going to work on. Within traditional structures, certain sub-units may have a flattened organization and undertake most projects by consensus. As illustrated in this chapter, this is often illustrated in investigative and research units where there is one supervisor and everyone has equal say.

The Crazy Environment

The organizational structure is composed of humans, and humans, as you know, can do all kinds of weird things and create or apply rules that make no sense. As a young police officer, the author learned this when he came out of a smoke-filled building looking for victims at a fire and was reprimanded for not having his uniform hat on. Thankfully, most student interns do not get introduced to too many dysfunctions that occur in the bureaucracy, but examples do abound. In one organization, full-time employees were not allowed to sit and have lunch with student interns in the cafeteria. The advent of new organizational structures is not without criticism in that working for certain companies is viewed as only of short duration. Writing about his experiences in a startup software firm, Lyons (2016) recounted that workers were required to achieve difficult monthly quotas and that productivity was closely monitored. A co-worker who failed to achieve results was fired and given a "graduation party" so that she could use her "superpowers in her next big adventure" (p. SR7).

Human Resource Administration

Another important consideration in any organization is human resource administration. Criminal justice organizations in the public sector are labor intensive; as much as 90 percent of agency budgets may be devoted to personnel costs. Human resource administration in either the public or private sector is a course of study in its own right and governed by a complex web of rules, regulations, and traditions. As an intern, you should be aware of hiring, training, evaluation, and collective bargaining.

Hiring

You should discuss with your field supervisor the processes by which candidates are recruited and hired for full-time employment. Police and security service personnel must go through a complex process in that they must successfully complete a series of written tests and background checks. For careers in law and public administration, and positions in certain criminal justice or social service organizations or the private sector, hiring is dependent on educational background and specific skill sets, work experience, and letters of recommendation. As discussed in Chapter 3, many positions require background investigations, physical agility and medical testing, psychological evaluations, and perhaps polygraph examination and drug testing. Both public- and private-sector organizations look at a candidate's interpersonal skills through individual and group interviews, as well as candidate presentations. In the public sector, hiring procedures are often defined by application dates, testing times, and the candidate's date of availability.

Today it is not out of the question for an organization to do a quick assessment of the candidate's skills. For example, candidates may be asked to bring writing samples or portfolios of college projects. In some cases, the candidate may be asked to address a problem using the technical skills required for the position. In one instance, candidates for a fraud unit were given a set of problems and told to solve them using a particular software program where knowledge and use was required for the position. It was very dramatic how many candidates were immediately disqualified from consideration even though they had stated they had experience with the program.

New employees receive training, be it formal or informal. Informal training includes on-the-job training, usually through an experienced employee telling a new person how to do something. Police and corrections agencies require formal training in a training academy and a probationary period, which involves the candidate being evaluated for on-the-job performance on a daily or weekly basis. The formal training may include classes in a school or academy setting and/or field training with a senior employee or a specially designated training officer. Other companies may follow a process in which an employee begins by doing simple tasks and works up to more detailed tasks of greater responsibility, under the supervision of a senior employee.

Whatever the procedure, training is an important element, not only for learning how to do the job but for learning about the traditions, norms, and attitudes of the people in the organization. It is a means of becoming socialized in the occupational subculture (i.e., the written and unwritten rules and expectations for employees). In many situations, training is not limited to new employees but is an ongoing process that provides in-service programs on current trends and topics, and retrains personnel who are promoted or reassigned to new positions. Very often, student interns become involved in training either as participants or as assistants in planning for training events as part of assigned duties. Quite recently a group of interns supervised by the author and assigned to a district attorney's office prepared the curriculum and helped to deliver a program to investigators on first response to economic and digital crimes. Another reviewed a software program for background investigations and scheduled a series of training sessions for a state-wide agency. Student interns assigned to a homeland security training center revised a general curriculum for responding to "active shooter" incidents for schools and businesses. Opportunities of this nature often arise during an internship and you are urged to take advantage of them.

Evaluation

Employees in public-sector agencies and private companies are evaluated on a regular basis. It may be a respected, formal process that is seen as important and essential, both by the employees and the supervisors. On the other hand, it may be perfunctory, involving simply filling out a form each year. If much importance or emphasis is placed on the process of evaluation, then it is likely that written evaluations are factors in promotions and salary raises. One financial institution rates employees and interns on a five-point scale related to job knowledge, quality of work, interpersonal skills and communication, customer service, leadership, and adherence to the mission and values of the organization. At the end of your internship you will also be evaluated on a number of factors, which are described in Chapter 13.

Collective Bargaining

Approximately 16.4 million workers, or 11.1 percent of the national workforce, are represented by labor unions (U.S. Bureau of Labor Statistics, 2016). Unions representing employees in negotiations with management have had an important impact on criminal justice operations and basic management decisions. However, not all states and agencies have collective bargaining for their criminal justice employees. If you are interning in an organization with collective bargaining, you should be aware of the following.

1. **The existing contract.** This is the agreement that defines wages, benefits, and conditions of employment. Contracts can include provisions for days off, disciplinary procedures, uniform allowances, and assignments by seniority, and so on.
2. **The agency grievance procedure.** A grievance is filed when either management or the union feels that the contract has been violated in some way. A grievance procedure is a multistep process intended to resolve the conflict within the agency.
3. **Contract negotiation.** Occasionally, student interns are assigned to an agency that is in the midst of negotiations. Before a contract ends, a new contract is negotiated between the union and management. The issues of wages and benefits are usually the most crucial. If negotiations are not going well, interns are exposed to poor morale and talk of strike or work slowdown. You should be aware that contract negotiations can be a stressful time for all involved.

A major trend that has occurred is the termination of collective bargaining rights for certain categories of public employees. In Wisconsin during April 2011, union members and their supporters staged a sit-in in the legislative chambers as both houses voted to remove collective bargaining rights for state employees. What this would mean is that benefits and conditions of employment would no longer be subject to negotiations. Sometimes interns have become involved in collective bargaining issues based on allegations that students are doing work reserved for full-time employees. This can become an issue if there is a perception or practice in which student interns are replacing regular employees. If this occurs in your internship, notify both your agency and faculty supervisor so that the issue can be addressed.

Changes in the Workplace

Since the first publication of this book in 1985, there have been quite a number of changes that have occurred in both the public and private sectors with regard to changes in organizational structures and delivery of services in an expanding global economy. Students are asked to comment on developments and trends as they affect their own internship sites. In the United States, the changes in our economy from one based on manufacturing to one geared to providing services continues unabated. This is all quite evident in your residence hall or home. Check your clothes, appliances, and electronic equipment and see what *is not* manufactured in China, India, or Latin America. Based on the financial realities brought on by the Great Recession of 2008, there are a number of new challenges confronting criminal justice organizations in both the private and public sectors that have an impact on students, both for their internships and future career plans. This is particularly evident in budget issues, as the economic downturn has resulted in reduced tax revenues, increased unemployment, and stalled job growth. Against this background, we are witnessing the following trends:

Growth of Technology

As discussed in Chapter 2, the growth of the Internet and wireless communications continues to have had a profound impact in many industries including entertainment, publishing, education, and retail sales. Who could have predicted the expanded growth of Internet mega-companies such as Google, Facebook, LinkedIn, Twitter, and Amazon? The applications of technology in criminal justice administration and crime investigation are discussed in greater detail in Chapter 12. From an organizational standpoint, there continue to be new ways of doing business such as working from home or through satellite locations globally connected to a central headquarters via the Internet. In fact, many of you may be taking this course over the Internet through a Web-based learning platform and may never have visited your campus. There have been a few instances in which student internships are taking place in "off-premise" sites as workers stay at home and projects are completed by phone and through the Internet.

Use of Contract Personnel

An increasing trend continues whereby contract or private-sector companies provide specific services once reserved for government employees, which is termed "privatization." Examples abound in adult and juvenile correctional services, security of government buildings, and security services and supply operations in war zones. The reason for this is simply cost; it is cheaper for the federal or state governmental unit to contract with an outside agency to provide the service for a specific period of time and not be tied to long-term payroll, benefit, and supply costs. There remains the serious jurisprudence question of contracting out certain powers of the state, such as arrest and use of force to obtain compliance, to private entities. A number of internships have obtained placements in these operations in such areas as crime analysis, cyber security research, and forensic work.

In recent semesters, interns supervised by the author were "contract" workers to private-sector or not-for-profit companies involved in cybersecurity and network protection.

The question that follows is how does this all impact employment opportunities? The answer is complex because it depends on the nature of the function, the length of the contract, and the terms and conditions for the service provider. As reported by one student, federally employed crime analysts at one agency worked side by side with contract personnel. There were significant differences not so much for pay but for benefits such as health care, retirement, and the lack of job security often found in regular civil service appointments. This must all be taken into account when students are seeking full-time employment after graduation.

Mergers, Consolidations, Regionalization

The pace of mergers and acquisitions in the private sector continues to be rapid in many economic sectors, especially in banking, publishing, and information technology. This trend has also entered into the public sector. In the state and local government area, many agencies are considering sharing support services or merging with each other to reduce operational costs. In some cases, small municipal governmental units are thinking about voting themselves out of existence to assimilate with larger townships or counties. The concept of regional support services in criminal justice operations is particularly evident in public safety communications, major crime investigation units, and forensic laboratories. Support services of this nature are very expensive and cannot be operated by smaller agencies.

Changes in Employee Health and Retirement Plans

Decades ago criminal justice agencies and most private-sector companies made most of the contributions to employee health and retirement plans. For health care, employees are being asked to take on greater responsibility for their health through agency and health provider wellness programs and greater contributions to health insurance programs. In many criminal justice agencies, 20- to 25-year retirement plans were once viewed as a major benefit for recruitment and retention purposes. Today employees are being asked to give greater contributions and to manage their own 401(k) and related retirement plans, and may be required to work beyond the traditional retirement brackets.

The Effect of the Organizational Structure on Your Internship

As mentioned previously, the success of your internship may depend on how well you adjust to the formal and informal organizational structure of your field site.

You will be asked at the end of this chapter to review the formal and informal organizational structures of your organization in relation to tasks and authority relationships. Upon your arrival at the agency or company, you should obtain an organizational chart and see how the hierarchy and the flow of communication is created from one office to another. An important concern for interns is the need to review the rules and regulations that govern the agency. For student interns, many rules address the need for confidentiality of case information, computer usage, personal safety procedures, and cell phone and Internet use on the job. In cyber-related internship sites, interns often have to sign nondisclosure agreements regarding product development and review. Your field supervisor will play a very important role in these matters.

Over time you will see how both the formal and informal organizational structures operate. Students have made many perceptive comments about the daily interactions and processes that take place. A common theme is the degree of informal communication that takes place in assignments, tasks, and getting the job done. Students are often surprised that they are able to discuss daily tasks or issues with the director or unit head of the agency. Another area that is sometimes amusing are informal rules related to minor issues such as cleaning your dishes in the lunchroom, parking, and watching out for evil employees.

Conclusion

Most likely, you will quickly identify and adapt to both structures, thereby ensuring an academically and personally rewarding experience. Your field supervisors will probably remind you that you are there as a student and neutral observer and that you should stay out of inter-office politics and cliques.

Knowing and understanding the formal and informal structure of your internship site is crucial to the learning that will occur during your experience. It will help you to adjust to the environment, the people, and your workload. The application of Weber's characteristics of a bureaucracy to your agency or company will give you a clearer picture of the dynamic forces that occur in both the formal and informal structures. This chapter also provided an overview of human resource administration issues as they relate to recruitment and selection, training, and collective bargaining.

■ ■ ■ ▬▬▬▬▬▬▬▬▬▬▬▬▬▬▬▬▬▬▬▬▬▬▬▬▬▬▬▬▬▬▬▬▬▬

Thinking About the Organization of Your Internship Site

1. Describe the formal structure of your site according to the concepts presented in this chapter. Using the main points presented by Max Weber, give examples in at least three of the following areas: division of labor, hierarchy of authority, rules and regulations, career orientation, efficiency, and effectiveness.

2. Obtain an organizational chart of your agency. Mark where your office or field supervisor appears in the chart.

3. Describe the flow of formal communication in your agency in relation to your place in the organization.

4. Review the personnel handbook or standard operating procedures of your agency. What are the formal rules for interns?

5. Describe the informal structure of your site, applying the concepts presented in this chapter. Give examples. How do they affect you in your capacity as an intern?

6. Sketch the informal organizational chart of your agency, showing links between various cliques or groups.

7. Review the job description of your field supervisor. What duties does the supervisor perform that are not part of this formal description?

8. What are the steps a candidate must take in order to be hired at your internship site? What training must he or she go through after being hired? How is an employee promoted? What job classifications exist at your agency or immediate work unit?

9. If collective bargaining takes places at your agency site, to what extent does the contract define pay, benefits, and conditions of employment?

10. Discuss with your intern supervisor or co-workers trends that they see occurring at your agency site with regard to the workforce issues discussed in the chapter.

11. Does your organization have any rules, regulations, or traditions that seem dysfunctional?

10

Political, Economic, and Legal Factors

This chapter focuses on general political, global, economic, and legal factors affecting the operations of criminal justice agencies and their personnel. In recent years, social movements to protest abuses in the criminal justice system have also come into play. As will be discussed, criminal justice agencies and organizations in the private sector dealing with justice administration issues do not operate in a vacuum. They are all tied to a wide range of variables that impact daily and long-term operations. One major factor affecting the delivery of services is the economic status of the community, state, nation, and increasingly, the global environment. As discussed in your coursework, the establishment of any criminal justice organization must be based on a perceived need, which is then redefined in a body of law. Personnel must develop a legal framework in order to perform their duties. This is a difficult task because daily business is affected by many laws, case rulings, and internal procedures. Thus, the major purpose of this chapter is for you to review the major impact these factors have on the criminal justice system and your internship placement site.

Politics and Power

Political scientists view power as the ability to control others. Power can be affected in several ways and can be limited by certain situations or circumstances. For example, the police department in any municipality usually has the power to enforce all the laws of the state. However, the department may not have the resources or expertise to investigate certain offenses, such as cyber crimes. Therefore, the department establishes priorities and does not enforce all the laws of the state. As a result, certain types of crimes and investigations are referred to other state and federal agencies. The extent to which certain laws are enacted, enforced, or prioritized reflects criminal justice policy, which is defined as the extent to which a government body takes action or does not take action. Similarly, in private companies, company policy also dictates activity dealing with a wide range of operational issues.

The political structure that exists in a community exercises control and influences criminal justice policymaking and administration. Many interns find this readily apparent in smaller communities in which one political party or group has control over the general political and economic life of the community. In private companies, corporate politics is commonly the main force in policymaking and personnel actions. This is also impacted by global events for multi-national corporations.

Special interest groups also can influence how policy decisions are made. In many areas, you will find several interest groups seeking to attain their goals through the governmental process. For instance, in any state, the following groups and associations actively lobby on criminal justice legislative issues: police chiefs, the state bar association, district attorneys, sheriffs, probation and corrections officers, unions representing criminal justice personnel, and various civil liberties groups. On the local level, you will find groups that attempt to influence criminal justice policymaking and administration (e.g., Citizens Against Brutality, law enforcement coalitions, criminal justice task force on corrections, Citizens to Stop DWI [driving while intoxicated], and others). Ironically, these groups are often supported by criminal justice agencies as a means of pursuing agency goals.

Many observers view public policy as decisions made by a political entity to take a course of action, to monitor a situation, or to do nothing at all. The decisions come about as a result of a series of activities related to a specific issue. According to Welsh and Harris (2016), these policy and planning steps include the following:

1. **Analyzing a problem.** This involves a detailed review of the causes of an issue and what has been done before to deal with them. During this time, various terms are defined so that all concerned are speaking the same language (e.g., community policing, product piracy). Here the role of advocacy groups must be reviewed in terms of their influence on how problems are defined.
2. **Setting goals and objectives.** In this stage, goals that broadly define what has to be done are established. Objectives are detailed steps that contribute to the attainment of the goals. For example, planners wishing to reduce crime in a high-crime area will define what steps will be taken to address such items as drug houses, street offenders, rundown homes, absentee landlords, and so on.
3. **Designing a program or policy.** This is essentially an intervention that comes about to address the issue. This also involves defining the target population and designating who is going to carry out the program or policy. For most criminal justice problems, this will involve multiple agencies and jurisdictions. Returning to the example in Step 2, addressing the problem involves the following agencies: police (local, regional, narcotics task force, arson task force), fire, codes, health, tax and finance, federal or state neighborhood grant program, and others.
4. **Developing an action plan.** This not only outlines how the activity is going to be carried out, but involves deciding what resources (money, people, and equipment) have to be allocated to the project. During this stage, a timetable is created to achieve certain objectives created in Step 2.

5. **Implementing and monitoring the plan or policy.** Here data will be obtained and used to ascertain that resources are being devoted to the policy or program. Data might include personal observations, structured interviews, and/or surveys. Monitoring also involves giving feedback to those involved in the project.
6. **Evaluating outcomes.** In this stage, the question is asked, "How will we determine whether the policy or program worked?" A research design is created to see if the project had any impact on the original issue that was defined. It also includes looking for unintended consequences that might occur. For example, in a high-crime neighborhood, reducing crime and improving on quality-of-life issues might, in the long run, increase property values and displace the original inhabitants of the area because of high rents or home prices.
7. **Reassessment and review.** In a perfect world, all of the above activities are addressed before the start of the program. Important questions that need to be addressed include program monitoring, data evaluation, and providing reports to major stakeholders. In some cases, changes may be needed in the program design.

Most program and policy planners outline the above steps in great detail before undertaking the program or policy. The number and extent of criminal justice programs and policies that can be applied to crime problems using these steps are endless. Using the above approach, projects undertaken by our students have focused on the following questions:

- How effective are sex offender registration programs?
- How well do Amber Alert (missing child) or student safety programs work?
- Are the efforts of corporate and government programs to reduce identity theft effective?
- How can independent audit firms control fraud?
- To what extent do federal regulatory statutes impact financial institutions?
- What school programs might reduce juvenile gangs or active shooter incidents?
- What is the overall effectiveness of DWI enforcement?
- What is the impact of legalizing marijuana for medical uses on justice administration?
- Do pro-arrest policies reduce domestic violence?
- Are laws named after crime victims effective in their impact?

During your internship program you may be asked to review a current program or policy for the agency. The steps cited above can be used for your analysis. You will, however, need to work closely with your supervisor because the problem identification area and the goals and objectives area often have a history that needs to be completely understood.

Some Considerations

In your community environment, does one external group define the power structure, or do a number of different groups influence the operations of your agency? Do many groups attempt to influence either agency operations or policymaking? For those students working with private-sector agencies, does one sector of the company have the greatest impact on company policy?

There is divided opinion regarding whether politics in criminal justice operations is a positive or negative feature of the system. Nonetheless, as most criminal justice organizations are part of the judicial and executive parts of government, and private companies are regulated by the government, politics is never going to go away. While there are many negative by-products, overall various political variables help to serve as checks and balances on agency activities and provide an avenue for citizen participation and review. Our students often do not agree with this. One wrote:

> *Everything around here is politics. Since the department does not have civil service, the sheriff hires people if they belong to the party. Therefore, there are many lugheads trying to act like cops.*

Another student, commenting on her rejection as an investigator at a district attorney's office, reported:

> *I don't believe they hired the other candidate. He doesn't know a damn thing about investigations. This week he was asking me, the intern, how to write an accusatory instrument and other papers. The reason they hired him was that he is the son of one of the political bigwigs in the county.*

Still another student in a private-sector company wrote:

> *There is a lot of politics around here in terms of who gets promoted or demoted. The finance people are at the top of the pyramid.*

As you go through your internship experience, in your role as participant-observer, you should observe and assess how politics affect operations, both positively and negatively.

Globalization

A current phenomenon affecting organizations is globalization. The term "globalization" refers to the worldwide exchange of ideas, culture products, and services, and the movement of populations from underdeveloped to developed countries (SUNY Levin Institute, 2012). This has been made possible by low-cost airfares, reduction in tariff and trade barriers, global wireless communication systems, and, most notably, the Internet. Many companies offer products and services around the world.

While globalization has created many positive results, there have been many economic and political consequences. The author's colleague, Kyung-Seok Choo, from South Korea, teaches about economic impact by asking students to check the manufacturing tags of the sweatshirts and hats they are wearing. This illustrates that much manufacturing, especially of durable goods, has been transferred from the United States to Mexico, Latin America, Southeast Asia, and China. Another related trend is the transfer of financial services to India, Ireland, and other English-speaking areas. The reason for this is simple: other nations have lower operating costs. This trend results in worker downsizing or layoffs in many communities and industries in the United States, particularly in manufacturing.

Crime, too, has become globalized through formal and informal criminal enterprises. Arms trading, manufacture of counterfeit luxury goods, the sale of body parts, all forms of prostitution and illegal drug manufacturing, and the illegal trafficking of humans for economic purposes also have become global in operation. As a result, many federal and state law enforcement agencies have offices in other countries or formal relationships with their counterparts there to deal with these crime issues. Interpol has become an important intelligence arm in the collection of data. There does, however, remain a need for a defined international policing and judicial system.

Related to the crime picture is international terrorism. As exemplified by the attacks of September 11, 2001, terrorism is the use of criminal acts and violence to advance a social or political cause beyond a region or a national border. As discussed by Combs (2001), while debate continues about the exact definitions and classification of terrorist groups, there is no question that terrorist acts have certain commonalities. These include the selection of nonmilitary targets, the use of the media to claim responsibility for the act and to spread fear, and overt and covert state support for funding, training, and organization. The threat of terrorism has many implications, including increased funding for security, armed interventions by nations against terrorist groups, an upheaval in commerce and tourism, the redeployment of resources for counterterrorism activities, and increased security of infrastructure sites (e.g., water reservoirs, utilities, and transportation and cyber systems) and national monuments. Perhaps the most significant result of the increased terrorist threat has been the creation of the Department of Homeland Security and related state homeland security departments and training centers.

Many of the author's students have been directly affected by globalization and issues related to terrorism. Two students were able to intern at Interpol in Lyon, France, where they worked on a worldwide antifraud payment (credit) card project. This project focused on Interpol's payment card web site and classification system, which is used by member countries as they investigate and combat payment card crime.

Where the impact of global developments in criminal justice is most evident is with those who have completed internships in the United States Department of Homeland Security agencies or state offices of public safety and emergency management. In basic terms, the term "homeland security" refers to all domestic and international activities to protect the United States from terrorist activities. It has also been expanded to include a number of related activities including emergency response to major natural and man-made emergencies (Curtis & McBride, 2011). For internships, students have been assigned to projects dealing with border security, airport security, money laundering, Internet security, and planning for situations that could involve weapons of mass destruction.

In light of the above, a recent class discussion by a group of interns yielded a wide array of comments and observations on the extent globalization impacted their field site. One student at a major bank spent a great deal of time tracking international financial transactions that were suspicious and possibly linked to crime groups. Another, assigned to a city criminal court, reported on the difficulty in finding translators for many newly arrived immigrants to the area. One student initiated a final project on steps to grant asylum for persons prosecuted in their home country for political and ethnic reasons.

Economics

Economics also plays an important role in your agency. Economics is defined as the acquisition and allocation of fiscal resources by an agency that results in the delivery of services or the acquisition of capital. As a student, you are acutely aware of how economics affects your personal life. A trip to the gas station provides a quick international perspective on how per-gallon prices are affected by international developments and trading. Your landlord may have raised the rent on your apartment recently to deal with a local tax hike. The employment decisions that you will make will be determined by various factors, such as the economic climate of a certain region, the need for skilled employees, and your own personal economic needs (e.g., tuition loan payments, car payments, and so on). As an intern, your perspective must focus on the economic conditions that affect an agency and the community in which it is located.

Because most criminal justice agencies belong to the public sector of the economy, their operations are financed by tax dollars, which are collected from federal, state, and local income taxes and sales taxes. At present, frequent changes are being made in the allowance of federal aid to state and local municipalities and the downsizing of bureaucracies. Many states are beginning to place taxation caps on property and school taxes of 2 or 3 percent or the rate of inflation, whichever is less. State and local governments today are addressing new ways to fund their services or discontinue them. As most criminal justice agencies are labor intensive (meaning that the main portion of their budget is for salaries and personnel benefits), critical attention is paid to the number of employees performing various jobs. Even during times when the economy is strong, most levels of government are cautious in the management of fiscal resources.

In the private sector, a business must make a profit in order to stay in business. For example, attorneys speak of billing rates and clients who have not paid their bills in full. Time is money; even a quick telephone call from a client is placed on the account. Many companies are very dependent on quarterly and annual profit-and-loss reports in terms of making short- and long-term capital and personnel expansions.

Fraud management or risk assessment units in large companies are created to deal with threats to assets or profits. The units themselves do not generate a profit through manufacturing, sales, or services. They exist to protect the assets of the corporation by reducing the amount of loss that occurs through internal and external fraud and theft. Unit managers, accordingly, must report progress or production in terms of the cost-benefit ratio related to fraud protection.

In like manner, not-for-profit organizations that deal with crime issues must rely on private contributions and state and federal grants in order to stay in business and deliver services to clients. National, state, or local economic conditions have an immediate impact on their ability to raise money. In difficult economic times, reduced funding results in personnel layoffs and reduction of services to client populations.

Budgets

The main tool of fiscal planning is the organization's or department's unit budget. A budget is the plan for operations based on expected income. Through an analysis of expenses, the agency or department is able to project its operating future. Good managers know that fiscal planning is an ongoing activity that is to be dealt with on a daily basis.

In the public sector, agency budgets are reviewed and approved by legislative bodies via a budgetary process. While the process varies among public municipalities, it generally has the following steps.

1. The department or agency head prepares submission forms for budgetary items. In preparing them, requests may be made for input from subordinate departments or personnel. Planning for submission of the budget is a continuous process that often begins several months before the budget is due. Internally, unit heads are required to defend their own proposals as they relate to the general agency budget.
2. The proposal is sent through a series of committees, discussed and revised, and then voted upon by the governing body.
3. By a specific date, the budget must be approved so that expenditures can be made.

In practice, the next budget cycle begins as the current budget is put into play and monitored. In some cases, the agency or certain departments will undergo a fiscal audit, which is a critical external examination of spending for either the current or several previous years. In public-sector criminal justice agencies, common areas that are often questioned are travel, staffing, overtime, and equipment purchases. This explanation is a simplified review of the actual process. In many cases, there are more than 50 different steps that occur before the budget is executed. Most large agencies have a budget-planning department whose functions are the planning, submission, defense, and audit of the budget document. It is important to find out the actual budget year for the agency. In some cases the agency may follow the calendar year or a specific time period, such as April 1 to March 31.

Types of Budgets

There are three main types of budgets: line-item, planned program budgeting (PPB), and zero-based. In line-item budgeting (see Table 10.1), each area of the organization is given a line and a general cost, and a comparison is made from one fiscal year to the next. Often the figures are accompanied by justification or a needs analysis. PPB requires that each unit in the organization be broken down in terms of specific functions and operational objectives. These are then measured in quantifiable terms in relation to fiscal costs and the stated objectives. The key to PPB is the use of an informational database on what the organization does. Each unit must justify both present and future expenditures according to how the objectives are achieved. In zero-based budgeting, an entirely new budget is prepared each year. Each unit administrator must justify every expenditure in terms of cost and the necessity of the service provided. Zero-based budgeting requires an examination of all programs and services, thus determining those that should and should not be continued.

Within the context of these three budget systems, there are several budgeting approaches. Concepts most often noted in budget discussions are open-end, fixed-ceiling, increase-decrease, priority listing, work measurement and unit costing, and line-item control. In the open-end concept, the administrator submitting the budget presents the request in terms of services performed or needed, with little or no justification. Under the fixed-ceiling concept, the legislature or some other higher administrative unit presents a department with a figure and basically says, "Do everything you have to do with this figure." The increase-decrease and priority listing concepts are used in line-item budgets and contain justification for noted increases and expenditures and/or present priorities for the fiscal year. Work measurement and unit costing programs pertain to PPB and zero-based budget programs in which each service is measured and justified. In line-item control, the executive or legislature has the power to control each budget line and to veto expenditures.

The most widely used budget type in public-sector criminal justice organizations is line-item, with local variations. The line-item budget is easy to construct and understand. Table 10.1 is a sample line-item budget for a fictitious village agency: the Caneyville Police Department. This is an open-ended budget, as there is no discussion of the expenditures. For example, about 85 percent of the budget goes to personnel and benefit expenditures. While not disclosed in the budget itself, the figures are based on several complex factors. Police officer salaries are determined by years of service and by the collective bargaining contract, which gave the officers a 2 percent increase in 2016. In addition to salaries, there is the employee benefit package, which includes health and dental insurance as well as retirement. This calculates to about 50 percent of overall personnel costs per year.

A county program based on fines collected from convicted drivers is called Stop DWI, and this pay for overtime is allocated to Stop DWI patrols. Based on memoranda from the county DWI administrator, this is what the Caneyville Police Department can expect

TABLE 10.1 Sample Line-Item Budget

Line	PUBLIC SAFETY: Police	2015	2016
100	PERSONNEL		
100	Chief of Police	95,000	98,000
103	Assistant Chief	88,000	93,000
110	Police Supervisors (2)	160,000	165,000
120	Police Officers (10)	750,000	765,000
122	Crossing Guards	14,500	15,000
123	Administrative Assistant	44,000	46,000
124	Stop DWI Overtime	18,000	20,000
125	General Overtime	25,000	30,000
127	Holiday Pay	65,900	70,000
	Sub Total	1,260,400	1,302,000
200	BENEFITS		
210	Retirement	189,060	195,300
220	Workman's Comp.	65,020	65,100
225	Medical/Dental Insur.	378,120	390,600
	Subtotal	632,200	651,000
300	EQUIPMENT		
315	Telephone	3,400	3,400
318	Internet	10,000	12,000
322	Utilities	21,000	21,800
325	Cell Phone	10,800	10,800
330	New Police Vehicles (2)	0	80,000
331	Vehicle Maint/Fuel	55,000	56,000
335	Liability Insurance	23,000	25,000
340	Computer Equipment	12,000	14,000
342	Building Maintenance	25,000	25,000
345	Communications	63,400	65,800
347	Ammunition	8,000	9,000
348	Firearms	4,000	4,000
350	Uniform Replacement	22,750	22,750
355	Training Supplies	11,000	11,000
357	Software Updates/Lic	5,000	5,000
360	Evidence Fees	5,000	7,000
	Subtotal	279,350	372,550
400	OTHER		
405	Travel	11,500	13,000
407	Conferences	10,000	12,000
410	Police Misc	15,000	15,000
412	Professional Fees	5,000	5,000
415	Accreditation	0	10,000
	Subtotal	41,500	55,000
	TOTAL EXPENDITURES	2,213,450	2,380,550
100	REVENUE		
105R	Parking Fines	10,000	12,000
110R	State Traffic Ticket	22,000	25,000
112R	Stop DWI	18,000	20,000
115R	Youth Grant	50,000	55,000
120R	Fingerprinting Fees	5,000	5,200
122R	Overtime Reimburse	7,000	8,000
125R	Homeland Security	10,000	10,000
	TOTAL REVENUE	122,000	135,200

to receive for the next fiscal year. Thus, these figures appear both as expenditures and revenue.

New Police Vehicles (line 330) shows an increase to replace two cars and their equipment (i.e., lights, computers, decaling, and safety items). If this request were submitted in a PPB budget, the police chief would have to justify this increase in terms of the size and age of the present vehicle fleet, miles driven, maintenance costs, anticipated mileage and fuel costs, potential savings if certain vehicles were refurbished, and how the cruisers contribute to the mission of the department.

Some areas of this budget appear to be fixed, such as uniforms, telephone costs, and evidence fees. However, some of the line items are actually approximations, as the chief did not know exactly how each area would be spent at the time of preparation. Note that police departments do generate income in the areas of fees, fines, and grants.

Although this may appear to be a static document, the department has great flexibility in moving the numbers around during the fiscal year. For example, if overtime can be curtailed, the extra money allotted can be used for areas that are short of funds or for a luxury item not included in the budget. One month before the end of the fiscal year, the chief collapses various areas and sends veteran officers to conferences and training programs. The bottom line in Caneyville is that for 2016 the chief must be able to stay within the confines of $2,380,550. His or her competency as an administrator is judged according to his or her ability to stay within the budget.

At the end of this chapter, you are asked to obtain a copy of your agency's operating budget and to discern how the approval process operates and the kind of budget planning that is used. Consider expenditures for personnel and personnel-related items (retirement, health insurance, uniforms, etc.) compared with equipment and hardware. Realize, also, that the figures presented often reflect the priorities the agency has set in order to meet its official goals. More often, however, these goals are defined according to the political realities of the community, and the budget is actually a document advocating the operating goals of the agency. In some cases, proposed budgets are completely altered during the approval process, reflecting political realities and social utility.

In addition to general economic trends and the budgetary process, there are a number of other dependent variables that affect the economic life of an agency. Returning to our earlier pronouncement that fiscal operations are based on tax dollars, a sudden increase or decrease of available revenue has an impact on the agency. Imagine if you were a criminal justice administrator and read the following in the newspaper:

> *The Smallville Corporation is closing next year. It created this town, built it, named it. It donated the land for the high school football field, the money for the ambulances, the pipe for the water system, and the brick and mortar for the town hall and two firehouses.*

Because of the loss in tax revenue caused by such a closing, the impact of the shutdown would be felt in all areas of the criminal justice system of this community. First to go would be special or fringe services followed by a reduction of essential services and perhaps the elimination of some probation officer positions.

Very often a catastrophic event will have dire consequences for an organization's operating budget. The terrorist attacks of 9/11 resulted in many agencies and companies making unplanned expenditures for physical security at transportation areas, water reservoirs, public buildings, historic sites, and other sites deemed critical to a local or regional economy. A major expenditure for many public- and private-sector organizations is computer security software to deal with the recent increases of viruses that threaten critical information systems. In the northeast United States, two hurricanes in 2011 and 2012 had a profound influence on immediate and long-term consequences for public safety in affected states and communities. In one community on Long Island, the police station and all police fleet vehicles were destroyed during a storm in 2012. In New Orleans after Hurricane Katrina in 2005, years of records and tons of equipment for criminal justice operations were wiped out.

In addition to tax dollars, department budgets in the public sector are often subsidized by government or private foundation grants. A grant is a sum of money that is issued by a state or federal agency to address a defined function, program, or public policy problem for a specific time period. For example, many police agencies receive Stop DWI/DUI (driving under the influence) funding, which is specifically directed to overtime for anti-drunk driving patrols during specific high-risk periods. Other agencies have received grants for personnel overtime and monitoring equipment to keep watch on sex offenders.

During your internship, when discussion focuses on budget matters in public-sector agencies, you may hear of new ways that agencies are attempting to raise funds. Most common are private donations, asset forfeiture, and fines. For donation programs, private companies and persons donate money or equipment to an agency. Very common is a donation of a car by a local dealership for an educational program or safety equipment purchased for patrol personnel through a private foundation. Forfeiture, on the other hand, is the confiscation of criminal evidence or proceeds related to the commission of a major felony crime and redirecting these items to the agency involved in the investigation. The most common items are money and vehicles used in drug transactions. In major cases involving multiple agencies, the money or vehicles are reallocated based on the percentage of agency involvement. Another method to augment agency budgets are fine monies paid to a governmental entity by a citizen or company as a punishment for specific offenses such as false intrusion alarms, loud noise, and parking violations. In many locations, fines for these and other minor offenses make a significant contribution to the budget.

Budget Considerations in the Private Sector

Many interns in the private sector have a difficult time procuring a copy of the corporation's operations budget. Because of proprietary concerns, such information is not generally available to many individuals in the organization. What supervisors can discuss is the budgetary process—how a budget is prepared, how the final budget affects the operations of the unit, and the major items in the budget. Some of the political concerns may also be shared. On the other hand, publicly traded companies report their earnings and losses on a quarterly basis, which in turn is reflected in public earnings reports. Reported compensation for executives, as well as ratings from independent economic reviewers, allow interns to obtain a picture of how well the company is doing in terms of profit and loss.

In certain private-sector operations, a fraud, compliance, or cybersecurity unit exists for controlling losses, monitoring compliance with federal and state laws, and protecting the digital infrastructure. Each unit would develop a budget within the context of company operations. In addition to personnel costs, important considerations are travel and equipment. You will not find costs for the unit in the consolidated balance sheet, which will list company assets, liabilities, and performance indicators. These units are generally found in such areas as other liabilities. One important issue in budgeting for this type of department is whether the amount of money saved justifies the expenditures to control fraud.

Legal Basis

During your internship, you may be asked to review the legal operations of a particular agency in terms of its powers and constraints. Criminal justice organizations are instruments of the state for carrying out crime control and prevention. The legal basis of these organizations and the rules that govern the execution of the agency mission, are found in myriad laws, statutes, state and federal court decisions, and administrative rulings by federal, state, and local governments. While we are aware that these foundations have been discussed in many of your courses, at intern seminars over the years we have posed the questions "What is the legal basis of your agency?" and "What laws affect the daily conduct of business at your internship site?" and have found that students are not always sure. We have also found that practitioners may be equally hazy when responding to students' questions. This section serves both to review and clarify the legal concerns you may have about the operations of your field site.

Every organization—whether it is a police department, a district attorney's or public defender's office, a probation department, or a private-sector fraud investigation or cybersecurity operation—is grounded in a legal framework. In essence, criminal justice departments or units are created either through the state constitution or a legislative act that grants the power for the agency to do something. Examples of constitutionally mandated agencies include the county sheriff's office, district attorney, justice of the peace, certain state and local courts, and most law enforcement agencies. Some state constitutions allow municipalities to establish agencies such as police departments or local courts if the municipality believes there is a need to do so.

Legislative enactments at all government levels provide the legal basis for the creation of the majority of criminal justice agencies and programs. At the federal level, congressional acts have established the Federal Bureau of Investigation; the Bureau of Alcohol, Tobacco, Firearms, and Explosives; the Secret Service; and other special investigative and intelligence agencies. After the events of September 11, 2001, the president established an advisory position on homeland security. This eventually became the basis for a cabinet-level position, Secretary of Homeland Security, and the reorganization of 23 separate agencies into the new department. This restructuring included agencies with long historical traditions such as the United States Coast Guard, United States Secret Service, and United States Customs and Border Protection. Thus, it is possible for agencies to be merged or have their missions directed toward a particular issue such as terrorism.

At the state level, you will find that many criminal justice departments (such as the state police or department of youth services) can trace their beginnings to a legislative act. Legislative enactments also provide the basis for the creation and termination of special criminal justice programs, special investigative bodies, and public study commissions on national and state crime problems.

A historical review of the background of these agency-creating statutes provides a fascinating study of politics in action. There must be a specific reason to establish an agency; namely, to address a particular criminal justice problem. Most state police agencies, for example, were created to address rural crime problems, to provide protection for state officials, to deal with labor strife events, and to act as special vehicles of the executive branch of government for law enforcement. Many federal agencies are organized for a specific range of offenses such as the Drug Enforcement Administration for narcotics violations or the Securities Exchange Commission for stock and bond-related frauds.

Federal and state legislative enactments related to criminal law and procedures have the greatest effect on criminal justice administration. Procedurally, legal rulings at the federal or state level can set guidelines or specify duties for criminal justice personnel (e.g., a police officer may not arrest or conduct a "stop and frisk" against a person unless he or she can demonstrate probable cause). For citizens, legislative enactments promulgate what kind of behavior will be deemed criminal, as well as specify or set the guidelines for punishment. Perhaps the best example of this is the USA PATRIOT Act, which was enacted weeks after 9/11. This act, which is formally titled the Uniting and Strengthening America by Providing Appropriate Tools Required to Intercept and Obstruct Terrorism Act, consists of 10 sections addressing a number of issues related to counterterrorism, including prosecution for electronic crimes, money laundering and banking regulations, foreign visa requirements, enhanced surveillance powers, and supporting victims of terrorism (Curtis & McBride, 2011). Concurrently, many states have enacted mini-PATRIOT Act laws that outlaw terrorism and possession of materials that can be used for weapons of mass destruction.

Equally legally potent are administrative rulings arising from regulatory powers legislatively given to state and federal agencies. A good example of a basis in administrative law is the organization of many state departments of motor vehicles. Generally, the legislative statutes regarding motor vehicle laws give the commissioner of motor vehicles the power to appoint deputies and hold hearings or inquiries into traffic-related matters. In many states, a driver can lose his or her license after certain motor vehicle hearings. While these hearings and rulings follow authorized standard procedures, they do not follow strict rules of evidence. Nevertheless, they carry the same effect as a rule of law. Other administrative rulings related to criminal justice operations include mediation procedures to resolve labor management disputes, due-process procedures on matters involving employee conduct and discipline, and agency standards on the granting of licenses.

The private sector is impacted by many types of regulations noted above. Corporations and partnerships are legal entities created by the state to raise capital and conduct business. While persons in private organizations serve the company, the legal basis to create the unit rests directly or indirectly with the state or federal government. For example, the Fraud Unit of Northwest Frontier Bank must conform to various state and regulatory policies in order to conduct investigations. The recent increase of corporate fraud in fiscal reporting, mutual funds trading, and outright theft of funds for personal use by corrupt executives has resulted in increased oversight by federal and state regulatory agencies. Another example is the passage of the Gramm-Leach-Bliley Act of 1999, which requires the Federal Trade Commission to enact safeguards to ensure the privacy and security of customer records and information, including unauthorized access that might result in harm to the customer. Still another example is the Health Insurance Portability and Accountability Act (HIPAA), passed in 1996, which requires all health care providers to provide information on security policies regarding patient records and hospital insurance claims. The Department of Health and Human Services is responsible for implementing these regulations (Curtis & McBride, 2011). Another important legislative compliance law is the Public Company Accounting Reform and Investor Protection Act of 2002, popularly known as the Sarbanes-Oxley Act, which requires publicly traded companies to certify their financial statements and to institute more effective internal accounting controls. This was brought about by a number of financial scandals between 2000 and 2002 that destroyed a number of major companies, including Enron, Adelphi Communications, and Tyco, and resulted in criminal convictions of many of their senior executives (Bainbridge, 2007). Today, financial institutions have to deal with further compliance related to the Recession of 2008–2009 and questionable practices related to lending and equity funds.

A Legal Framework

What laws affect the daily conduct of business of an organization? This question is difficult to answer in view of agency rules and federal, state, and local laws. How does the practitioner perform his or her duties within this complex legal scenario? First, each official has to review the overall scope of the laws that directly and indirectly affect the performance of his or her duties. For example, laws affecting a police officer include the penal code, criminal procedure law, family court acts, vehicle and traffic laws, and department policy manuals and rules. Those laws affecting a probation officer include corrections law, family or juvenile court acts, penal law, criminal procedure law, and department rules and regulations. In private-sector operations, personnel must be trained in institutional procedures and federal and state regulatory laws.

In addition, each official is obliged to keep abreast of new legal developments in the field. There is no systematic way to do this. Many departments address this problem through in-service training sessions, webinars, legal aid bulletins, or special memoranda. While many organizations do not go out of their way to remain informed on legal updates except when a revised annual edition of the body of law is issued, many practitioners do attempt to stay current through self-study. Realistically, it is impossible to remain up-to-date on all legal developments in one's immediate field. Therefore, the practitioner is forced to consult with other experts. The practitioner develops a legal framework of the laws, simplified into three lists: dos, don'ts, and standard practices.

External Controls on Agencies and Personnel

How are criminal justice organizations and personnel controlled so that rights of citizens are not abridged? At first glance, it might appear to many that there are few legal controls. However, high-profile cases on alleged official corruption and misuse of force, show that there are both formal and informal systems of checks and balances on governmental agencies and their personnel through the following means. The following are the key factors that have both an impact on criminal justice administration and influence daily activities.

Politics

As previously discussed, political action can have a direct and indirect effect on all criminal justice operations. Citizens displeased with agency heads or services have the option of not reelecting the political officials who are responsible for providing those services. Politicians who are confronted with this possibility usually shift the blame to the agency heads. A domino effect may occur as these agency heads begin placing pressure on subordinates to rectify the problem.

Political action also has a direct effect on the agency through the budgetary process. For example, a state agency responsible for juvenile delinquents found its budget slashed by the legislature when a youth in an outreach program murdered an elderly woman while on leave. This focused critical attention of the public, the media, and elected officials on the wide range of rehabilitative programs sponsored by the agency.

In corporate life, company boards of directors and stockholders have a great say in policymaking. The annual meetings of company stockholders can become feisty affairs if there is a need to change corporate leadership or direction because of financial losses. At this time, many chief executive officers of major corporations are under attack by shareholders for commanding high salaries and stock options despite poor economic performance by their companies.

Departmental Policies

As is discussed in Chapter 11, the organizational manual, or standard operating procedures, is based on organizational considerations, environmental conditions, and the laws the organization deals with most frequently. Taken together, these policies have the most immediate effect on the actions of employees because they outline procedures that personnel should follow in everyday situations. One shortcoming is that they may result in personnel having very little discretion in dealing with unusual situations or in situations for which policies do not exist.

Traditional and Social Media

It is often said that criminal justice officials have every move watched by the outside world. Because of technological advances such as cell phone cameras, and the long-term effect of national and local scandals, the public has more access to criminal justice information through freedom of information statutes and up-to-the-minute news information services such as CNN, MSNBC, local 24-hour news channels, and local cable stations. The news media, particularly television, has a profound impact on how criminal justice agencies and personnel perform their duties because events are up to the minute. This is amply illustrated by immediate coverage of recent spree killings that occur at schools and shopping malls. As discussed in Chapter 2, there is more transparency than ever before in the vast arena of criminal justice administration.

Today every mobile device has a camera, and complaints against criminal justice personnel—particularly police officers—can be broadcasted on YouTube and other social media outlets in seconds after an event.

Internet

The increase in Internet use for communications has had a profound impact on criminal justice policymaking. Both individuals and public advocacy groups have created web sites that advocate a wide range of views on criminal justice policymaking. For example, the American Civil Liberties Union web site (www.aclu.org) provides legal cases and viewpoints on issues such as racial profiling, the need for the USA PATRIOT Act, and corporate fraud control.

Most large criminal justice agencies and security service units have their own web sites to present their agency missions and programs. The Department of Homeland Security site is updated very frequently to report on antiterrorist programs and issues. The Federal Emergency Management Administration (FEMA) offers disaster assistance information and certification courses through its web site at www.fema.gov. Returning to the discussion of technology in Chapter 2, a number of groups and individuals have blogs that attempt to influence criminal justice policy. More recently, the power of the Internet for personal communication and social media shows how information can or cannot be controlled.

Legal Action

The 1964 Civil Rights Act states that citizens have the right to redress in cases in which their civil rights have been violated. This is particularly important to criminal justice managers, as it has been the basis for scores of lawsuits filed by aggrieved citizens over brutality, incompetence, and nonfeasance by government officials. In such claims, a citizen alleges that a government official deprived a plaintiff of some right secured by the constitution or the laws of the United States, and that the deprivation occurred under color of law. Illegal searches, false arrests, assaults, and malicious prosecutions are examples of civil rights violations.

In the private sector, civil claims can be filed for a number of issues by plaintiffs for such issues as negligence, defamation, acquiring property under false pretenses, failing to honor contracts, and failing to comply with various compliance functions mandated by law. The former has much implication for various corporations. For example, the Gramm-Leach-Bliley Act requires credit and lending institutions to notify consumers on the privacy of their information. HIPAA requires health providers to secure the information of patients including digital information. Your own campus is required to comply with the Jeanne Clery Act to report policies for campus safety and certain crime statistics. Perhaps the most controversial is the Patient Protection and Affordable Care Act, also referred to as "Obamacare," which was passed in 2010 and is intended to provide health care to millions of uninsured Americans and lower health costs. The impact of this complex legislation continues to be argued in Congress, the courts, and the media after the law went into effect in 2014. For these and many other federal and state laws, there can be fines and negative media publicity for noncompliance.

Related to compliance is regulation of business and public activity by various governmental agencies. Hundreds of books could be written on the vast number of regulatory bodies on the state and federal levels. The Securities and Exchange Commission, for example, is the federal agency that regulates the stocks and bonds industry. On the state level, many state attorney's offices regulate commercial activities and either mediate or file lawsuits against individuals and companies involved in unlawful business practices. The Civil Rights Division of the United States Department of Justice receives complaints and may take legal action on complaints relating to civil rights abuses against law enforcement agencies. The Better Business Bureau is a private organization to which consumers can make complaints about shoddy work or failure to perform or provide a service. In many large cities, there are police-citizen commissions that monitor law enforcement activity. On the state level, those agencies related to criminal justice operations include commissions that review detention facilities, consumer complaints, the sale of alcoholic beverages, the issuance of motor vehicle licenses and registration, public transportation operations, and educational safety. Of note, all of these agencies are potential internship sites. Most recently, a very interesting internship was undertaken by a student with the New York City Taxi and Limousine Commission which regulates taxis, limousines, and for-hire vehicles in that city.

Professionalism

This term has become an important part of the vocabulary of criminal justice personnel and organizational leaders. Although there are many questions regarding what actually constitutes a professional police officer or probation officer, it is safe to say that the profession denotes an occupational group that has a distinct body of knowledge, a desire to serve the community, and the skills needed to perform certain tasks. The bottom line here is that members of an occupation who feel that they are professionals strive to do the best job possible (reflected by quality arrests, not abusing prisoners, not covering mistakes, producing quality reports, etc.). Whether many criminal justice occupations, such as police officers, probation officers, correctional officers, and youth counselors, are indeed professions is a topic of some debate. Regardless, we find that the concept of professionalism has brought about positive results because of higher community and peer expectations in terms of performance of duties.

Customer Satisfaction

In the private sector, a dissatisfied customer can simply walk to another company for the product or service needed. Customer satisfaction and quality services are the main goals of many major corporations; public-sector agencies have similar concerns. For example, the main tenets of community policing programs are establishing closer relationships with the people served by the police, improving communication with the community, and providing good overall service by establishing ties and working together. In the private sector, consumers are constantly filing reviews of services via social media sites on dining, transportation, vehicle repairs, and other services.

Social Movements

Social movements can have an important impact on organizations. By basic definition, social movements are created by groups of people to address and reform an important social issue. With the use of social media, groups of people can be brought together over an issue in rapid fashion, often within hours. For example, within the past two years, national and local movements have arisen over the deaths of African American men at the hands of police, the treatment of juveniles as adults in criminal proceeding, and the death of prisoners in correctional facilities. Other well organized protests were focused on corporate investments in the tobacco and fossil fuel industries. On campuses, protests emerged over benefactors' historical involvement in the slave trade, campus policies related to sexual assault victimization, residence hall safety, and police tactics used in an enforcement action.

When this occurs, the organization is placed on the defensive in terms of justifying its policies, or the courses of action taken in a situation that spurred the protest. These all can have an impact on organizational behavior in terms of altering operational policies and changes in leadership.

Conclusion

This chapter directed your attention to general political, global, economic, and legal factors affecting the operations of criminal justice agencies and their personnel. Within the first week of your internship you may see how the administration of justice is affected by politics. Agency heads are required to be political actors because they often must be elected or appointed and compete for staff and equipment resources.

Politics and globalization are distinctly tied to the economic policies of the agency. Through review of an agency budget, you will see the factors that must be dealt with in administering the labor-intensive agencies of the criminal justice field. The economic health of your community, as well as the state and nation, all affect the manner in which your agency is able to provide services.

Lastly, the legal basis for criminal justice administration was reviewed. The establishment of any criminal justice agency must be based on a perceived need, which is then redefined in a body of law. Personnel must develop a legal framework in order to perform their duties. This is a difficult task because daily business is affected by many laws, case rulings, and agency procedures. As an intern, you should be aware of the legal framework of your organization.

■ ■ ■ ▬▬▬▬▬▬▬▬▬▬▬▬▬▬▬▬▬▬▬▬▬▬▬▬▬▬▬▬▬▬▬▬▬▬▬

Political, Economic, and Legal Factors at Your Site

1. How do federal, state, or local politics affect the operation of your organization?
2. Apply the program or policy planning approach presented in this chapter to an issue currently being addressed by your internship site.
3. Obtain a recent copy of your organization's budget, and review personnel and equipment expenditures. Interns in the private sector may have difficulty procuring a budget because

of the proprietary concerns of the organization. In these cases, it may still be possible to learn about the major expense categories and the budgetary process. If the organization is publicly traded, what were the overall earnings and profit and loss for the last fiscal year?

4. Explain the process your agency uses in preparing its budget. For those students in public-sector or not-for-profit agencies, to what extent does politics affect this process?

5. To what extent have national, state, or local economic developments affected the operation of your agency?

6. How has your agency or unit been affected by globalization?

7. Why was your agency or organization created? If applicable, what is the legal basis of your agency? Present a brief history of your agency.

8. List and discuss the main bodies of law that affect your field supervisor in the daily performance of his or her duties.

9. How have recent court or administrative rulings affected the operations of your agency? How do personnel in your agency stay current on legal developments?

10. What are major federal or state laws that your agency must comply with or face civil penalties?

11. Explain, where applicable, how customer satisfaction, Internet, media, professional standards, and regulatory oversight affect the daily actions of agency personnel. Give examples from your internship experience.

11

Organizational Goals and Relationships

This chapter reviews some basic concepts in administration and management related to goals and the organizational relationships that exist with the external environment. All criminal justice organizations have official and operative goals that serve as guidelines for day-to-day operations and long-term planning. These are tied to the vision, mission, and core values of the organization. These goals also help the organizations to compete and survive in the competitive global environment. Related to goals is the issue of effectiveness—the degree to which an organization attains its goals. However, effectiveness is often difficult to measure, in either qualitative or quantitative terms. In addition, organizational outcomes, or what the organization actually does, may have nothing in common with either category of goals. In recent years, however, goals and degree of effectiveness have become common in the lexicon of criminal justice administration, due to public demands for accountability and productivity.

As you go through your program of study, you should be able to review the scope of organizational relationships in their sphere of the criminal justice system. This chapter also discusses the issue of relationships in the criminal justice system. Regardless of formal legal, economic, or political ties, organizational relationships are often determined by the personalities of individual administrators and staff members.

Official Goals versus Operative Goals

In discussing the importance of organizational goals, Hall (1999) distinguishes between official goals and operative goals. Official goals can be defined as the general purposes of any organization as stated by statute, charter, mission statement, or official pronouncement. Operative goals, on the other hand, are the policies of the organization that dictate what the agency actually does. Operative goals become the real standards by which day-to-day decisions are made. They reflect human interest, competition, and available resources. As you will see, these goals may or may not be related to the organization's official goals.

Organizations create their goals based on a number of factors. These include:

1. political pressures from various segments of the community;
2. availability of economic resources;
3. legal decrees set by legislators, courts, administrative offices, and common law;
4. personal desires of organizational leaders and followers;
5. historical precedent (e.g., the agency has always provided a certain service or function);
6. influence of technology; and
7. demographic trends such as population growth/decline.

Private-sector companies must also establish official and operative goals as a means of staying in business. The majority of large companies today have adopted mission statements that outline the underlying philosophy for offering goods and services to customers.

An example of a mission statement appears in the duty manual of the Flanders County District Attorney's Office:

> *The Office of the District Attorney will prosecute crimes, obtain victim relief to provide for a safe environment for all citizens of Flanders County, and provide a people-oriented work environment where all the staff members may enjoy their jobs, utilize their talents, respect one another, and grow as individuals.*

The goal-setting process can be either planned or done by the seat of one's pants. The Flanders County District Attorney's Office (see Chapter 9) specified the following official goals:

1. Bring all criminal matters to trial in the proper court.
2. Review felony arrests through the grand jury process and secure indictments against suspected persons deemed probable to have committed offenses.
3. Initiate criminal investigations through the grand jury process.
4. Extradite criminals who committed crimes in Flanders County and fled to another county, state, or country.
5. In cooperation with county police agencies, apply and execute electronic surveillance devices for criminal investigations.

From reviewing annual reports, however, we find that the following are the operative goals for this agency:

1. Prosecute in an efficient manner driving while intoxicated (DWI) cases in order to reduce alcohol-related deaths on the county's roads.
2. Reduce the backlog of cases in the county court system, especially those related to traffic offenses.
3. Increase the effectiveness in solving identity theft cases.
4. Reduce arson via the arson task force.

Do the operative goals reflect the official goals of the agency? Generally, they do. The efforts by the agency directed at arson, DWI, case management, and the like are related to the constitutional mandates for the district attorney's office. However, operative goals do not have to be written or stated in official pronouncements. For example, the following unwritten operative goals affect the operations of the agency:

1. Do a good job so that the district attorney can be reelected, enabling the party to hold on to the office and maintain jobs and power in the county.
2. Do a good job with the arson task force so that we may be able to obtain more federal funding.
3. Be realistic in plea bargaining. We cannot take every case to trial because it is too expensive.

In similar fashion, Northwest Frontier Bank Corporation has the following official goals:

1. Maintain a leadership role within the financial services industry by providing customers with innovative services.
2. Provide shareholders with ongoing enhancement of their investment.
3. Provide employees with an improved quality of life through career and professional advancement opportunities.
4. Share the bank's talents and resources to improve communities served in the market area.

This mission statement provides the cornerstone for operations in every unit of the corporation. Based on this, the operative goals for the bank's Fraud Unit are:

1. Reduce the amount of loss through fraud.
2. Identify employees who are involved in fraudulent activities and prosecute them to the fullest extent possible.
3. Maintain a positive relationship with federal and state law enforcement agencies.
4. Serve as a deterrent to nonemployees who wish to commit fraud against the company.

In certain criminal justice organizations, you will find that goal displacement occurs; that is, the official goals are not reflected in the operative goals, or the official goals are completely changed. The rape crisis center of Flanders County provides a case study on goal displacement. The original official goals of the crisis center were to help victims cope with their situation and, if possible, help the police apprehend the rapists. The crisis center was fairly successful in its endeavors and, within a few years, rape incidents decreased radically. Reviewing their operations today, we find that the center now deals with child abuse, spousal abuse, and general crime-victim assistance. The organization has directed its efforts toward other social problems. Such situations are commonplace for several reasons. First, encouraged by its effectiveness, the organization is able to work on other problems in the community. Second, the organizational structure is intact, which is important for directing personnel, acquiring fiscal resources, and maintaining a public image. Finally, and depending on whether the agency staff consists of paid employees or volunteers, personnel in the agency may want to continue their employment. Therefore, they expand their scope of interest and operations.

Vision and Mission

The term "organizational vision" is often used in agency planning sessions to define how the organization views itself in the present and its potential directions in the future. Organizational planners argue that vision is important because organizations continually have to review ever-changing markets, client needs, funding, and technology in order to survive. For example, sophisticated database analysis and pattern recognition is being used increasingly in money-laundering investigations and tracking of terrorist financing. In criminal investigations, many states are developing DNA databank programs for sample testing of arrested violent offenders. Will DNA replace fingerprints, the mainstay for personal identification for the past 100 years?

Related to organizational vision is the defined mission of the agency. As already presented with the Flanders County District Attorney's Office and Northwest Frontier Bank, a mission statement is a statement of purpose of what the organization does and the issues it tries to confront.

Mission statements can be found on organizational web sites and in publications and duty manuals. Tied to both mission and vision are the core values of the organization that define the essential operating philosophies for dealing with clients or customers. Many of these value statements cite ethical behavior, providing assistance to crime victims, quality services for the community, and protection of the rights of citizens in enforcing the laws. In the private sector, the same holds true with regard to providing quality products, dealing honestly with customers, and confronting the realities of the marketplace.

Strategic Planning

To remain competitive, many organizations have conducted strategic planning exercises to review their mission, vision, and official goals. As discussed by King (2003), strategic planning is a detailed review of current operations, with a look to how they might change in the future. Strategic planning challenges the organization to review what it does, its current resources, and resources that might be needed in the future. If undertaken correctly, this form of planning involves all units of the enterprise participating in the process. One common method for this type of analysis is a SWOT (strengths, weaknesses, opportunities, threats) review. Included in the SWOT review process are a number of questions or issues concerning internal strengths and weaknesses and external opportunities and threats that a private- or public-sector organization might have to address.

Strengths. What do we do right, and how do we outperform our competitors or like agencies? What do we have in terms of assets (people, equipment, buildings, and money reserves)? What are our positive internal aspects?

Weaknesses. What do we not do well, and how do our competitors outperform us? Why is this so? Is it due to a lack of funding, not having enough people, or are we trying to do too many things? Are our assets in poor shape or are we using outmoded technology? What are our negative internal aspects?

Opportunities. What does the future have in store for us in terms of daily operations? How will the federal and state budget affect us if there is an economic upturn? Will our tax or customer base increase? What will be our workforce needs in view of a growth cycle? What are our external positive aspects?

Threats. What are the dark clouds on the horizon? If there is an economic downturn, how will we be affected? If in the private sector, are we a target for a takeover? If so, what happens to our current staff and operations? What are our external negative aspects?

From this SWOT analysis the organization's mission is reviewed and long-term plans are formulated to deal with the future. A SWOT analysis will also review the organization's core values to determine if, in fact, they are applied and operational in daily activity.

Organizational Effectiveness

Effectiveness is the degree to which an organization attains its goals. This statement is somewhat complicated when both official and operative goals are involved. In the technical sense, effectiveness relates to both types of goals. Realistically, however, there are organizational goals that cannot be achieved because they are unattainable. In some cases, it is impossible to gauge effectiveness because the achievement of goals is not quantifiable. Added to this is the fact that some organizations have conflicting goals. The Flanders County District Attorney's Office has provided a glimpse of this dilemma. Officially, the agency is supposed to prosecute all criminal cases in an effective and efficient manner. On the other hand, there is an operative goal that says, "Do not bust the budget over unimportant cases." The Fraud Unit at Northwest Frontier Bank will not deal with fraud cases that involve sums lower than $15,000.

Most criminal justice organizations have official and operative goals that are unattainable or not quantifiable. First, let us say a word about attainability. Officially, it is nice to say that an agency will do all it can to fight crime and send wrongdoers to jail. However, the reality in this complex world is that not all criminals are caught, not all crimes are reported, and not all criminals who are caught go to jail. This is a reality that both interns and practitioners have to accept.

Measurability is a separate but related issue. Most criminal justice goals are not quantifiable. It would be difficult, for example, to evaluate whether an agency had fulfilled the official goal of administering justice. Operative goals are often not easily measured either. Sometimes, however, administrators and planners must quantify (reduce to numbers) certain operations as a step toward measuring effectiveness. It would be fairly easy, for example, to evaluate the effectiveness of the Flanders County Arson Task Force by comparing previous rates of arson, arrests, and convictions to current figures. The danger is that department heads tend to forget that numbers can be deceiving. They may make short-sighted pronouncements about program effectiveness. For example, in claiming that the arson problem is under control, a director may cite higher rates of arrests and convictions in arson cases, as well as a reduction in arson reports. However, there is always the chance that the arson rate will increase drastically, thus decreasing effectiveness.

Although the achievement of an organization's goals cannot always be discussed in quantitative terms, and many of the goals cannot be fully attained, goal development provides a guiding path for the organization. Priorities can be established in the execution of the agency mission according to the official and operative goals.

Organizational Relationships

The term "criminal justice system," while used in several contexts and general discussion, is actually a misnomer. There is no true system because the various organizations that comprise criminal justice administration do not actually interface with each other. Instead, the criminal justice system is a social process that occurs after a crime has occurred. It has emerged as a convenient way to describe the entirety of processes, actors, and organizations that can affect the disposition of a criminal case. Many textbooks attempt to describe this vast complex social system through organizational and flow charts. Such schemes cannot take into account the vast variety of interchanges and procedural nuances that occur in every community in the United States. For example, consider the relationship chart for the Canal City Police Department (see Figure 11.1).

The Canal City Police Department enforces all state and local statutes within a 12-square-mile limit. The police force is composed of 40 officers who provide services for a resident population of 60,000. Because of local industry, county and state offices, and a community college within the city limits, the population of the city during the day is estimated at about 80,000.

The left side of the agency relationship chart illustrates the major social and educational service institutions with which the police department interacts on a daily basis. For example, victims of sexual assault receive counseling through a special unit funded by the Department of Social Services. The Department of Social Services also sponsors a program to deal with offenses and situations related to the homeless. The city school system has many active programs with the police department, including crime prevention programs and juvenile offense interdiction, where at-risk students receive counseling and guidance.

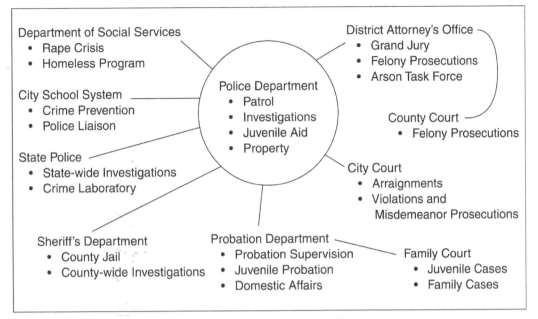

FIGURE 11.1 Police Department and Agency Relationships: Canal City Police Department.

The right side of the chart shows criminal justice offices that have a systematic relationship with the police department for the prosecution of criminal cases. These include the District Attorney's Office, City Court (for violations and misdemeanors), and County Court (for felonies). The District Attorney's Office intercedes between the Police Department and the County Court for the prosecution of major felony cases. The Probation Department has a similar role in juvenile delinquency cases.

The chart also illustrates the relationship between the city police department and both the state police and county sheriff's departments. The sheriff's department and police department are in close contact because the sheriff maintains the county jail, the population of which is comprised primarily of people arrested by the police department.

As shown in Figure 11.2, the Fraud Unit at Northwest Frontier Bank has a number of relationships with federal, state, local, and even international police departments. These include:

1. **U.S. Secret Service.** Works with the unit to investigate credit card fraud.
2. **U.S. Postal Inspectors.** Interacts with the unit when the mail is used for scams or credit card theft.
3. **U.S. Marshal's Office.** Through its warrants section, identifies and actively seeks persons with outstanding warrants filed by Northwest Frontier Bank as the complainant.
4. **U.S. Attorney's Office.** Prosecutes all interstate fraud cases involving the company.
5. **Interpol.** Liaises with police agencies around the world.

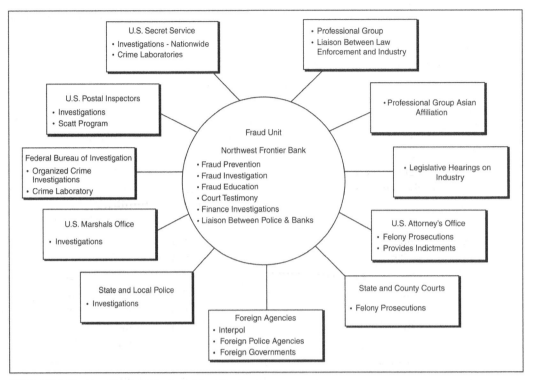

FIGURE 11.2 The Fraud Unit At Northwest Frontier Bank.

Added to this list are a whole host of professional organizations that comprise the bank security network in the United States and around the world. This network provides training sessions and intelligence on fraud trends.

While the extent of the relationships has not been fully discussed here, it is evident from the discussion above that the entire system is extremely complex, even for a relatively small community or for one company. Each organization operates in a community network that includes schools, social service agencies, and other criminal justice agencies in a local or national network. The relationships may be different, depending on the type of organization at the center of the chart, but they are inevitably complicated.

Discussing this arrangement, Ismaili (2011) points to the public policy concept of "subgovernments" to characterize the complex relationships between criminal justice organizations and their stakeholders. This relationship consists of three main groups that constitute the subgovernment: elected heads of government and the legislature, the bureaucracy, and public interest groups. For example, applying this model to a county sheriff's department, the department would be influenced by the county executive, the county legislature, and the various legislative committees that oversee general policies and funding for law enforcement and corrections (most county jails are operated by the sheriff). For purposes of this discussion, policy refers to general courses of action that are taken to meet agency goals. The bureaucracy, which executes policies for both law enforcement and correctional operations, constitutes both the leadership and members of the department. The extent to which goals are achieved depends on a number of factors, including priorities by agency leadership, numbers and types of activities, staffing levels, and funding. The bureaucracy includes those units of government that are not in the department per se, but are concerned about its daily operations, such as county offices of audit and control, planning, and probation and the court system. For example, the county court system has a strong relationship with the sheriff's department because court security, prisoner transports, and the jail are provided by the sheriff's department and are critical for the daily operations of the various courts. As with many criminal justice heads, the office of sheriff is an elected position and successful bids for future reelection depend on goodwill and positive relations with all three groups.

Interest groups are those individuals and groups that have a stake in department policies and practices. These might include labor unions, civil liberty organizations, crime reduction groups such as Stop DWI, and those businesses that have contracts with the department for goods and services. Included as an interest group is the "attentive public," which can suddenly be created as the result of an unpopular action broadcasted on the social media. As discussed by Ismaili (2011), this term is difficult to define because public interest in criminal justice is defined by specific events and issues in a community. Public opinion on crime and safety is often obtained through the media and personal interactions with criminal justice actors, such as police officers, judges, and attorneys. All three parts of this subgovernment play a significant role as to how the agency, in this case the sheriff's department, achieves its short- and long-term goals.

The same model can be applied to many private-sector companies. For example, the general operating plan and policies for the Fraud Unit at Northwest Frontier Bank would be influenced and directed by senior management and the corporate board of directors. This would not be legislative per se but constitutes senior policymakers. The bureaucracy would be the Fraud Unit itself, which takes in, prioritizes, and investigates cases. Interest groups for the Fraud Unit would be both internal to the corporation, such as the legal department and customer services, and external, such as the federal, state, and global law enforcement and prosecutorial agencies noted above. For major cases involving the theft of large amounts of data or funds, stakeholders might also include stockholders, federal and state regulators, and professional fraud prevention groups. The attentive public would include the media, which reports on business activities, and, of course, investors.

At the end of this chapter, you will be asked to describe the agencies that interact with your organization and their impact on daily operations and apply the subgovernment model. This interplay of agencies in the criminal justice system is affected by the political, economic, and legal variables discussed in Chapter 10. You will find that your organization has a certain sphere of influence in justice administration in terms of its impact on and role in the course of a criminal case or the prosecution and punishment of an offender.

For example, it is the primary role of the police to investigate crimes, gather evidence, and arrest suspected criminals. Some would argue that the police also have the duty of deterring crime. An intern in a district attorney's office might also argue that the primary role of his or her organization is to investigate crimes, gather evidence, and arrest suspected criminals, as well as try to deter crime. Many organizations have overlapping roles, a frequent problem in this so-called system. Consider the following reports from our students when asked, "How does your agency interact with other agencies in the criminal justice system?"

In the district attorney's office there are many problems with the coordination of the agencies that the office deals with. One very good example of this occurs with the state police. In the county, the district attorney's office is the only one that has the expertise and the resources to initiate any major investigation other than the state police, who have the manpower and the economic resources which the smaller departments do not have. It seems that the goal of the state police is to become the only major investigating public police agency. Additionally, the state police dispatch all the other smaller police departments other than the city police. When a call regarding a major crime comes in, the state police naturally take it. But when a garbage offense is reported, then the state will give it to the smaller department where the offense took place. Very often, when a small police department comes across a major crime, the state will come in and take over. This has caused much bad feeling between these departments and the state police. Also, the district attorney and the local state police commander will not talk to each other about the dilemma of who should control major investigations. Additionally, the sheriff's department will not talk to any other agency when a major case occurs. Believe me, it's a real mess down here.

Another student wrote:

There is a barrier between the police and the probation department. The police generally feel that the probation officers are nothing but a bunch of bleeding-heart liberals who want to help the dirtballs stay on the street. The probation department will not do anything to interact with the cops. Usually, when probation is violated, a warrant is issued. The probation officers will take the violator in personally, rather than call for assistance.

You will find that these interagency relationships may be based on the personalities of agency personnel. As one student wrote:

I really have not had any problems dealing with people from the other agencies we deal with. I did learn from my field supervisor that as long as you treat other criminal justice workers in a professional manner, they will return the same attitude in their

dealings with you. But when you talk down to other workers, or don't share informa-
tion, then the problems begin to happen.

We are totally dependent on the federal agencies. Without them we cannot prose-
cute cases or track down bad guys.

You can see that these students became somewhat biased about the role of their internship agency and its relationship to other agencies. It indicates that one's viewpoint on criminal justice is often affected by one's environment, which is natural. However, it is surprising that this is so strongly rooted in just one semester. You can easily lose sight of the fact that other criminal justice agencies have goals and obligations that differ from yours. For example, some police officers condemn district attorneys, public defenders, private attorneys, and judges when suspected criminals are acquitted or receive relatively minor punishments after pleading guilty to reduced charges. They may not see the situation from the perspective of the constraints and rules imposed on other agencies.

This does not mean that conflict and competition are dysfunctional. One of the positive features of the American criminal justice system is that each agency can act as a check and a balance for another. This helps guard against one organization establishing too much power. We often lose sight of this important notion in the quest for effectiveness and efficiency.

Conclusion

All criminal justice organizations have official and operative goals that serve as guidelines for day-to-day operations and long-term planning. These are tied to the vision, mission, and core values of the organization. These goals also help the organizations to compete and survive in the community environment. Related to goals is the issue of effectiveness—the degree to which an organization attains its goals. However, effectiveness is often difficult to measure, in either qualitative or quantitative terms. In addition, organizational outcomes, or what the organization actually does, may have nothing in common with either category of goals. In recent years, however, goals and degree of effectiveness have become common in the lexicon of criminal justice administration, due to public demands for accountability and productivity. In this chapter we have also discussed the issue of organizational relationships in the criminal justice system. Regardless of formal legal, economic, or political ties, relationships are often determined by the personalities of individual administrators and staff members.

■ ■ ■ ————————————————————————————————

Thinking About Your Organization

1. Based on a review of the annual reports or documents, such as departmental manuals, define the mission of your internship site and list at least five official goals of your organization.
2. Based on your experience, what are the operative goals of your organization? How do these reflect the official goals or mission? To what extent does goal displacement occur?
3. What are the core values and vision of your internship site?
4. Has your organization conducted strategic planning? If so, what changes are forecast? If not, based on your experience, do a quick analysis and predict what changes might occur in terms of SWOT.
5. Explain how your internship organizational goals are measured in terms of effectiveness.
6. How does your organization interact with others in the criminal justice system? Chart these relationships (see Figures 11.1 and 11.2).
7. Apply the subgovernment model described in the text to analyze your organization's relationships and their impact on daily operations.

———————————————————————————————— ■ ■ ■

12

Using Information and Technology as Crime-Fighting Tools

Technology plays a key role in the prevention, detection, investigation, and prosecution of crime. Employees and student interns who are well versed in technological advances through coursework in computer forensics and network protections are highly valued by their organizations. It goes without saying that those interns who bring technical skills to the internship setting or who can develop these skills during their internship become attractive candidates for openings in a wide variety of organizations. There are many new and exciting career areas in criminal justice and the private sector. Many organizations provide extensive training to individuals who show an interest and capability in technological areas. Therefore, it is imperative that students be exposed to as much of this technology as possible during their internship.

Introduction

The use of technology in the prevention, detection, investigation, and prosecution of crime has continued to evolve and become more sophisticated since the last edition of this book. The technology used in the Crime Scene Investigation (CSI) television series and other programs is becoming more of a real option for law enforcement investigations. A few years ago, it would have been unimaginable to think that DNA testing would be used to solve property crimes, which is now possible through collection and analysis of cellular or "touch" DNA (Hunt, 2013). Great strides have also been made with mobile phone forensics. With mobile phones having more and more functionality, there is a wealth of probative information that can be downloaded, including global positioning system data, call logs, text messages, contacts, and much more. Facial recognition software has advanced to the point where it is being used in detecting fraudulent bank activity at the teller window and to catch identity thieves who are using multiple identities. The latest trend in physical and personal security is the use of iris recognition technology for education and banking.

The typical police patrol vehicle today has been transformed by the addition of multiple technologies. Cars equipped with wireless computers allow officers to receive complaints, run data checks, enter reports, and give copies of reports to crime victims. Vehicles can now be equipped with automatic license plate readers that scan license plates on roads and in parking lots for stolen vehicles, suspended registrations, or wanted persons. As shown on many television programs that focus on police-citizen encounters, many cars now have video cameras and audio devices that can be used to review major incidents. Today law enforcement agencies are taking this technology one step further with the wearing of digital body-worn cameras that can be used for any police-citizen encounter. Computer-aided dispatch is able to complete tasks including address verification, suspect identification, call logging, case number assignment, and call priority. The data from each call is used for administrative reports to monitor police activity statistics and crime mapping. The major trend is to increase wireless interoperability between law enforcement, fire departments, and emergency medical services. The use of unmanned aerial vehicles (UAV) or drones has become very commonplace in law enforcement and private-sector operations, and it has increased surveillance capabilities and raised new questions regarding privacy.

Most public agencies and organizations in the private sector use technology to assist in the day-to-day operations in responding to crime incidents. As a result, interns are exposed to more technology and are able to apply the skills they have learned in the classroom to the tasks at their site. Even though technology use is on the increase in a number of settings, interns—as a result of their education and personal knowledge— often bring skills to the position that are at least equivalent to many of the workers in the organization. This knowledge base may allow interns to be involved with significant projects. Expertise in analytical tools (e.g., link analysis and mapping software, statistical software such as SPSS or SAS, knowledge of different operating systems, computer and network security, digital forensics, and the Internet) will be welcomed by host organizations.

Commenting on the vast array of technology being used in criminal justice and related organizations, Byrne and Rebovich (2007) map their applications according to categories of "hard" and "soft." Hard technologies refer to those materials, devices, and equipment used for crime offending, prevention, detection, or control. These would include such items as weapons, devices for identification, video surveillance, detection systems, computer systems in offices and patrol vehicles, and construction of facilities. Soft technologies generally refer to computer software applications for criminal histories, paperless processes, crime mapping, threat assessments, training simulations, and monitoring of offenders. In like manner, crimes are committed with the same kinds of hard and soft applications and often at the workplace. It seems that every technological development results in a new form of criminal enterprise as illustrated by the expansion of cybercrimes and attempts to steal information from networks. The most recent is the use of bitcoins, which is a term used for virtual currency which can be exchanged through online exchanges. Goods and services then can be exchanged between the consumer and a merchant. As with any other economic activity, bitcoins can be used to purchase illegal goods and services. Bitcoins are also being used as the currency for ransomware transactions, whereby information in a computer is held hostage by malware and will not be released until a payment is made.

One of the criteria for picking an internship site should be the extent to which the organization uses technology. What can you learn by interning there? How can your technical skills be used and enhanced by the organization? Some colleges and universities have long been preparing their students in these technology areas, while others have just begun the process. Regardless of your preparation, your internship should be viewed as a means of learning new technology, sharpening existing skills, or gaining experience with tools and methods to which you have already been exposed.

Information as a Resource

The quantity and quality of information available to practitioners have grown exponentially each year and will greatly expand in the near future. Information is used to prevent, detect, investigate, and prosecute criminal behavior. It can be found in a variety of public and private databases, on the Internet, and through associations. Organizations that provide their employees with access to this data are better able to combat the wave of technology-based crimes. As an intern, you may be asked to complete tasks for which you need to use information provider services or internal data systems that track offenses, stolen property, or potential suspects. Even if you have little or no experience in using such tools, most agencies can provide you with introductory training based on your coursework and data searches. For example, one student assigned to a federal agency became very adept at tracking down stolen firearms and applying this information to regional locations after a brief on-the-job overview on how the system worked, given by her supervisor. You also need to be aware of privacy issues and your agency's information-sharing policy, so that you will be in compliance with laws and regulations. There are now numerous examples illustrating the benefits of information sharing and the use of data mining to search vast amounts of data for information to combat crime.

Other examples of information sharing focus on fighting identity theft or identifying sex offenders who are located in an area where a child was abducted. The Identity Theft Assistance Center (ITAC) was formed in 2004 to provide assistance to the customers of the 45-member financial institutions who were victims of identity theft. ITAC also shares data with law enforcement and the Federal Trade Commission (FTC) to assist in the investigation, prosecution, and conviction of identity thieves. Because of this information sharing, cases involving numerous victims in multiple jurisdictions, across the United States and beyond, can be investigated and prosecuted.

The system developed by LexisNexis to track sex offenders who do not comply with registration requirements incorporates access to multiple databases and analytic visualization technologies including mapping and link analysis. Being able to find offenders who have purposely moved off the grid, or to locate all sex offenders of a particular level near a crime scene, allows police to respond rapidly to criminal activity. This linking of information and technology illustrates the ways in which the criminal justice system is using more sophisticated technologies to fight crime.

Prevention

Ideally, organizations would like to prevent crime from occurring. In the public sector, crime prevention strategies have been deployed at many levels. The ability to provide timely information on clusters of crime in specific areas through mapping programs has assisted police in the reduction of crime. The success of the CompStat programs and intelligence-based policing in New York and other cities is illustrative of this methodology. Computer analysis can provide detailed crime data in order for police managers to predict crimes and deploy police resources. However, historically, public-sector organizations have been reactive rather than proactive in addressing crime issues. Although there are several reasons for this, one critical one has been the lack of real-time or near-real-time data for decision making. With the addition of computer systems using sophisticated statistical analysis, this gap has begun to close, at least in large departments and in some progressive smaller ones.

As discussed by Thibault et al. (2014), many cities, schools, transit centers, retail outlets, and shopping malls have installed closed-circuit television (CCTV) systems to deter criminal activity and to assist investigators for review purposes when an incident occurs. With the rapid development and use of CCTV systems, legal and procedural questions often emerge as to the authenticity and quality of receptions (Kuntz, 2013). Emergency notification to law enforcement is available by cell phone applications and personal fobs. They are common today at most college and university campuses and they are being expanded to a wide range of businesses. Many public criminal agencies also use the Internet to relay crime information and upcoming events through their own web sites or via social network sources such as Twitter and Facebook.

The private sector has initiated several technological methods to prevent fraud or computer intrusions from occurring. Some examples of these methods include neural net technology, intrusion detection software, and new industry-specific technologies to prevent money laundering, counterfeiting of identity documents, and abuse of debit and credit cards. The difficulty is that while it may be possible to prevent most fraud, it would require limiting business opportunities and inconveniencing customers. The fraud-to-sales ratio does not often provide a strong rationale for spending large sums of money for prevention. However, there are many industry-specific techniques that help to prevent crime from occurring. For example, prior to issuing credit cards, shipping goods ordered from a catalog company or Internet site, or issuing a contract for a mobile phone, verification and authentication programs that check the relationship among an individual's name, phone number, and address can eliminate a number of fraud cases. Recent major cases involving data breaches at a number of major retailers and the subsequent misuse of fraudulent credit cards has forced card providers and retailers to adopt smart chip technology used in other countries.

Data breaches by external intruders remains a major issue in all fields particularly in health care and finance.

Detection

Crime that slips through prevention efforts can be solved at a higher rate if it is detected quickly. Early detection can help to minimize potential losses. Just as the old-fashioned burglar alarm is a good example of a method that can be used to help prevent crime or to detect it when it has occurred, law enforcement is developing methods to detect crimes quickly. For example, when dealing with hot spots, the strategic deployment of personnel can both prevent crimes from occurring and detect them quickly when they do occur. With increasing frequency, law enforcement personnel have assumed digital identities in an effort to detect pedophiles who are surfing the Internet. In a number of cases, pedophiles have communicated with police officers whom they believed were underage girls. Either on their own accord or through being lured by the police, pedophiles often travel to meet their potential victims. The detection, location, and subsequent arrest of pedophiles is a good example of how technology can be used as a detection tool.

High-technology crime has resulted in a need for law enforcement officers to be versed in digital forensics, as well as computer crime-scene seizure procedures. The private sector utilizes a variety of methods to alert analysts that someone has committed a fraud or has violated their systems. These technologies include pattern recognition software, neural net technology, scoring software, link analysis software, intrusion detection software, and databases of individuals or organizations that have attempted such fraudulent activity in the past.

As financial crimes have become increasingly complex, analysts and investigators have had to develop methods to find patterns and links among vast amounts of data. Frequently, several investigators may be working on pieces of the same case without even realizing it. One tool that has been successfully applied in this situation is link analysis. In link analysis, data is either imported into a special software program or an analyst/investigator uses the software as they build the case.

Neural net technology has helped to detect vast amounts of fraud before the victimized companies have lost much money. Neural net technology is capable of tracking the spending behavior of credit card holders and can recognize potential aberrant patterns. For example, if someone uses his or her credit card only to purchase gas and clothes, a number of computer equipment purchases on that account would be viewed as a red flag. The program would give a high score to the transaction and put it in a queue to be reviewed by an analyst.

Anti-money-laundering solutions have also undergone considerable development. As a result of compliance requirements and increased sophistication of criminals, software that searches through vast numbers of transactions to discern patterns of suspicious activities is being used by financial institutions.

The same efforts are directed in the social media world, by which software programs can identify potential major crime threats and criminal behavior in a certain geographical area. These programs are particularly aimed at major city schools, and college and universities to pre-empt major shooting events.

Investigation

Crime that is neither prevented nor detected early requires the ability of a skilled investigator to close the case. This is a time-consuming and costly process. In the public sector, where resources are limited, technology can assist in the reduction of the time necessary to solve the case. The recent availability of an extensive array of databases has provided the public-sector investigator with a wealth of information that is accessible by computer. These databases can be used to collect background information on individuals and organizations. While not every organization has been able to afford or see the value of this information, the situation appears to be changing. Public records from many states are now online, making it possible to investigate individuals or corporations who are doing business in multiple jurisdictions, without leaving the office.

As cases become more complex, tools such as link analysis software assist investigators in building their cases and analyzing large amounts of data already collected. This software identifies relationships between or among people or organizations that might otherwise be missed because of the complexity of the case.

Botnets (collections of Internet-connected computers that interact to accomplish a specific—often malicious—task), WiFi data breaches, key loggers, and other cybercrimes are current problems that have been identified by investigators. Learning about such new schemes is usually accomplished through investigations and by interviewing suspects. This new information can be fed back into the front end of the system (i.e., prevention and detection) to help stop similar types of crimes. The same can be done with information gathered in other investigations. The knowledge gained can assist in revising the models and making them more effective.

In many cases, interns have to be closely supervised if they are involved with investigations in their organizations. This occurs partly because they may not be available to testify if the case goes to court. However, interns often have technical skills that are welcomed in this process and can make a significant contribution. In recent semesters, several of our students were able to track down suspects using social networking web sites. Students have also used link analysis software to show the relationships among suspects and events in complex fraud cases.

Prosecution

As a result of high-technology or complex financial crimes, prosecutors have begun to rely on sophisticated methods of presenting evidence in a courtroom. Federal and major city courtrooms are being wired so that electronic evidence can be presented. Both the public and private sectors will have to become more adept at packaging the evidence, using technology to convince prosecutors of the significance of their cases and to assist juries in understanding the evidence presented.

As law enforcement organizations develop new methods for fighting technology-related crimes, they must be able to defend these methods in a court. Law enforcement personnel must have expertise in the techniques used for testifying in court. These methods and tools are being validated and standardized. For example, in the area of digital forensics, guidelines have been developed to ensure that procedures can be defended. Legal issues must also be resolved, as technology is challenging traditional evidentiary requirements.

Many private corporations have difficulty convincing overworked prosecutors with limited resources to take their cases. Therefore, it has become important to package cases that are easily understood and ready for prosecution. Link analysis diagrams quickly communicate relationships in complex crimes. In a similar way, audit logs from computer systems can provide detailed documentation of a suspect's behavior regarding computer use. Detailed analysis of financial records and transactions can also help make a case. Generally, law enforcement personnel and prosecutors require the technical expertise of the victimized organization to assist them in investigating and presenting the case in court.

Training

With the advent of new technology comes a critical need to provide training to the personnel who will use it. In a number of cases, new technology has been purchased but, because of a lack of training, has remained unused for a number of months. In the public sector especially, there often is a heavy reliance on the few technologically sophisticated individuals in the organization to deal with all the technical problems. While at one time this may have been a good stopgap measure, rapid developments in technology-related crimes have made this solution impractical.

A concerted effort is now taking place both in the private and public sectors to provide key personnel with the training necessary to use new technologies effectively. Law enforcement personnel receive specialized training in cybercrime, computer crime, digital forensics, and identity theft from the following organizations: the FBI's Regional Computer Forensics Laboratories, the National Computer Forensic Institute, the U.S. Secret Service's Cell Phone Forensic Laboratory, the International High Technology Crime Investigation Association, Visa, CSI, the Association of Certified Fraud Examiners, FTC, and the National White Collar Crime Center (NW3C). In many cases, interns have been able to participate in such training sessions. If, as an intern, you learn that technological training will occur, it is wise to request permission to participate. Usually, if the training will not result in a cost to the organization, interns are allowed to attend. Demonstrating an interest in learning about technology and participating in this type of training is advantageous for future employment opportunities.

Many private-sector organizations have developed computer training sites where employees or interns can learn how to use software through tutorials or by attending classes. A manager and internship supervisor once asked a student if he knew Microsoft Excel well enough to work on a major project during his internship. The student responded that he knew how to do the basics but needed to hone his skills to do the type of work that would be required. The supervisor told the student that he had 24 hours before the initial project meeting was to occur. The supervisor sent him to the computer training room to work on Excel until the meeting the next afternoon. The student wrote in his journal:

I have never been under so much pressure in my life. I wished I had listened to my professor who said how important knowing spreadsheets such as Excel would be when I was working in the field. I learned enough to answer the questions in the meeting and spent the rest of my free time over the next week learning Excel. I now use it every day and have become the resident expert in my area. Looking back on the experience, I am really glad that my supervisor forced me to learn it in a short period of time. I now have the confidence to handle a similar situation in the future.

Future Use of Technology

Technology continues to play a key role in the operations of public- and private-sector organizations fighting crime, and digital evidence has become part of most investigations. The investigation, detection, and prevention of Internet and technology-based crimes, as well as web sites that facilitate criminal activities, require cutting-edge technology. Technologies such as smartphones continue to be less expensive and, therefore, more accessible to the general public, as well as the criminal element who might use them for committing financial crimes, identity theft and medical identity theft, cyberbullying and cyberstalking, and document fraud. The increase in electronic commerce over the Internet and the explosion of social media provide new opportunities for crime. The availability of information on the Internet has already increased the volume of crime. People who did not previously have the requisite knowledge or skills are now able to commit fraudulent acts. For example, point-and-click programs allow individuals to program computers to generate computer viruses. The exponential rise in data breaches has resulted in the increased threat of identity theft, in which a person creates a fraudulent or fictitious identity by stealing someone else's identity or using fraudulent identifiers such as a driver's license, passport, Social Security number, or birth certificate. Criminal elements from around the world are selling full portfolio identities online, complete with birth certificates, Social Security numbers, credit card and banking numbers, date of birth, and much more. For example, the Internet Crime Complaint Center's Internet Crime Report, a joint effort by the FBI and the NW3C, indicates that the top five reported Internet crimes of 2015 were non-delivery of payment/merchandise, 419/overpayment scams, identity theft, fraudulent auctions, and miscellaneous fraud. This growing pervasiveness of online crime can be observed by the near linear growth of reports received since the creation of this complaint center (United States Department of Justice, 2015).

Cognizant of the vast financial gains possible, criminals have developed increasing sophistication with regard to cybercrime threats and have dramatically increased the number of these attacks. The annual *Symantec Internet Security Threat Report: Trends for 2010* showed five significant trends that continue to develop:

1. Targeted attacks continue to evolve. Targeted attacks, while not new, gained notoriety from high-profile attacks against major organizations (Hydraq) and significant targets (Stuxnet).
2. Social networks + social engineering = compromise. The ability to research a target online has enabled hackers to create powerful social engineering attacks that easily fool even sophisticated users.
3. Hide and seek (zero-day vulnerabilities and root kits). Targeted attacks depend on their ability to get inside an organization and stay hidden in plain sight. Zero-day vulnerabilities and root kits have made this possible.
4. Attack kits. Innovations from targeted attacks will make their way into massive attacks, most likely via toolkits.
5. Mobile attacks increase. All these types of attacks are moving to mobile devices, limited only by attackers getting a return on their investment (Symantec Corporation, 2011, p. 3).

A review of past annual Symantec reports and the annual reports of the CSI indicates that the above threats are evolving, becoming stealthier, and pose a serious danger to our financial system, public safety, and homeland security. Whether the goal is to protect the public, secure critical information, or ensure the viability of our critical infrastructure, public and private organizations will continue to invest in both a strong, technologically sophisticated workforce and the necessary resources to meet this cybercrime crisis.

Conclusion

Technology plays a key role in the prevention, detection, investigation, and prosecution of crime. Employees who are well versed in technological advances will be highly valued by their organizations. Therefore, it is imperative that interns be exposed to as much of this technology as possible during their internship. Those interns who bring technical skills to the internship setting or who can develop these skills during their internship will be attractive candidates for openings in a wide variety of organizations.

There are many new and exciting career areas in criminal justice and the private sector. If in the course of your internship you are able to develop or hone your technology skills, you may want to consider pursuing these areas. Be sure to update your résumé to reflect these skills. Many organizations are providing extensive training to individuals who show an interest and capability in this area. There is a growing gap between the number of technological jobs available and the pool of candidates. This area will be further addressed in the final chapter on career planning.

Thinking About Your Agency

1. What role does technology play in your organization's ability to prevent, detect, investigate, and prosecute crime and fraud?
2. What "hard" and "soft" technologies are used at your internship site? How often are they used? Who are the technology experts?
3. Based on the mission and goals of your organization, to what extent do criminals use technology to commit offenses that are investigated?
4. What is the extent of technology training in your intern site? Are personnel sent to training programs? How much of a priority is this for the organization?
5. What technologies could your organization be using? What are the impediments to introducing this or any other technology at your site?

Thinking About Yourself

1. How have you been able to use technological skills at your internship site?
2. What opportunities has your internship site provided for your technological development?
3. As a result of your internship, what new skills would you like or need to learn in order to enhance your job opportunities?
4. What recommendations would you make to your faculty regarding technology coursework for your degree program?

Assessment and Career Planning

13

Assessing Your Experience

This chapter discusses how to assess personal growth and professional development during an internship experience, how faculty and agency supervisors will appraise you, and how to evaluate an agency site. Assessing the internship experience is an ongoing process throughout the experience. A detailed assessment of an internship will make the experience more meaningful. This process provides an opportunity to focus on personal growth and professional development. Evaluations by agency and faculty supervisors give interns a good indication of their professional and personal progress as well as an index of their potential as professionals in the criminal justice field. Learning how to assess performance is one of the most important skills an intern can develop in an internship.

Assessing Personal Growth and Professional Development

You can be certain that your internship will effect some change in you, personally as well as professionally. How much change occurs depends on many factors, especially the amount of time you spend at the agency. While many interns have an intuitive feeling that they have gained a great deal from the internship, they find it difficult to assess the changes in other than the most general terms.

In order to complete a self-assessment, you must determine whether and how well you have met your own expectations. What you hope to gain from your experience (your goals and objectives) and your first impressions are important benchmarks for assessing growth and development. These should be recorded carefully for later reflection. The expectations of others, such as field or faculty supervisors, can also be important assessment points. This may be the first time that you have had to meet the expectations of professionals in the field. Their appraisal of your performance is discussed in detail in the next section of this chapter. The issue is also raised here because you should evaluate how well you have met others' expectations as part of your self-assessment. Evaluating yourself is not an easy task, however. You can use a purely subjective and intuitive approach as a first step, but if you go no further, you will lose a valuable learning experience.

Besides the careful documentation of your pre-experience expectations and your initial impressions, it will be important to keep field notes, as discussed in Chapter 6 on participant observation. This is advantageous for two reasons. First, notes document your experience so that you can look at your personal and professional development at particular times or as you move through the stages of the experience described in Chapter 5. Second, they allow you to review key personal or professional issues to determine how well you resolved them and which ones you need to pursue further.

If you have set goals and established learning objectives to help you meet those goals, you will then have more definitive areas to assess. Your progress on the goals can be evaluated based on the following criteria.

The Willingness of the Organization to Allow You to Take Action on Your Goals

Although you may have certain expectations, internship supervisors may be unsure of whether you can perform certain tasks. They may be unwilling to allow you to accomplish your learning objectives because they are unsure of your ability to perform or because they are limited by the internal policies of the agency.

If you have set a goal that you can attain only toward the end of your internship, be aware that you may have difficulty fulfilling it. You may not reach the level of competence that agency personnel deem necessary to handle a particular task. However, you should not be discouraged from setting goals of this type, for they give both you and the field site something to strive toward. For example, when beginning work in a juvenile detention center, one intern stated that she wanted to have responsibility for one of the female groups herself. The field supervisor was pessimistic about this ever happening with an intern. Two weeks before the end of the internship, however, the intern was handed the keys to the unit and told that she was to run it that day. The field supervisor stated in her final review that the intern would never have had that opportunity if she had not stated it as a professional goal. Therefore, it is important to share your goals and objectives with the field supervisor at the initiation of the internship.

Your Ability to Accomplish Your Learning Objectives

Your goal attainment and the assessment of your progress on your goals are dependent on how well you complete your learning objectives once the agency allows you to take action toward your goals. If you are given the opportunity to perform these learning tasks, you will be in a position to determine whether you have selected appropriate and realistic means for meeting your goals. Your assessment should answer these questions:

1. Was I able to complete the tasks that I set as learning objectives for my goals?
2. If not, was it a problem with personal motivation, organizational policies, my supervisor's feeling that I was not sufficiently competent, or time limitations?
3. Was completing the tasks sufficient for developing certain competencies?

4. If I completed the tasks but did not attain the specified goals, was it because the learning objectives were not sufficient?
5. Were the tasks I set as learning objectives realistic?
6. Knowing what I now know, how would I change my learning objectives? What new goals would I set?

In assessing his performance at his internship, one student wrote the following:

I discovered a huge weakness in my on-site performance during the beginning of my internship. I was not self-motivated, and I often waited for my superiors to assign me work rather than finding it when I was not busy. This was brought to my attention during my professor's site visit. Following the visit I immediately corrected the issue by approaching the staff and offering my assistance. I feel that by turning my weakness into strength, I made the best out of my experience while learning a valuable lesson in being productive within the workplace even when I do not have any work.

Discussions with Your Agency Supervisor on Your Progress

A mid-semester internship meeting and a final evaluation meeting with your supervisor should focus on progress you made toward your goals. This should help identify additional areas that need work. Weekly supervision sessions or less formal ad hoc discussions can be useful for planning or evaluating learning tasks. Careful note taking during or after these discussions will be extremely helpful in your final assessment.

Written Documentation

Besides the notes you may take during and/or after evaluation sessions, you may keep a log or write weekly or biweekly memoranda to your faculty supervisor. Reviewing this regularly will afford you an overall perspective of your internship experience. This process will be enhanced if you have carefully documented problems, issues, successes, and failures. It also addresses a main issue in evaluation in that evaluators tend to focus on items that are more recent before the formal evaluation.

Your Professional Development

Once you have assessed your professional development over the course of your internship, it is necessary to contemplate the next phase of your professional growth. What you have learned and accomplished during your internship will provide the foundation for developing new goals consistent with the categories described in Chapter 4 on setting goals and identifying educational objectives. For example, goals in the area of professional development may lead you to a specific job search or graduate program, or influence you to seek certification in a specialized area. One student noted the following in discussing his professional future:

> *My newfound knowledge derived from this experience has enabled me to be more confident in the work I am doing. I feel as if the work I am doing is very valuable to the overall picture of the industry. This experience has raised the bar for me, and forced me into seeking deeper understandings of why things occur. This is the fundamental doctrine of forensics. Seeking this understanding is a valuable skill that is transferable into any type of industry. I will seek out careers and establish goals that enable me to learn while I work.*

Field and Faculty Supervisors' Evaluations

Generally, interns are evaluated by both their field and faculty supervisors. The supervisors' expectations and the criteria for evaluation should be spelled out for you before you begin your internship. While expectations and requirements may vary depending on the site and the supervisor, there are certain general areas of evaluation you will encounter.

Field Supervisor

Each supervisor has a set of broad expectations for interns, based on past experiences working with interns and/or helping new staff members develop in their jobs. Your field supervisor will be concerned about all or some of the following:

1. General performance as a member of the staff.
2. Performance on assigned tasks.
3. Professionalism and ethical behavior.
4. Ability to work with others.
5. Potential for continued work in the field.

There are often organizational performance standards that apply to all personnel, including student interns. Specific variables are identified as ratings are often given based on the following items:

- Significantly exceeds expected job standards and accountabilities.
- Exceeds expected job standards and accountabilities.
- Meets job requirements expected.
- Needs improvement.
- Fails to meet most expected job standards and accountabilities.

Performance as a Member of the Staff

Specific characteristics you exhibit, such as attendance, initiative, promptness, punctuality, appearance, reliability, resourcefulness, and self-reliance, will be evaluated. In general, students do very well in this area, and evaluators can always give examples. They are also quick to point out major issues in this area when they occur during the course of the internship. An important element here is your willingness to learn and take on assignments and the level of supervision that is required. Often brought to light are tasks and assignments undertaken with little or no prompting by the field supervisor. For example, on his own, one student created a listing and a map of locations where crime victims could go to obtain assistance. Another created a proposal for registering law enforcement trainees taking homeland security courses via iPad and thus eliminating paper scanning of required paperwork.

Performance on Assigned Tasks

Your ability to complete assigned tasks in a timely fashion will be evaluated by your field supervisor. He or she will be concerned with how well you handled progressively more difficult tasks over the course of the internship. While you hopefully will receive feedback after the completion of each task, the overall development of your ability will be evaluated at the end of your internship. Here it is important to keep copies or a list of the major assignments that you completed over the course of the semester. The same is true for any major papers or projects completed for academic requirements.

Professionalism and Ethical Behavior

This is one category in which you will be directly compared with other agency employees and previous student interns. Chapter 8 on ethics in practice spells out the conduct and expectations of interns in this area. Most supervisors will tell you what they expect. If yours does not, or if you have questions during your internship, you should ask for clarification. Overall, very few students have had problems with this category. Those that have major issues generally do not complete the program.

Ability to Work with Others

How well you interact with your fellow workers, the public, clients, and administrators is an important evaluation item especially in the ever-changing workforce. The willingness to work with those who are different from you, who have authority over you, and who require service from your agency is an important aspect of your professional development. An important element here is how well you treated clients. Here supervisors may also comment on how well the student maintained appropriate relationships with staff and clients. Additionally, there may be comments on how open you were to constructive feedback.

Adherence to Company Values

As discussed in Chapter 11 on Organizational Goals and Relationships, many organizations have adopted mission and values statements and have incorporated those into the evaluation of employees. Such items slated for performance reviews might include respect shown to employees and clients, dealing with customers, delivering exceptional service, knowledge of company policies and procedures, professional development and training, and commitment to diversity.

Your Potential for Work in This Field

The quality of your performance in your internship and the extent of your development will strongly influence your supervisor's assessment of your potential. Both of you may feel that you are very well suited to the type of work you have done in your internship. On the other hand, for a variety of reasons, you and/or your supervisor may feel that you should not pursue a career in this field. This should not be misconstrued as meaning that the internship was a meaningless or negative experience. An internship is the time and place to experiment—finding out what you do not want to do is just as important as finding out what you do want to do.

Faculty Supervisor

Faculty supervisors are concerned with some of the same issues as field supervisors, but they are at a disadvantage because they rarely see an intern's performance in the field. Therefore, faculty supervisors rely heavily on field supervisors' comments and their own impressions gleaned from the few times they are able to visit the sites.

Because of this, your faculty supervisor will evaluate you on the basis of his or her expectations of interns, the reported progress you have made on your goals, your written assignments, your participation in seminars, discussions with you, and the evaluation received from your field supervisor. The weight that each of these has in your final evaluation will vary according to the policies of your college and the particular professor supervising you.

The class syllabus should contain the elements for the final grading. For some programs, internship is graded either "Satisfactory" or "Unsatisfactory," while in others a letter grade is assigned based on percentages given to the agency evaluation, weekly reports, participation at seminars, and submission of a final project or major paper.

Assessing Your Internship Agency

As part of your internship, you may be required to assess your agency. This can be accomplished in two ways. First, you can evaluate how well the agency met your needs as a learning environment. Second, you can evaluate how well the agency meets its goals and objectives.

Your faculty supervisor will be interested in knowing how well the internship agency met your expectations and needs so that he or she can assess whether future interns should be placed there. This will help to determine what types of students would profit from an experience at that site. You may be asked to write a brief statement about the site to be placed on file for future interns.

From a personal perspective, you should evaluate the agency to determine what characteristics you liked and disliked. This will aid you in making decisions about future career options. For example, how were you treated by the field supervisor and coworkers? Were you allowed to become a full participant, where possible, in agency operations? Were you challenged by the tasks assigned? How did you like the work environment and the daily tasks that needed to be completed by you and your coworkers?

Finally, you may be asked to assess the organization's performance. Through discussions with personnel and by reading the official publications, you should be aware of the goals and objectives of your organization or unit by the end of your internship as described in Chapter 11. Your assessment should include a discussion of how well your organization meets its goals and objectives. The following questions are intended to guide you in your assessment.

1. How realistic are the organization's goals?
2. Which goals does the organization actually attempt to fulfill and which ones are merely for public relations?
3. What are some of the difficulties the organization faces in attaining its goals?

A discussion including explicit proposals on how your field site might be able to attain unmet objectives and goals should conclude your assessment. Interns often have been reluctant to share these thoughts during the internship placement because they have been there for a short time and do not view themselves as having sufficient expertise to critique professionals. However, your field supervisor and others might welcome review from interns because it allows them to see the problems from a fresh perspective. One supervisor stated in an evaluation:

> While it is difficult to encourage interns and even new employees to critique the operations of our agency, I have found the few that are able to do this to be extremely helpful. [Name of intern] has given us something to think about. After working in an agency for many years, you tend to overlook or take for granted too many things.

Conclusion

A detailed assessment of your internship will make the experience more meaningful for you. This process offers you an opportunity to focus on your personal growth and professional development. Evaluations by your internship and faculty supervisors will give you a good indication of the professional and personal progress you have made as well as an index of your potential as a professional in the criminal justice field.

Learning how to assess your performance is one of the most important skills you can develop in an internship. Your ability to be a self-directed learner will help you continue to grow and develop after you leave college, regardless of the quality of supervision you may receive on a job.

■ ■ ■ ━━

Assessing Your Internship

1. Write a detailed analysis of the progress you have made on the goals you set for this internship.
2. What strengths and weaknesses have you discovered in yourself during your internship? Give several examples to illustrate your points.
3. What new goals would you like to set in your next position? Why are these important to you?
4. How do you think your coworkers and supervisor(s) viewed your work?
5. How do you think your new knowledge, your increased understanding of the criminal justice system, the new skills you have acquired, and the personal growth you have experienced will affect your future in terms of academic achievements and career goals?
6. Do you want to continue to work in this area of criminal justice? Do you want to work in any facet of criminal justice? Why or why not?
7. How has your internship made you a better self-directed learner? Give examples.
8. Having assessed yourself in the above questions, to what extent is the agency where you interned performing its goals?
9. To what extent did the organization meet your expectation as an intern? Did you receive adequate supervision from your field and academic supervisors during the experience? Would you recommend this agency to another student for internship purposes?

━━━━━━━━━━━━━━━━━━━━━━━━━━━━━━━━━━━━━━━ ■ ■ ■

14

Career Planning

The decision to major in criminal justice is usually based on a desire for a career in some area of the field, such as law enforcement, corrections, cybercrime investigation, forensics, fraud investigation, law, or something related to the public administration or social services. By the conclusion of the internship experience, you should have a general understanding of the level of credentials needed for a particular group of positions that you have an interest in, the job responsibilities, and salary and benefits. It is important to keep one's career goals in sight. Working in any criminal justice position is difficult in terms of legalities, peer pressure, long hours, and seeing human beings at their worst. If a person has the right attitude, philosophy, and personal stamina for coping with the myriad of emotions and frustrations inherent in this field, a criminal justice career can be very rewarding.

Introduction

The question "What should I do after graduation?" is a difficult one. It is a question that should be initially addressed at least two semesters before graduation, both for completing course requirements and making internship plans. Most internship advisors will try to create a placement that has something to do with your general career goals. However, at the conclusion of your internship, you will have to consider several questions related to your career goals. Did you enjoy the work in which you were involved? Would you be happy and satisfied working in that type of organization environment and with the people you have come to know? Would you have the credentials necessary for the position(s) that the organization has to offer? Do you see a position with your internship site or some similar organization as a stepping-stone to something else or as a final position? Considering these questions and the points outlined below will help you to further define and/or finalize your career goals and assist in the planning process of procuring your next position.

The Current Picture

In his book *There is Life After College,* Selingo (2016) writes that today's graduates will have to face various challenges for employment. Competition for positions in all fields is high, and there are extenuating factors that today's graduates have to face—one being student debt, which is estimated between $25,000–35,000 or more per graduate. Debt, he writes, has an important impact on job selection and living expenses, especially in major metropolitan areas such as New York and San Francisco. To no one's surprise, deciding to live at home with parents to save money has become a popular trend. For job placement after commencement, he presents three types of graduates: Sprinters, Wanderers, and Stragglers. Sprinters knew what they wanted to do very early into their college career. In addition to coursework, they completed several internships with a certain career target and have done a number of interesting leadership and work activities throughout college. More often than not, they graduated on time. He notes that the acceptance of a job immediately after graduation will be only one of several career moves that will take place during the first decade of full-time employment.

Wanderers are not quite sure what they would like to do after graduation, and they will take two to three years before starting a meaningful career. In the meantime, they will work at various kinds of lower-paying positions to make ends meet and often will live at home with parents. Very often graduates in this category have switched majors during their undergraduate years. Frequently they decide to continue on to graduate school for something to do, which often adds to their debt burden for both graduate and undergraduate education.

The last group identified by Selingo are Stragglers. Stragglers' search for employment that fits their economic needs will take some time. For many Stragglers, college was a four-year vacation (i.e., party), and school work often was not very important. Often they chose majors in which they had no real interest. Note that these are typologies that may or may not apply to you or your peers. However, they do capture some realities of dealing with today's job searching realities.

Using Your Own Network

Professors, intern field supervisors, co-workers at the agency site, and others are all important sources on regional, state, and national and international hiring based on their experience and memberships in professional associations. The discussion on state, national, and global economic developments discussed in Chapter 10 has an important impact on hiring trends. It is important to have an understanding of these so that you can realistically prepare for a job search. One source that is regularly reviewed is the *Occupational Outlook Handbook*, which provides information on employment trends based on data collected by the United States Department of Labor's Bureau of Labor Statistics (2016). An update in 2016 showed the following projected hiring trends:

1. Hiring for public- and private-sector personnel in the Protective Service Occupations is projected to grow only by about 4 percent. The rate of growth will vary based on geographical location.

2. The need for financial accountants and examiners and investigators is projected to be strong based on the need to address fraud in both the private and public sector.
3. It is projected that information system and cyber analysts will have strong job potential based on the need for all organizations to plan and carry out security measures for network systems. The need for this expertise continues to increase just as the number of cybersecurity problems expand each year.
4. Probation officers and correctional treatment specialist job titles are expected to have slower than average growth between 2014–2024. It was noted that these positions do experience a high rate of turnover.
5. Substance abuse and behavior disorder counselor job titles were expected to grow by 22 percent based on the increased coverage of services by insurance companies.

Not reflected in the data are the job opportunities that are available in the private sector as many traditional public-sector job responsibilities in corrections and national security are transferred to the private sector. Another area is in the area of compliance and fraud detection in such areas as health care, financial services, and consumer protection.

Realize that job searching is a full-time task. A specific career goal or a range of goals can be set after the following issues are addressed: personal assessment, skills capability, and geographic considerations.

Personal Assessment

Personal assessment issues are those that relate to personal likes, dislikes, strengths, weaknesses, and needs for work satisfaction. In other words, you need to generate a list of factors that will make you happy and fulfilled in the workplace. Some questions to consider as you are engaged in your internship experience include:

1. What are your financial concerns and lifestyle needs?
2. What do you really like to do?
3. Do you like working indoors, outdoors, or a combination of both?
4. Reflecting on Chapter 7, with how much supervision are you comfortable?
5. How do you feel about work-related travel?
6. What are your job security needs?
7. Are you looking for an entry-level position that provides opportunity for advancement and/or transfer?
8. Are you willing to continue your education in order to be qualified or to advance in your position?
9. Are there certain things you cannot or will not do (e.g., drive at high speeds, shoot a gun, lock someone in a jail cell, be instrumental in sending someone to prison, spend long hours in front of a computer, etc.)?
10. Are you able to adhere to deadlines or schedules? Are you a procrastinator?

11. Do you need specific instructions on a task in order to feel confident in your ability to complete it?
12. Do you have geographic limitations for your employment considerations based on climate, family, and economics (which will be discussed in further detail)?
13. Do you like to work within the confines of an office or facility for an 8- to 10-hour day, or would you rather work at home and make your own schedule?
14. Is the career path defined or does one have to find their own way for promotions and greater income?

Once you have determined the answers to these questions and any others that are applicable to your personal situation, you can begin to match your criteria to those of various careers in which you are interested. You will be able to eliminate some career choices and (perhaps) compromise on others, and thus begin to determine a career or careers that will meet your needs.

Realize that salary should not be the only determining factor. Other related factors are organizational benefits, which include health insurance, dental insurance, vacation days, and contributions to a retirement fund. In some organizations, this can amount to about 50 percent of defined salary.

Another important factor is the work culture and the nature of work in the organization. Most criminal justice agencies are formed in fairly traditional organizational structures, which can be a "turn-off" for potential job applicants. As discussed by Morgan (2014), many "millennials" want to have a say in company operations and collaborate on projects.

Skills Capability

The next step in matching yourself to a career is to consider your strengths and weaknesses related to the required skills in various professions. Assessing your performance at your internship site will help you as you consider:

1. Do you have good interpersonal skills?
2. Do you have good written and oral communication skills?
3. Are you well organized? Are you able to multitask?
4. What are your strengths and weaknesses with regard to field, Internet, and library research?
5. What are your strengths and weaknesses with regard to accounting, problem analysis, detail work, and computer usage?
6. Do you have good analytic and intuitive thinking skills?
7. What technological skills do you have?
8. Would you be able to work in a virtual location?

Once again, you will have to match your skills profile to the requirements of the career or careers you are considering. You will then be able to see what strengths you already have and what ones you have to refine. You will find out if your weaknesses are such that you are not suited to that profession. Campus career services offices often sponsor seminars and online programs that allow you to assess your personal qualities in relation to potential careers.

Geographic Considerations

Where you are willing to live is a very important element in job placement. You have to consider whether you want to remain in your home town or home state, what climate you prefer, what social and cultural considerations are important for you, in what region(s) of the country you are willing to live, what type of living you prefer (urban, suburban, or rural), and where you can afford to live. Serious consideration must be given to geographic regions that are either experiencing job decline or growth. In addition, in view of the global economy, students should consider opportunities with multinational companies or government agencies with international operations. Once you have a general idea, you can determine if the career option you desire is available in the geographic location(s) you have chosen. This is one of the most important considerations in career planning after graduation.

Using Your Internship to Plan and Execute a Job Search

Your first professional position may be the first step in a number of career moves. Working for one organization for a 25- to 35-year period is no longer the norm. For example, many of our colleagues made three or four career changes before attaining their present positions. Some made career changes within the same field, while others made drastic career changes. You should not feel locked into your first professional position or the area of criminal justice you have chosen for your internship site.

Full-Time Employment at the Internship Site

At the start of your internship, you should be aware of professional opportunities and become informed about career opportunities, entry procedures, and requirements for the positions in your organization through formal and informal discussions with supervisors and work associates. The same can be done with the other potential employers with which your department or unit has contact. For example, although the compliance unit of a financial organization may not be hiring investigators, the fraud unit of another competitor may be holding an entry examination during your internship. In like fashion, students should not overlook the opportunities in the private sector for investigators, analysts, and compliance monitoring.

Often students are fortunate in obtaining jobs upon completion of their internships with their internship site. Those who have been successful usually began the hiring process by discussing employment opportunities with their supervisors. They also have been in the right place at the right time. As discussed by Huhman (2011), an intern picks up a certain skill or niche needed by the organization and becomes indispensable.

In some cases, interns are able to be placed into a temporary position on a contractual basis. This has occurred for students who were placed as legislative aides or under a subcontractor for certain federal agencies. While this is positive, you need to know the exact date when the position will end as part of your overall job or graduate school plans.

As is discussed in this chapter, interns are able to network within their area of interest and subsequently use those professional contacts and references as they seek employment. Before you leave your internship site, you should ask your supervisor, associates, and those you have worked with in other departments if you may contact them in the future regarding job openings or if you may use them as references on a job application. It is important to discuss this before terminating your internship; as discussed in Chapter 3, protocol requires that you request permission before using someone's name. You may also request a general letter of recommendation immediately before terminating your internship, so that it can be included in your placement file. Ask your supervisor to include in the letter the dates of your internship, your assigned duties, your ability to carry out those duties, and a statement concerning your viability as a candidate for a position in the general field of the agency. This will be important during background investigations or reference checks for future employment if you list the person's name on the application. Additionally, as Berger (2012) suggests, write a number of personal thank-you notes to the staff members who helped you and stay in touch from time to time with them to give an update on your career progress.

Letters of Reference

You should be aware that letters of reference in your college placement file, whether from a professor or a field supervisor, become outdated as your career intentions and prospective job requirements change. You may have to ask your references to rewrite the letters in order to add specific information about your personal and professional characteristics based on the requirements of the job, or the specific requirements of a graduate education program.

Having taught many students, the author requests that students include their most recent résumé and specific information on the program of study being undertaken. If the letter is for employment considerations, it is best to also include the advertised job description so that the letter can point to the requirements of the position. With regard to letters of reference or recommendation, apprise the person writing the letter of the outcome of the job or graduate school placement. For graduate or law school, it is not uncommon for letters to be submitted to national data banks for distribution to a pool of schools.

Résumé Update

In addition to obtaining letters of reference, you should update your résumé as the end of your internship nears. Any name or address changes should be included, as well as the addition of any new part-time jobs, extracurricular activities, and so on. The most important changes will be those relating to your internship experience. If, as a result of the internship, your professional objective has changed or been refined, be sure to incorporate that information as well. Using the sample résumé in Figure 3.1 in Chapter 3, let us assume that Mary Douglas has had a positive internship experience with the Livingston Police Department and, as a result, has decided that she would like to be a law enforcement officer in the area of juvenile justice. She would want to include that new professional objective in her résumé. In the educational background section, under Remsen College, she would add to the related courses: "Internship at Livingston Police Department (see 'Criminal Justice Experience,' below)." A more detailed account of the internship would then be added to the Criminal Justice Experience section; for example, 1/2017–5/2017 Criminal Justice Internship, Livingston Police Department, 159 Main St., Livingston, MA.

- Worked with the juvenile officer, primarily in public schools, after-school programs, and the Boys and Girls Club.

The final item to consider in planning seeking employment is a cover letter to prospective employers to include with your résumé (see Chapter 3). While changes will have to be incorporated depending on the position for which you are applying, it is helpful to have a basic letter on file. In your cover letter, you should introduce yourself as a recent (or prospective) college graduate who has majored in criminal justice. You should mention any double major, minor, or area of concentration as well. Be sure to refer to your recent internship experience. Finally, state your reason(s) for seeking the particular position. Figure 14.1 is a sample letter of application. Your college career services office should have a number of cover letter samples for you to consider.

Job Sources

Once your cover letter, résumé, and placement file are in order, the next step is to investigate employment opportunities that fit your career goals. You should consult several sources in order to explore all possibilities, including web site classified advertisements, civil service position announcements, classified advertisements in journals, college placement office files, criminal justice faculty, the Internet, and the professional network you have developed during your internship. You should be aware that approximately 10 percent or less of the available criminal justice positions are advertised in local newspapers and their web sites; however, it is still worth following the papers, particularly those from the geographic locations you are willing to consider. Most government position announcements are posted on public bulletin boards and web sites and in public

James Barton
384 Running Brook Drive
Old Lynne, NE 87654

June 25 2017

Mr. Robert E. Harding, Director
Department of Probation
4074 S. Washington Ave.
Hartford, NE 87653

Dear Mr. Harding:

Enclosed please find my résumé in application for the position of Probation Officer currently open in your department. I am a recent graduate of Wayne State College, where I majored in Criminal Justice with a concentration in Corrections. I have completed a fifteen-week full-time internship with the Campbell County Probation Department, where I was oriented to all phases of probation practice. I have taken several relevant courses, including a course dedicated to the study of probation and parole.

My internship experience was both challenging and rewarding. As you can see from the enclosed documents, I received excellent evaluations from my supervisors. I feel confident that my interests, education, internship experience, and interpersonal skills provide an excellent foundation from which I can become a valuable addition to your department.

I am available for an interview at your convenience. If selected for this position, I could begin immediately. My placement file from Wayne State College, including transcripts, will be forwarded to you at your request. I can be reached by telephone at (402) 555-1234 or e-mail at jbarton@mail.com.

Thank you for your consideration. I look forward to hearing from you.

Sincerely,

James Barton

James Barton

FIGURE 14.1 Sample Letter of Application.

employment offices. A civil service examination is required for most of these positions. The time, date, and place of the test, as well as a deadline for applying to take the examination, will be posted; the deadline must be strictly adhered to. Other requirements, such as residency, education, age, and experience, need to be considered in addition to salary ranges. You must also become aware of the other tests that accompany many of these positions, such as physical agility, personal health, psychological, polygraph, drug use, and background investigation. Candidates who pass these steps may also have to undergo a series of interviews that may include a session before an oral review board. As discussed in Chapter 3, the types of interviews and questions vary from agency to agency and can range from the conversational to stressful situations in which you have to make decisions. You will have to match your personal and professional goals and needs to these positions and apply the skills that you gained from your internship experience.

Several professional criminal justice journals, newsletters, and web sites include advertisements for jobs all over the country. While many of the positions require post-graduate work and/or more experience than you may have, it is worth exploring these sources. You will find a selection of criminal justice journals and newsletters available through your college library site.

The private sector is also a good source of jobs for criminal justice students. Students who are interested in fraud analysis and investigation may seek opportunities with banks, credit card companies, cellular and other telecommunications organizations, insurance companies, and securities firms. These organizations are especially interested in students who have a background in accounting and computers.

The career services office at your college is likely to have a range of resources to assist you in seeking employment. Among these are trained counselors to advise you, position announcements, print directories, and electronic sites of criminal justice and related agencies (local, state, and federal) that include the agency addresses and names of key personnel, names of companies that have employed alumni of the college, graduate school and law school information, and announcements of job fairs and agency recruiters visiting campus. The position announcements will provide the same information as civil service postings and will include a person to contact. The directories can be used as a means of finding appropriate agencies, particularly in other areas of the country, so that you can write to them inquiring about employment possibilities. Companies and agencies that already employ graduates of your school may look favorably upon you as a potential employee. In addition, you can contact the alumni personally to gain information about the organization. Catalogs and databases are available for graduate and law schools, as is information regarding graduate school and law school examinations (such as Graduate Record Examinations and Law Scholastic Aptitude Tests). Counselors may be aware of recent position openings; they can also review and critique your résumé, letters of reference, and cover letter. Agencies and companies often send recruiters to college campuses so that they can have preliminary interviews with interested students. Job fairs bring together several recruiters for a day on campus. The programs offered by career services might also include free business cards and special presentations on cocktail party and dining etiquette and trends in professional attire (e.g., dress for success). These and other services are often extended to alumni seeking employment or career changes well after graduation. Social media sites such as LinkedIn offer a number of possibilities, as job candidates are able to learn about positions in discussions and, in some cases, organizations recruit via the medium.

The majority of criminal justice professors are either former agency personnel or active researchers who have strong ties to the criminal justice community. As faculty, they often attend national and regional conferences and workshops and often have established strong professional networks. Thus, it is not uncommon for faculty to hear of job openings before they are officially posted. You should use your faculty as a resource for employment opportunities both before and after graduation. They will be happy to hear from you and willing to do what they can to help you procure a position.

Internet Leads

An Internet search can identify current job opportunities in the public or private sector. The following are the general steps that you should take:

- Identify key words to describe the type of job you want. For example, you could use "criminal justice jobs" or "fraud investigator."
- Using a variety of search engines (e.g., Google, Yahoo, etc.), search using key words. It is important to use several search engines, as they tend to locate different information.
- Refine your search as you review your results. As with all information on the Internet, you will need to assess the sources of information.

Social media sites, such as LinkedIn, are increasingly being used for professional networking and for job leads. Some organizations have begun recruiting on social media. Many career services departments have increasingly advised students to create a professional identity for networking and job seeking. It is important to create and keep an updated profile that would include your résumé. This has become an important tool for recruiters as well as for companies.

The federal government has an official web site for employment opportunities at www.usajobs.gov. At this web site you can create and store a résumé, as well as search the USAJOBS database for openings. The site also provides a Career Interest Center, which can help you assess your interests and capabilities and refine your search to an appropriate position. To search for jobs, you are asked to enter information such as geographic location, job category, and salary range. The position listings include information about who may apply, the opening and closing dates of the position announcement, and the salary. Other services provided by this web site include guidance on procuring a government position and information on the application process. At the time of this writing, the author is advised that this site is being upgraded. Note that not all federal law enforcement agencies use USAJOBS. Instead, many will advertise openings and accept a maximum number of applications and then close the site. When this occurs depends on the whims of the agency, budget issues, and the need for new applicants.

There are numerous web sites for state civil service jobs and other state employment opportunities. You should do an Internet search for civil service postings or employment opportunities in a particular state. For example, the New York State Department of Civil Service web site (www.cs.ny.gov) provides information about required examinations for positions in state government, local government, and the City of New York. Sites of this nature include information on careers in state government, how to take a civil service examination, and employee benefits.

Another possible course of action, and one that is very controversial, is a postgraduate internship. There are many opportunities available in government and the private sector that may or may not be paid. There are certain foundations that are fee-based programs that place qualified students in government positions in the United States and overseas. Your career services office will have information on legitimate programs of this nature, which can be a stepping stone to full-time employment. However, this leads to the issue of the "perpetual intern syndrome" that is often discussed in the national media. In a *New York Times* article, "All Work and No Payoff," Williams (2014) discusses a number of situations where graduates have been in two or more non-paid internship positions, particularly in the publishing and media fields. It is often not the issue of pay. He writes, "Millennials, it is often said, want more than a paycheck; they crave a meaningful and fulfilling career, maybe even a chance to change the world" (p. 14). Returning to the discussion of nonpaid internships, there appears to be a counter-trend whereby private-sector companies will not offer internships unless they are paid.

Once you have contacted an agency about an employment opportunity, you should receive a response within a month. If you do not hear from them, you can write a follow-up letter, as discussed in Chapter 3. If you are invited for an interview, you should follow the guidelines outlined in Chapter 3. In addition, go into the interview with a positive and confident attitude, write a thank-you note a day or so after the interview, and, if you are not offered the position, look upon the interview as a learning experience. Each interview you have is practice for the next. If you question why you were not offered the position, it is acceptable to write to the person with whom you interviewed and ask him or her (in a polite fashion) why you were not selected, indicating that you wish to know so that you can be better prepared for the next employment opportunity you pursue.

Creating a Professional Network

At a meeting of graduates, former students were asked what advice they could give upcoming graduates about career planning and job searches. In addition to the above items, many reported that developing a professional network was important. What is a professional network? A professional network is nothing more than a web of contacts that you have developed during your college career. They may include friends, teammates, or colleagues from sports, projects, clubs, plays, and so on, who are now working in the field. Your network might also include immediate family, relatives, cousins, and in-laws working in the criminal justice field. Joining national and professional associations related to your career goals is another way to expand your network. Many national groups—for example, the Academy of Criminal Justice Sciences, state associations of criminal justice educators, the National Association of Certified Fraud Examiners, the American Society for Industrial Security, and many others—have student memberships. All of them also maintain web sites that can be readily located. Annual dues are usually discounted for undergraduate and graduate students.

In her book on criminal justice careers, Peat (2004) writes that the internship experience provides direct entry into a professional network that can have positive results. She cautions that it is important to be professional at all times in your dealings with people at your internship site and in interactions with the people (both inside and outside the agency) with whom coworkers communicate on a frequent basis. "It is important to keep in mind that your reputation is likely to follow you wherever you go. I have always found it interesting that criminal justice professionals within a community, state, or even at the national level are a relatively small network," she states (Peat, 2004, p. 106). In short, your dealings on the job will make lasting impressions, especially when you are applying for future positions and related reference or background investigations.

Creating and Monitoring Your Online Identity

As discussed throughout this book, the use of social media has become an important tool for both job candidates and employers. Career counselors generally agree that it is important for students to both create and monitor their online presence. The main resources for what is called "personal branding" are LinkedIn and Brand Yourself. These are recognized as reputable sites that allow you to create a professional Web appearance and network with trusted colleagues. As discussed by Korkki (2010) and in Chapter 2 of this book, employers routinely check out job candidates through Google profiles, LinkedIn, and at other sites. Thus, it is important to edit out questionable behavior postings and photos and to monitor, as you would with your financial credit rating, your online reputation. According to Korkki: "You may never know why you weren't hired, but be aware that background checks can make or break a job application. And in a data-rich world, the person with the fewest red flags may get the job."

Continuing Your Education

Law school and graduate work in a variety of disciplines are options open to criminal justice majors' immediately after graduation or after a few years of work experience. It is important to have career goals in mind before considering a specific graduate program. Criminal justice majors may be interested in graduate degrees in criminal justice administration, public administration, business administration, social work, psychology, or sociology, among others. Once you know in what area you want to continue your education, you should consult graduate and law school directories and web sites to see which schools meet your needs in terms of program focus, academic requirements, cost, and geographic location. Many programs have specific grade point average and letters of recommendation requirements. If you plan to go to law school or graduate school immediately after graduation, you will need to plan ahead in terms of taking the required examination(s) and meeting application deadlines. Most graduate schools in criminal justice and related fields require the Graduate Record Examination (GRE), which is offered by the Education Testing Service several times a year at various locations. The purpose of the GRE is to measure analytical writing, critical thinking, quantitative reasoning, and verbal reasoning. Specific information on the GRE in terms of test areas, scoring, and costs can be found at www.ets.org. Law schools require the Law School Admissions Test (LSAT), which is offered four times a year by the Law School Admissions Council. The LSAT measures analytical reasoning, logical reasoning, and reading comprehension. Useful information on the LSAT and law school admissions is located at www.lsac.org.

Each school has its own procedures and requirements. As stated above, the college career services office is a good source of information on graduate schools and law schools, as well as the prerequisite examinations. Many offer seminars and practice sessions in preparing for the GRE and the LSAT. A criminal justice faculty and/or pre-law advisor can help in evaluating your potential for such endeavors, selecting an appropriate school, and providing you with information on pre-examination preparation courses and how to secure letters of recommendation.

Successful Students

The author is often asked on what were the general qualities or traits for those graduates who were deemed "successful" after they left college. There are many faces and experiences, but the following observations come to mind:

They were good students. This does not mean that they were on the dean's list every semester but they were prepared for class and there were no problems with attendance or behavior issues. They enjoyed learning about the topics at hand and submitted assignments and papers on time. They also had good research and writing skills.

They had a successful internship. As discussed throughout this book, internships have a profound impact on a person's career in many ways. Internships open up endless possibilities and networks for future employment and professional development. Not surprisingly, students who successfully completed internships are remembered by the faculty supervisor and many organizational personnel.

Great interpersonal skills. Criminal justice positions and related areas are "people-oriented" types of endeavors. This means that you need to deal with a variety of populations in a professional and empathetic manner and often with people acting at their worst.

Above average on technology. As administrators and faculty, we constantly learn about many trends in technology through items and applications purchased and practiced by our students. These students are by no means computer geeks. Yet, they understood the strengths and weaknesses of a particular application and software and were willing to use it and share their knowledge with others.

Active on campus and in the community. The majority of students either had part-time jobs or were on athletic teams and thus had to have good time management skills to survive. Many were volunteers with various helping and social service agencies. Those with special academic success records were recruited to become student or teaching assistants. Additionally, there were those who were elected leaders of the criminal justice or economic crime investigation clubs. As faculty we got to know them better and, no surprise here, would often notify them of special events or intern placements that came to our attention.

Willing to try new things. Some favorite intern experiences come from those students who took risks and obtained placements beyond the normal agency placements or had to compete nationally or statewide for limited placements with nationally competitive internship programs. Sometimes they were not successful but at least they learned from the undertaking. There was one student who was supervised by a religious community and taught women in a prison in Nicaragua. Another had to wait 2 months before starting her program in the summer due to the time-consuming federal background check, but managed to graduate on time. They all showed drive and persistence in their undertakings.

Success in the Field

Based on the above discussion, the questions often loom of how long it took to find employment after graduation and whether graduates stayed in the field. For the first question—employment after graduation—it all depends on a number of factors as discussed earlier in this section. The main issue is what was the main postgraduate goal and when did this take shape? Some students have specific career goals and they start on these immediately a year before graduation. For others, it takes time—months and years beyond graduation. Again the main issue is geographical location and the filing of applications and résumés for examinations or positions months before graduation.

As for staying in the field as a career, my faculty colleagues seem to agree that most successful graduates who were interns used their experiences to pursue and remain in criminal justice and related positions and went on to become agency heads or persons in major policymaking positions. They often continued their education in graduate or law school or took extensive certifications and training courses related to their positions.

However, the traditional career path of staying with one agency or firm for 20 years or so is not typical anymore. Recent graduates tend to move from one organization to another. This reflects the nature of the new economy and the mobility that occurs in many occupations. For example, a recent graduate who was named the state's law enforcement officer of the year had transferred from two other agencies before landing a position with a major department in the central part of the state. Another student who majored in cybersecurity started as an analyst with a federal agency and then moved to a private-sector firm.

There are also those students who start in the criminal justice field and then move to other occupations. One in particular began in criminal justice planning after graduation and then decided to go into hospital equipment sales where he is now a senior administrator. "People skills, problem solving, and being able to respond to a client's emergency are readily applicable to a number of occupational fields," he remarked.

Final Considerations

No matter how well prepared you are for employment, job hunting is hard work and a full-time endeavor. You must be assertive and enthusiastic but extremely patient and always polite. You will have to wait for responses to initial inquiries, for test results, for interviews to be set up, and for semi-final and final decisions to be made. You should have realistic expectations about the responsibilities and salary offered to an entry-level employee.

As a recent college graduate, you do not have the experience you need to get what you might see as your ideal job. Your first position, however, can be a step toward that ideal. Some students are so sure they can earn a high salary, and it is so important to them, that they are seduced into a position that offers more money without considering the job itself or its potential as a stepping-stone. For example, one student was hired by a large corporation, at a salary higher than most of his professors, to check the license plates of the cars in the parking lot and identify those that did not have clearance. He was making a lot of money, but the job was not challenging and, most notably, it was a dead end. Do not lose sight of the career goals you have set.

As you move along your career path, be aware that the assessment of your personal needs, your skills, and your geographic limitations may change as you gain experience and as your personal situation changes. Therefore, you should periodically assess your career to determine if your personal and professional needs are being met.

Above all, in whatever criminal justice career you choose, you must be able to have a passion for the job and to live with yourself and with the daily issues of justice, fairness, and punishment. As discussed in Chapter 8, you must constantly review your values and the behavior you exhibit in the workplace. Working in any criminal justice position is difficult in terms of legalities, peer pressure, and seeing human beings at their worst. If you have the attitude, philosophy, and personal stamina for coping with the myriad emotions and frustrations inherent in this field, then a criminal justice career can be very rewarding in terms of the assistance you will provide to fellow citizens in need.

I wish you well in your future endeavors.

References

Academy of Criminal Justice Sciences (2005). Certification standards for college/university Criminal Justice Baccalaureate Degree programs. Retrieved July 1, 2008, from www.acjs.org/pubs/167_667_ 12021.cfm.

Association of Certified Fraud Examiners (2004). The Tampa Bay chapter. Code of ethics for certified fraud examiners. Retrieved February 3, 2004, from http://www.tampabaycfe.org/our-chapter.php.

Bainbridge, S. (2007). *The complete guide to Sarbanes-Oxley: Understanding how Sarbanes-Oxley affects your business.* Avon, MA: Adams.

Berger, L. (2012). *Finding an internship, building your resume, making connections, and gaining job experience.* Berkeley: Ten Speed.

Bump, B. (2016, January 12). SUNY students gain path to internships. *Albany Times Union.* Retrieved April 1, 2016, from http://www.timesunion.com/tuplus-local/article/SUNY-students-gain-path-to-internships-6749752.php.

Burns, J. (2016). How the overtime rules could impact your summer internships. *Pulse.* Retrieved June 5, 2016 from https://www.linkedin.com/pulse/how-overtime-rules-could impact.

Byrne, J. M., & Rebovich, D. J. (2007). *The new technology of crime, law and social control.* Monsey, NY: Criminal Justice Press.

Combs, C. C. (2001). *Terrorism in the twenty-first century.* Upper Saddle River, NJ: Prentice Hall.

Curtis, G., & McBride, R. B. (2011). *Proactive security administration.* Upper Saddle River, NJ: Pearson Prentice Hall.

Frankfort-Nachmias, C., & Nachmias, D. (2000). *Research methods in the social sciences.* New York: Worth.

Fuller, J. (2001). Street cop ethics. Originally published in The Law Enforcement Trainer. Retrieved February 3, 2004, from www.commfaculty.fullerton.edu/lester/ethics/street_cop.html.

Gibson, J. L., Ivancevich, J. M., & Donnelly, J. H., Jr. (1997). *Organizations: Behavior, structure, processes* (9th ed.). Boston: Irwin.

Gilbertson, S., & Eilts, S. (2011, May 24). Internship and externship programs under the Fair Labor Standards Act. *NACUA Notes,* 9 (11).

Glatt et al. v Fox Searchlight Pictures, Inc. et al. (2014). 13-4478-cv (L). United States Court of Appeals (2ed Circuit). Retrieved June 1, 2016 from http://www.nysd.uscourts.gov/cases/show.php?db=special&id=300.

Hall, R. H. (1999). *Organizations: Structures, processes, outcomes.* Upper Saddle River, NJ: Prentice Hall.

Huhman, H. R. (2011). *Lies, damned lies & internships: The truth about getting from classroom to cubicle.* Cupertino, CA: Happy About.

Hunt, T. (2013). Communication, context, and crime scenes: Enhancing opportunities to identify and collect touch DNA evidence. *The Police Chief,* (September 2013), pp. 42–3.

International Association of Chiefs of Police (2004). Law enforcement code of ethics. Retrieved March 22, 2004, from www.theiacp.org/documents/index.cfm?fuseaction=document&document_id=95.

Internet Crime Complaint Center (2010). 2010 Internet crime report. Retrieved May 20, 2011, from www.ic3.gov/media/annualreport/2010_IC3Report.pdf.

Ismaili, K. (2011). Thinking about criminal justice policy: Process, players, and politics. In K. Ismaili (Ed.), *U.S. criminal justice policy: A contemporary reader*. Sudbury, MA: Jones & Barlett Learning, pp. 1–18.

Jones, G. (2007). *Organizational theory, design, and change*. Upper Saddle River, NJ: Pearson Prentice Hall.

Jordan, W. T., Burns, R. G., Bedard, L. E., & Barringer, T. A. (2007). Criminal justice interns' observations of misconduct: An exploratory study. *Journal of Criminal Justice Education*, 18(2), 298–310.

King, J. (2003). Strategic planning. Presentation to Executive Development Institute of the International Association of Campus Law Enforcement Administrators, San Antonio, TX.

Korkki, P. (2010). Is your online identity spoiling your chances? *The New York Times*. Retrieved May 30, 2014, from www.nytimes.com/2010/10/10/jobs/10search.html.

Kuntz, S. (2013). Video evidence is everywhere: Training and respect are needed. *The Police Chief*, (September 2013), pp. 38–9.

Lockheed Martin (2006). Setting the standard: Code of ethics and business conduct. Retrieved May 28, 2008, from www.lockheedmartin.com/data/assets/corporate/documents/ethics/setting-the-standard.pdf.

Lotyczewski, H. (2011). *Resume writing & interviewing workshop*. Utica, NY: Utica College.

Lyons, D. (2016). Congratulations! You've been fired. *The New York Times*. Retrieved April 10, 2016, from http://www.nytimes.com/2016/04/10/opinion/sday/congratulation-youve-been-fired.html?_r=0.

Maxfield, M. G., & Babbie, E. (2008). *Research methods for criminal justice and criminology* (5th ed.). New York: Thompson/Wadsworth.

McLeod, M. (n.d.). *Preparing for life after college: A short guide for enhancing success*. Troy, NY: Forensic Mental Health, The Sage Colleges.

Morgan, J. (2014). The future of work: Attract new talent, build better leaders, and create a competitive organization. New York: Wiley.

Myren, R. A. (1982). A second view. In *Joint Commission on Criminology and Criminal Justice Education and Standards, Two views of criminology and criminal justice: Definition, trends, and the future*. Chicago: University of Chicago.

National Association of Colleges and Employers (2010). Position statement: U.S. internships: A definition and criteria to assess opportunities and determine the implications for compensation. Retrieved April 27, 2016, from http://www.naceweb.org/advocacy/position-statement/united-states-internships.aspx.

O'Connor, T. R. (2005). Police deviance and ethics, megalinks in criminal justice. Retrieved May 28, 2008, from www.policecrimes.com/police_deviance.html.

Office of Career Services at Utica College (2010). A guide to services offered. Retrieved June 10, 2011, from www.utica.edu/student/career/cs/services.pdf.

Olson, A. (2008). Authoring a code of ethics: Observations on process and organization. Center for the Study of Ethics in the Professions at Illinois Institute of Technology. Retrieved May 28, 2008, from www.ethics.iit.edu/codes/Writing_A_Code.html.

Patten, D. (2013). Fox searchlight scores partial win in "Black Swan" interns lawsuit. Retrieved December 21, 2013, from http://deadline.com/2013/08/fox-searchlight-scores-partial-win-in-black-swan-interns-lawsuit-573011/.

Peat, B. (2004). *From college to career: A guide for criminal justice majors*. Boston: Allyn & Bacon.

Peat, B., & Moriarty, L. (2009). *Assessing criminal justice/criminology education: A resource handbook for educators and administrators*. Durham, NC: Carolina Academic Press.

Perlin, R. (2012). *Intern nation: How to earn nothing and learn little in the brave new economy*. London: Verso.

Permaul, J. (1981). *Monitoring and supporting experiential learning*. Washington, DC: National Society for Internships and Experiential Education.

Policies compared: today's corporate blogging rules (2005). *Corporate blogging blog*. Rerieved January 16, 2008, from http://corporatebloggin.ino/2005/06/policies-compared-todays-corporate.asp.

Ross, L. E., & Elechi, O. (2002). Student attitudes towards internship experience: From theory to practice. *Journal of Criminal Justice Education*, 13(2), 297–312.

Schawbel, D. (2012). How recruiters use social networks to make hiring decisions now. Retrieved February 11, 2014, from www.business.time.com/2012/07/09/how-recruiters-use-social-networks-to-makehiring-decisions-now/.

Scheiber, N. (2016). President Obama's overtime pay plan threatens the "Prada Economy." *The New York Times*. Retrieved June 2, 2016, from www.nytimes.com/2016/05/31/business/for-harried-assistants-overtime-rule-may-have-its-downside.html?_r=0.

Schmidt, E., & Cohen, J. (2013). *The new digital age: Reshaping the future of people, nations and business*. New York: Alfred Knopf.

Segroi, C. A., & Ryniker, M. (2002). Preparing for the real world: A prelude to a fieldwork experience. *Journal of Criminal Justice Education*, 13(1), 187–200.

Seidman, D. (2007). *How: Why how we do anything means everything, in business (and in life)*. Hoboken, NJ: John Wiley.

Selingo, J. J. (2016). *There is life after college*. New York: William Morrow.

Singer, M. C. (2011). Roundtable on internships: Issues, concerns and best practices. Presentation to Northeastern Association of Criminal Justice Sciences 2011, Bristol, RI, June.

Stichman, A. J., & Farkas, M. A. (2005). The pedagogical use of internships in criminal justice programs: A nationwide study. *Journal of Criminal Justice Education*, 16(1), 145–65.

SUNY Levin Institute (2012). *New York in the world: The impact of the global economy on New York State and the City*. New York: Levin Institute/Center for an Urban Future.

Symantec Corporation (2011). Symantec Internet security threat report: Trends for 2010. Retrieved May 4, 2011, from www.symantec.com/business/threatreport/index.jsp.

Thibault, E., Lynch, L., McBride, R. B., & Walsh, G. (2014). *Proactive police management* (9th ed.). Upper Saddle River, NJ: Pearson Prentice Hall.

United States Department of Justice: Federal Bureau of Investigation (2015). *2015 internet crime report*. Retrieved June 3, 2016 from https://pdf.ic3.gov/2015_IC3Report.pdf.

United States Department of Labor. Fact Sheet #71: Internship programs under the Fair Labor Standards Act: United States Department of Labor, Wage and Hour Division. Retrieved December 1, 2013, from http://www.dol.gov/whd/regs/compliance/whdfs71.htm.

United States Department of Labor, Bureau of Labor Statistics (2016). Economic News Release—Union Members Summary. Retrieved May 2, 2016, from www.bls.gov/news.release/union2.nr0.htm.

United States Department of Labor, Bureau of Labor Statistics, Occupational Outlook Handbook (2015). Retrieved May 31, 2016, from http://www.bls.gov/ooh/.

United States Postal Inspections Service (2012). *Memorandum of agreement*.

Urbina, I. (2014). Social Media, A Trove of Clues and Confessions. *The New York Times*, SR5.

Welsh, W. N., & Harris, P. (2016). *Criminal justice policy and planning* (5th ed.). New York: Routledge (Anderson Publishing).

Wetfeet.com (2013, January 9). Top 3 internships challenges and how to solve them. Retrieved May 14, 2016, from www.wetfeet.com/articles/top-3-internship-challenges-and-how-to-solve-them.

Williams, A. (2014). All work and no payoff. *The New York Times* (February 16), pp. 1, 14.

World Wide Web Foundation. *History of the Web*. Retrieved August 9, 2016 from http://webfoundation.org/about/vision/history-of-the-web.

Index